Miracles
and More

Chicken Soup for the Soul: Miracles and More
101 Stories of Angels, Divine Intervention, Answered Prayers and Messages from Heaven
Amy Newmark

Published by Chicken Soup for the Soul, LLC www.chickensoup.com
Copyright ©2018 by Chicken Soup for the Soul, LLC. All Rights Reserved.

The publisher gratefully acknowledges the many publishers and individuals who granted Chicken Soup for the Soul permission to reprint the cited material.

Front cover artwork courtesy of iStockphoto.com/Yuri_Arcurs (©Yuri_Arcurs)
Back cover and Interior artwork of dove courtesy of iStockphoto.com/DNY59 (©DNY59)
Photo of Amy Newmark courtesy of Susan Morrow at SwickPix

Cover and Interior by Daniel Zaccari

Distributed to the booktrade by Simon & Schuster. SAN: 200-2442

Publisher's Cataloging-In-Publication Data
(Prepared by The Donohue Group, Inc.)

Names: Newmark, Amy, compiler.
Title: Chicken soup for the soul : miracles and more : 101 stories of
      angels, divine intervention, answered prayers and messages from heaven
      / [compiled by] Amy Newmark.
Other Titles: Miracles and more : 101 stories of angels, divine
      intervention, answered prayers and messages from heaven
Description: [Cos Cob, Connecticut] : Chicken Soup for the Soul, LLC,
      [2018]
Identifiers: ISBN 9781611599756 (print) | ISBN 9781611592757 (ebook)
Subjects: LCSH: Miracles--Literary collections. | Miracles--Anecdotes. |
      Angels--Literary collections. | Angels--Anecdotes. | Providence and
      government of God--Literary collections. | Providence and government of
      God--Anecdotes. | LCGFT: Anecdotes.
Classification: LCC BL425 .C452 2018 (print) | LCC BL425 (ebook) | DDC
      202.1/02--dc23

Library of Congress LCCN: 2017962939

PRINTED IN THE UNITED STATES OF AMERICA
on acid∞free paper

25 24 23 22 21 20 19 18   01 02 03 04 05 06 07 08 09 10 11

Miracles
and More

**101 Stories of Angels,
Divine Intervention,
Answered Prayers and
Messages from Heaven**

Amy Newmark

Chicken Soup for the Soul, LLC
Cos Cob, CT

Changing your world one story at a time®
www.chickensoup.com

Table of Contents

❶

~Divine Coincidences~

❷

~Messages from Heaven~

❸

~Answered Prayers~

❹

~Divine Guidance~

❺

~Miraculous Healing~

❻

~Divine Timing~

❼

~Everyday Miracles~

8

~Dreams and Premonitions~

9

~Divine Intervention~

10

~Signs from Above~

⑪

~Heavenly Strangers~

Chapter 1

Miracles and More

Divine Coincidences

Finding My Truth

We do not create our destiny; we participate in its
unfolding. Synchronicity works as a catalyst toward
the working out of that destiny.
~David Richo, The Power of Coincidence

I'd been seeing a gifted healer named Kathy as part of a holistic approach to treating the symptoms of my traumatic brain injury. She gave counsel and did energy healing. I'd been seeing her monthly for about a year and I always felt better after each session. Then one day, as the session ended, she asked me suddenly, "Could you possibly be adopted?"

I laughed and said, "I don't know. I have a birth certificate with the names of both parents who raised me on it. However, I have always felt different from everyone else in the family, so I wouldn't be surprised."

I had said that to make light of the question. Still, later that night, I decided to call my parents. When I questioned my father, he started stammering, and my mother's response was odd, too. I began to search for more information. After several frustrating months with no results, I decided to stop searching and "let go and let God."

Six months later, I was on the phone with Kathy complaining that my mother expected me to go to a three-hour Christmas celebration. I didn't want to attend, but felt obligated. She reminded me I was "grown" and had been considered an adult for more than thirty years. Then she asked, "What do you want to do?"

I responded, "Sit on an island somewhere." She encouraged me to do what would make me happy, and she added that if I decided to go to the islands, she would go with me.

I decided to do it, even though Christmas was only a month away and most places were already fully booked. I told my travel agent that I was flexible as long as the flight wasn't more than three hours, and she said that if I was willing to drive 100 miles to Philadelphia, fly out on Christmas Day and return on New Year's Eve, she could get us to St. Thomas in the U.S. Virgin Islands.

We set off on our adventure on Christmas Eve, but our first day on St. Thomas was disappointing. The beach near our hotel was small and crowded.

We decided to travel to the other side of the island the next day, and we randomly chose a restaurant in another hotel to have breakfast. The restaurant was practically empty, so we were surprised when the waitress sat two women right beside us.

Soon, we were chatting and sharing stories about how we arrived at this isolated location. We were so engrossed in conversation that an hour passed before we exchanged names. When I handed them my business card, which said Sheila Quarles on it, one of the women stared at it. And then she said, "I had a sister who was adopted by a Quarles family in Washington, D.C."

I answered, "I'm from D.C."

She looked at me and said, "I remembered hearing the adults discussing how this family promised to take care of her feet, which needed special attention."

"I had trouble with my feet and had to wear special shoes," I answered.

She then said, "We heard she was modeling. We didn't understand how with her foot problems."

I told her I had been a model for a department store, and my picture had been in the newspaper. Everyone gasped.

I began to cry. I was sitting next to my biological sister.

She had started looking for me six months earlier because our mother had died, and I was the only missing sibling. She further explained that she actually lived in St. Croix and was visiting her friend on St. Thomas when they decided to try this restaurant.

My sister was returning home that day, and I agreed to go with her to St. Croix. I packed my bags and met her at the small plane that would take us there. She held my hand, and I cried as I looked out the window.

When I arrived at her home, we actually had some of the same items. We had also sent out the same holiday greeting cards. We had so much in common that I felt as though I was home. She called my aunts, sisters, and brothers and told them I had been found.

That year, by deciding to do something very different for Christmas, I set off on a miraculous journey and I discovered my truth. And if you're wondering what happened to my friend Kathy, who helped to create this miracle, after I met my sister at the breakfast table, Kathy said, "my job is done." She booked the next flight home. Five years later, I offered to lend my skills to assist Kathy with her business, Inner Journeys, and I've been her business partner for ten years now.

~Sheila Quarles

Warily We Roll Along

I could not have made it this far had there
not been angels along the way.
~Della Reese

The ink had barely dried on Joe's discharge from the Navy when we rolled out of the driveway in Fortuna, California and headed for home sweet home in Philadelphia. This little adventure took place in 1986 when we were driving our old Pontiac LeMans, which was ugly, faded, and lacked both air conditioning and a radio.

At least the old girl was reliable… mostly. We had both chosen to ignore the quirky little hiccup sound that happened occasionally on hills. But after about three hours on the road, still in northern California, we noticed that the odd little engine hiccup had developed into a full-blown cough. The car lurched its way up every hill, teetered at the top, and then wheezed down the other side. Clearly, we weren't prepared for the streets of San Francisco, let alone a cross-country trip over mountain passes.

In San Francisco, the car did that thing that cars do, behaving perfectly on hills for two different mechanics. With our attempts to repair the car thwarted, we set off again on our trip, pretending not to notice the road rage of the drivers forced to follow us on single-lane mountain passes. To remedy this, we flipped our daily routine and began driving from midnight to daybreak so as to slow down fewer of our fellow travelers.

That kept us out of heavy traffic, but still didn't solve the problem. Our crippled engine continued to wheeze its way over hill and dale.

One morning, as a huge hill loomed ahead of us, we pulled over to let a peppy little vehicle pass us. Much to our surprise, the driver pulled over behind us.

As he stepped out of his vehicle and headed in our direction, all I could think about was how long it might take the highway patrol to find our bodies.

"Hello," the driver said with a smile. "Looks like you two are having some car trouble."

"Just a little," Joe said. "That's why we pulled to the side. Sorry for any inconvenience."

"Don't worry. I think I can help. My name is Tom."

Joe got out of the car, and they shook hands.

A few minutes later, Joe stuck his head in the window.

"Annie, have you got a pencil?"

I rooted around in the glove compartment and plucked the stub of a pencil from between the folds of our road map.

"Will this do?"

"Perfect," he said, and off he went toward Tom, pencil in hand.

Tom grabbed the pencil and shimmied under the car. A few minutes later, he emerged. By this time, I'd joined Joe on the side of the road.

"That should do it," Tom said.

"Do what?" I asked.

Our new friend explained that the fuel system of a Pontiac LeMans engaged two separate fuel lines. One hose carried gasoline to the engine; the other siphoned off the excess and returned it to the tank. This saved gas when it worked, but the design was flawed. As the car aged, the tubing deteriorated, and the siphon hose wound up extracting most of the fuel needed to fire the engine up a hill. The warmer the engine, the more pronounced the problem.

"I plugged the siphon hose with the pencil. That should take care of the problem," Tom said.

"You're a genius!" I exclaimed.

"Not really," he said. "But I *am* a retired automotive engineer."

We wanted to pay Tom, buy him breakfast, walk his dog—something, anything to show our appreciation—but Tom would have none of it.

He just laughed and offered to follow us for a bit to make sure we were okay. After a while, Tom waved as he headed toward the exit, and we tooted our horn in thanks.

Later, Joe told me that while chatting with him, he'd learned that Tom wasn't just a retired automotive engineer. Tom was part of the original team that designed the Pontiac LeMans, and he knew his way around that engine like a heart surgeon knows his way around a chest cavity. And there he was driving along behind us that morning, realizing that we might be having trouble with hills. What are the odds? The hair on the back of my neck still stands on end when I think of it.

We traveled home without any further worrying. Along the way, we enjoyed the excitement of Las Vegas, the vistas of Yosemite National Park, and the majesty of Mount Rushmore—all because an angel in our path knew exactly what to do with an old pencil stub.

~Annmarie B. Tait

What Are the Odds?

Coincidences mean you're on the right path.
~Simon Van Booy

he scheduling desk of the imaging center where I worked as a Nuclear Medicine Technologist hadn't allotted enough time for my patient's exam. I could tell the woman was frustrated — she had taken off work for the test — but she remained pleasant as the front-office staff arranged to reschedule her visit. I introduced myself and let her know I would be the one performing her test when she returned. I apologized for the inconvenience, and we made small talk as the receptionist clicked through the calendar looking for the next available time slot.

When the woman was offered an appointment nearly three weeks away, I decided that would not do. I volunteered to open the nuclear-medicine department two hours early the following day. I didn't want her to have to miss another day of work. She was extremely grateful and left the clinic with a smile.

The next morning, the imaging center was just coming to life as I helped my patient off the exam table following her test.

"I don't suppose you'd be interested in another job, would you?" she asked, her hopeful tone catching me off-guard.

I'd grown quite fond of my co-workers. I was not, however, fond of the fifty-mile drive to work every day.

She had connections at the city's military hospitals and told me they were always looking for good people. She handed me her business card and asked me to call her. I thanked her, and she was on her way.

It didn't take long for me to decide to call the number on that card. Before I knew what was happening, I was scheduled for an interview at a local military base.

Within hours of leaving the interview, I received a phone call. The job was mine if I wanted it. I couldn't believe my luck! The benefits package was amazing, and my drive would be cut in half, not to mention civil service jobs were highly sought after and extremely hard to come by.

There was a hitch, though. My college degree was in radiology technology, not nuclear medicine, and while I had completed all of the additional training as mandated by the Nuclear Medicine Technology Certification Board, I had never taken the time to actually sit for the test. I would need to successfully complete the Nuclear Medicine exam within a few months of my hire or risk losing my dream job.

I decided to take a chance. I turned in my resignation to my employer and began the application process to sit for my boards. I had two weeks left at my current job, and I wanted to get the test application all tidied up so I could start my new position feeling confident.

There was a lot more paperwork than I had anticipated. I would need to submit an affidavit signed by the radiologist under whom I had performed the majority of my training. He needed to attest to the fact that I had completed the required hours of on-the-job training. Luckily I had done nearly all the training under the watchful eye of one doctor. All I had to do was find him.

I thought it would be easy to find Dr. Smith, but I discovered he no longer worked for the clinic where I had done my training. The company had been bought out by a large corporation, and their human resources department offered me no help in locating him. It was a dead end.

The radiology community is a small one, and I felt pretty confident that I could call around to a few area clinics and find Dr. Smith, or someone who knew where he was currently employed. When I struck out yet again, I turned to the Internet. A Google search of his name and profession turned up nothing. I had exhausted every avenue I could think of. My co-workers, many of whom had tried to help me find the elusive doctor, were as stumped as I was.

If I couldn't find this man, then I couldn't sit for my boards. If I couldn't sit for my boards, then I could say goodbye to the amazing job opportunity that had basically fallen into my lap.

I was becoming increasingly stressed over the situation. I woke up one morning well aware that I only had two days left with my current employer and no hope of getting my test application approved without Dr. Smith's signature.

There was still one thing I could try. I began to pray: "God, I give up. I'm handing it over to you. I don't know where Dr. Smith is, but I know that you do. If you could please help me find him, that would be great. If not, I'll accept that this job was not your will for me."

I got dressed and made the fifty-mile drive to work. I'd give it one more day before I spoke to my boss about rescinding my resignation. I was at peace with it — mostly — although I would be lying if I said I wasn't disappointed.

I started the morning QC tests on the equipment and stood in the doorway of the nuclear-medicine suite while I waited. That spot happened to give me a view of the clinic's long hallway, and that turned out to be very fortunate, because who rounded the corner just then but Dr. Smith! I charged toward him, talking so fast I don't think he understood me at first. I told him about the events of the last two weeks and how I had been desperately searching for him.

Dr. Smith laughed at my animated account and explained that he was now working for a temp agency for doctors. He told me he had been sent to my clinic to fill in for our staff radiologist.

I returned to my office and picked up the phone to call my husband, Joey. "You're not going to believe who just walked into the clinic!" I said when he answered.

"Wow, what are the odds of that?" Joey said after I told him the good news.

I hung up the phone and noticed a movement in the doorway. I looked up to find Dr. Smith.

"Melissa, I have to leave." He handed me a piece of paper. "Here's my contact info."

"You're leaving now? Already?" I asked, confused.

He nodded. Dr. Smith explained that he had driven to the wrong clinic. That day, he was scheduled to work at our south-side location, thirty miles on the other side of town.

What are the odds, indeed?

~Melissa Wootan

An Unexpected Gift

One does not play the piano with one's fingers;
one plays the piano with one's mind.
~Glenn Gould

My grandfather married his first wife, Edith, when they were both nineteen years old. When she was twenty-one and heavily pregnant with twin sons, she bent over the oven and her apron caught on fire. She panicked and ran from the house to find my grandfather, who was out working in the fields. By that time, she was engulfed in flames. The babies were stillborn the next day. Although the doctor, my grandfather and their family tended to her in the upstairs bedroom of their farmhouse, Edith died about two weeks later.

Grandpa rarely spoke of Edith. He lived alone in their home for five years before marrying my grandmother and having a family. My father and his siblings knew nothing about their father's first wife until they were playing one day and ran through the cemetery of a little church located in the middle of their farm. There they happened upon the headstones of Edith and the twins.

That farm became a refuge for me after my father died when I was only five. This year, on his birthday, I was looking for a way to honor and remember him. It was a lovely day, warm and sunny, so I spontaneously decided to drive down to the old farm.

Once I reached the farm, I didn't quite know what to do with myself. My cousin owns it now, but he and his family weren't home. I had my two Golden Retrievers with me, and I let them run for a bit in the field behind the church. Then I decided I would visit the old church and graveyard to "look for Edith."

In all the time I had spent at that farm, I had never looked for Edith's headstone. I found the boys first — "twin sons of Foster and Edith McDonnell." Although I had always known it was there, I felt a twinge upon actually seeing it. The larger headstone was just behind the first. *Edith Little McDonnell, 1905–1926.* A white plastic flower had been placed in front of the stone — the only flower I saw in the cemetery. Apparently, someone else was remembering Edith, too.

I wandered for a while, enjoying the quiet, the sound of the birds, and the fresh air. I could see my cousin's home where Grandpa's house had once stood down the hill. I was happy to see that the new home fit in, and by closing my eyes, I could imagine the old farmhouse as it looked all those years ago. I put the dogs back in the car and prepared to leave but decided to walk to the front of the church and look over the hill one more time. Just as I did, a truck pulled in, and the man inside looked at me. I wavered, thinking I should jump in my car and run away, but then decided I had as much business to be there as anybody. So I continued standing on the steps looking out over the view.

The man came over to inquire as to why I was there. I told him I had just been exploring the old cemetery and what I was looking for. His name was Tim, and his interest was caught immediately. He walked back through the cemetery gate with me to see the headstones I had been looking for. I told him who Edith was, and we began to put some pieces together. He had known my aunt and uncle, had grown up nearby, and was lovingly restoring the old church and caring for the cemetery. He invited me in to see the progress he had made inside the old church. The inside of the building looked well cared for. An altar from the late 1800s still stood in its place.

Tim played me a hymn on the old piano in the church. I complimented him, adding that it reminded me of my grandma, who had lived in the old house down the road and used to pound out those hymns on the piano in her living room. That piano had been there when my grandma moved in, as it had belonged to Edith.

Tim turned and looked at me. That moment is frozen in my mind. He said, "I know where that piano is." I couldn't believe it. I had not thought about that piano in years.

It seems that when my cousin tore down the old house, he didn't know what to do with the piano. He knew that Tim loved music, so he put the piano on a forklift and drove over to Tim's house. Tim did not need the piano, but he refinished it, put on new keys and pads, and tuned it up. Eventually, Tim gave away the piano, and the man to whom it had been given had called him just a few months ago. He said he was moving and asked if Tim wanted the old piano back. He did not, so the man moved, leaving behind the piano for whoever moved in after him.

I couldn't believe it. The piano from the home I loved was still in existence, in a town about twenty miles away, right next to the one where I live.

I left the old church and headed straight for New Philadelphia, stopping only to drop off the dogs. Tim had said that the house was on High Street, on an alley and close to another old church. We had visited that church just a few months before; I could not believe I had been so close. I found the house and jumped from the car. I went up the steps, feeling a little foolish, not quite sure what I was going to say when I knocked on the door. No one answered, so I began to look around, and I realized the house was still unoccupied. Not knowing what else to do, I returned to my car. A neighbor was outside, so I asked if he knew anything about the owner of the house. He said the church actually owned the house and it was going to be torn down.

I walked over to the church and met the director of music. She knew about the piano. The church had tried to sell it, but the two people who had been interested had decided it was too heavy to move. Now she just wanted to get rid of it.

That piano now sits in my house. After the movers brought it to me, I sat down to play. There was an echo when certain keys were hit, and when I heard that sound, I began to weep. It was the echo of my childhood.

~Sara Conkle

Home for the Holidays

There's no place like home.
~Dorothy, The Wizard of Oz

J ust after Thanksgiving, I awoke to the sound of footsteps in the kitchen followed by the aroma of freshly brewed coffee. Home from college, my daughter, Carolyn, surprised me with a special birthday celebration beginning with breakfast in bed. On a tray adorned with fresh flowers were my favorites: an omelette, hot coffee, and a homemade muffin, along with handmade cards revealing the day's events, including "Picking out a Christmas Tree."

On the way to pick out our tree, I surprised Carolyn and myself by suggesting that we stop at Petco and look at the dogs that were up for adoption. I had been saying that I traveled too much to get a dog, and I was trying to focus on my freelance writing career, but something was nudging me to look anyway. Nevertheless, I confidently announced to Carolyn that we would not be getting a dog that day. We were just looking.

All that changed when I held tiny Ebenezer in my arms. He was a two-year-old Yorkie-Chihuahua mix and he fit perfectly in the crook of my arm as his big brown eyes stared up at me. As I cradled him like a baby and rubbed his tummy, he dozed off, completely oblivious to the chaotic surroundings.

After about twenty minutes of cuddling, I asked the 4 Precious Paws rescue representative, Julie, for more information. She shared Ebenezer's story, explaining that he had been in a hoarding situation with fifteen other dogs. They lived in a small partitioned area of a patio and, at the time of their rescue, were filthy, flea-infested, and in need of heavy medication for parasites. She added that Ebenezer was a sweet dog with a delightful personality. The more I heard and the longer I held him, the more difficult it was to let him go.

After my questions were answered, I remained curious, asking, "Ebenezer seems like an odd name for this dog, especially since he's so sweet. He's definitely no Scrooge."

"Oh, that was just the name we gave him when we rescued him a couple of weeks ago," Julie explained. "We gave all the dogs Christmas names. Jingle is right over there."

"So what was Ebenezer's original name?" I asked.

"His name," she said, "was Toto."

With that, Carolyn broke into a grin and said, "Looks like you found your dog, Mom." I had recently launched my blog called "Tales of Oz," inspired by my nickname "Oz" (for my last name — Osborne) as well as The Wizard of Oz.

As I finished the adoption paperwork, I gave Julie my "Tales of Oz" business card, complete with its yellow brick road theme. She smiled and said, "Looks like it's a match made in heaven."

And it was.

Since Toto's arrival, we have enjoyed a smooth transition, and I can't imagine my life without him. My quiet empty nest is now filled with a new energy as well as occasional barking, and my exercise routine has improved with our mile-long walks each morning. Toto is the inspiration for many of my stories as he sleeps on my lap while I write. He even has his own column in our local newspaper called, "Toto Around Town." There's no doubt in my mind that we were destined to meet — not in Kansas, but in Indiana.

And so there is a happy ending for this tiny, lovable dog. Just as

Dorothy landed in Oz in her dream, a rescue dog named Toto landed in Oz, too — Oz's lap, that is.

I'm sure Toto would agree: "There's no place like home."

~Julie Osborne

The Boomerang Bible

Coincidences are spiritual puns.
~G.K. Chesterton

One of my favorite pastimes is shopping at yard sales and flea markets. I never know what kind of treasures I'm going to find, whether it's toys for my grandkids or a blouse with the price tag still attached. But one memorable summer day, I came home with something better than a bargain — I came home with a miracle.

I was at a popular flea market in my Wisconsin hometown where I was looking for some good deals on books. When I came upon a stall filled with shelves and shelves of books I was in heaven. There were so many — big books, little books, old books, new books — but something guided me to a specific one: a compact book, with a protective cover made from a brown paper grocery bag. I smiled, thinking back to all the schoolbooks I had covered with brown paper bags as a child. It was a fall tradition, sitting at the kitchen table with scissors and tape and the bags my mother had collected all summer.

Both the spine and the front of this book had a cross drawn in red marker. I slipped the brown paper off and admired the black leather cover with "Bible" stamped in gold. It was just like the Bible I had as a parochial school student. Intrigued, I started flipping through the pages. I came to the very first page of the book — a blank page that came before the title page. There, in the shaky cursive writing of a young elementary student, was my maiden name: Judy Torgerson. It took a few seconds to sink in. This didn't just *look* like my Bible; this *was* my Bible!

My amazement quickly gave way to being mystified. Where had my book been for the last thirty or so years? What road had it traveled from parochial school to flea market?

Unfortunately, the bookseller did not have any information for me. I have warm memories of sitting at my school desk, following along as my teacher read us Bible stories. I hope that somewhere in those intervening years, the Bible helped another child's faith grow the way mine had.

My husband was initially speechless at my find. At most flea markets, he sees me coming with my arms full of finds, ready to check out, and tries to talk me out of buying most of them. But that Bible was one purchase we both agreed on. It was the best deal of my whole life. For just a dime, my Bible was returned to me.

We've dubbed it the "Boomerang Bible." I'm not letting that book out of my sight ever again! It has become a treasured family heirloom and a part of new family traditions. A few years after being reunited with my Bible, my daughter Cassandra was married, and instead of carrying a bouquet of flowers, she carried our special Bible.

~Judy Fleming

Mistaken Identity

Timing is everything. If it's meant to happen, it
will, at the right time for the right reasons.
~Author Unknown

It was a hot and humid summer Friday, and I was looking forward to the weekend. I had only managed to get one new customer for my parcel delivery service all week; it was one rejection after another.

It was almost 5:00 p.m. but I decided to make one more sales call.

Hmm, a book distribution warehouse. Yes, that would be a good prospect, as they must send out a lot of parcels each week, I thought to myself. I walked along the driveway to the side of an old house that had been converted into an office. I could see their warehouse at the rear. Putting on my brightest smile, I asked to see the dispatch manager, only to be told, "Bob is away sick today. Can you come back Monday?"

I was there Monday at 9. A large truck was blocking the driveway, so I went through the front door instead of going directly to the warehouse.

I was greeted by the receptionist. "Good morning, how can I help you?"

"I've come to see Bob in dispatch," I answered.

"Oh, I'm so sorry, but Bob is still away sick," she replied. "Perhaps you could speak to our general manager, Claude?"

"Oh, yes, thank you, that would be great." I waited a few minutes until a charming French gentleman emerged from his office and ushered me in.

"Good morning," he said in his rather pronounced French accent.

"Good morning to you, *bonjour*," I replied with my schoolgirl French, and my brightest smile. I was mentally rehearsing my sales pitch, thinking of all the reasons why Claude's company should use our superior parcel delivery services.

"Well, thank you for coming. Tell me, what do you like reading?"

This was a bit different, but I guessed publishing types had their own way of doing things. I had adored reading since I was a small child, so I was happy to chat with him about books. "Well, I do like crime and biographies, even some science fiction."

I was very polite and had always been taught never to interrupt, but I did wonder what this had to do with parcel delivery logistics.

"Where did you go to school?" *Oh, well,* I thought, *I will just humor him for a little longer, and then go for the sales pitch!*

"Can you sell?" *Well, if you just give me the chance, I will show you our wonderful deal on parcel delivery.*

"You know, the book trade is addictive. Once you get that printer's ink into your blood, it will never let you go."

Oh dear, where is this all going? When will I get the chance to tell him about our excellent parcel delivery service, great prices, quantity discounts and, of course, my company's superior reliability? This has to be the strangest sales call I have ever made!

Claude asked me many more questions, and I politely answered all of them.

Still rather confused, and not knowing quite when I should start telling Claude about our wonderful delivery service, he opened his diary and asked me if I could come back Friday morning. I thought, *Maybe he is expecting Bob to be back at work by then.* Of course, I agreed.

"Second interview!" stated Claude with his lovely French accent.

"Oh, but I didn't come about a job. I just wanted to talk to you about our parcel delivery service!"

At that moment, Claude and I finally realized that all the while we had completely misunderstood each other.

"Oh, so your name is not Jacquie?"

"No, it's Fay."

"*Mon Dieu*, I am so sorry. I thought you had come for the interview. Please forgive me."

"Oh, that's quite alright. I have always loved books and would absolutely love the opportunity to work here."

And so began my thirty-year career in bookselling and publishing!

Yes, the love of the written word and printer's ink continue to course through my very being to this day.

Was this meant to be? Yes, I believe it was!

~Fay Peterson

An Abundant Blessing of Watermelons

*Accept the things to which fate binds you, and love
the people with whom fate brings you together,
but do so with all your heart.*
~Marcus Aurelius

I was driving down the highway, in the left lane, when I felt a sudden urge to get off at the next exit. Something told me that I needed to visit my favorite thrift store. When I got this kind of feeling, I almost always discovered a treasure.

As I made my way through the store, I noticed a giant wicker basket that was hidden behind various odds and ends. After some pulling and maneuvering, I was able to extract it and open the lid, finding an abundance of watermelon plasticware. Inside were watermelon plates, cups, sauce containers, pitchers for tea and lemonade, and baskets to hold food or carry dishes. All of this, perhaps more than 100 pieces, was wedged into this gorgeous basket — everything one could need for a picnic.

I had just purchased a lake house and was looking for something quirky and simple for entertaining and this would be perfect. There was no price listed on the basket, so I went off to find a salesperson. I found one who was just returning from lunch, and when she noticed the name badge I was wearing, from a hospice, she started talking. Her mom had been one of our first patients many years ago, and she told me this was a difficult time of year for her because of the upcoming holidays. I let her know that I was a grief counselor, and I had some upcoming programming that dealt with how to cope with the holidays. I invited her to attend. We talked for a little bit longer and settled on a price of ten dollars for the picnic set, and then I made my way back to the car.

On my drive back, I spent some time thinking about everything that had to fall into place in order for all of those connections to be made. For instance, I just happened to be on that side of town, when I could have been anywhere within a fifty-mile radius. Then, I stopped at that particular thrift store and was drawn toward a bottom shelf with a basket that was partially obscured and hidden in the back. And because there was no price tag on the basket, I had to find a salesperson, and she happened to be a person who needed to talk to someone with my expertise. If I hadn't left on my name badge, she wouldn't even have known that I could help her.

Smiling, I made my way back to work, content that something amazing had just happened. I was eager to share with my co-workers about how all things are connected and how powerful that connection can be. Little did I know that the story would not end there.

The next morning, I shared the experience with my peers, and I described my treasure — the basket full of watermelon plasticware. And then I noticed a look on my friend's face — a look that went from surprise and wonder to peace all in one moment. Her mother-in-law had recently passed away, and she and her husband had painstakingly sorted and organized and donated items to the thrift store just that previous weekend. Her husband had grown up with — you guessed it — a giant wicker basket filled with watermelon plasticware, but he figured that someone else could benefit from using it more than they could.

I got chills as I understood what had happened. Because I had listened to that "message from above" — that urge — I was given an unexpected gift that was threefold: an amazing picnic set that was perfect for my new house; a chance encounter with someone who needed to receive grief support, which allowed me to be present for her in her time of sadness; and, lastly, I was able to give a gift to a friend and her husband — the knowledge that his mom's watermelon set had found a new home and would be cherished by my family for years to come.

~Jenny Filush-Glaze

Blue Eyes

*I have always believed, and I still believe, that
whatever good or bad fortune may come our
way, we can always give it meaning and
transform it into something of value.*
~Hermann Hesse

My family and I often feed the homeless in our community. It actually feels more like spending time with friends. We hug them, give them something to eat and drink, and sit and talk with them.

We hadn't been doing this too long when we met a tall, thin gentleman I refer to as Blue Eyes. His blond hair was turning gray, and his eyes were as bright and piercing blue as the summer sky. Blue Eyes smiled a lot. Even when he was crying, he would smile. He knew that what he was doing on the streets was wrong. His addictions had taken hold of him, and he couldn't pull away, though he never failed to let us know how thankful he was for us.

Blue Eyes was a business owner at one time, married to a beautiful woman. But his wife got sick, and he used all his money for her treatment. When she died, not only did Blue Eyes lose the love of his life, but he was also out of money. Then his beloved dog passed away. Sometime during all that heartache Blue Eyes turned to drugs and alcohol to numb his pain. His life became a downward spiral, he lost his home, and he ended up on the streets.

On one particular Sunday afternoon, one of the guys he shared the streets with advised us that Blue Eyes was sick and needed help getting a prescription filled. When we mentioned this to Blue Eyes, he put down his head, ashamed to make it seem that he had to ask for help.

We learned that he had esophageal cancer and various other ailments. His prescription would cost sixty dollars — an amount that he didn't have. We assured him that we would get it filled for him.

Walking away from him that day, I wondered what we had just done. As much as we loved spending time with our homeless friends, the amount of money we were spending on the food and snack bags made our budget tight. We kept on week after week, trusting that God would make sure we had all we needed. But sixty dollars extra for a prescription? I didn't see how we were going to pull that off. Something told me to just have faith, though.

We went to the pharmacy and dropped off the prescription to be filled. Because we were aware of the addictions among the population we were dealing with, we made sure to discuss the situation with the pharmacist, who confirmed that the medicine was legitimate and not associated with any type of street drug. Then he confirmed the sixty-dollar price.

We left with the confidence that everything would work out. We didn't know how or when, but we knew that God would see to it that we would be able to afford this prescription when it was ready.

The very next day, walking into work, I saw an envelope on the ground. It was folded in half and looked as though it had been stepped on a dozen times. I kicked it aside, but then I felt guilty for not picking it up, so I turned around and went back to throw it in the garbage.

As I picked it up, I decided to open it. I felt my legs go a bit numb, and I had to lean against the wall when I saw what was inside. There was only one thing in that envelope — a $100 bill.

~Michelle Blan

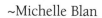

Special Delivery

I always interpret coincidences as
little clues to our destiny.
~Ann Brashares

My husband and I had been trying to start a family for several years with no luck. It was a difficult time of doctors' appointments, hormone drugs and injections, acupuncture, waiting, fighting back tears at friends' baby showers, and a growing sense of hopelessness. We spent far too much time asking the universe and ourselves, "Why?"

Around that same time, my husband visited with a woman at the school where he was being trained in massage therapy. She was known as a highly spiritual person. My husband mentioned our pregnancy difficulties and she smiled reassuringly and told him that she felt certain we would have a baby. But not soon.

When he asked her to explain, she told him she was getting a strong message from my husband's grandfather, whom we all called Grandpa Mac. He had passed away a few years earlier, and we missed him dearly. She said that quite possibly Grandpa Mac was holding the spirit of a child for us in heaven, and that he would send us this baby's spirit when he felt we were ready.

Mostly because we needed to laugh so we wouldn't cry in those days, we joked on and off about this revelation.

First of all, we weren't sure we believed in this sort of thing. A

Greater Power — maybe. But anything else was a stretch.

Secondly, Grandpa Mac had been an all-out jokester. He was the kind of man who would give you an empty box to open, watch for your disappointment, and then lead you outside to see the new car he'd bought you.

Frankly, it would have been just like him to tease us unmercifully — to know that we wanted something so badly and to say, winking, that he was waiting for the right moment to give it to us.

We even laughed (a little bit) when our expensive fertility treatments continued to fail. We'd shake our fists at the sky and say, "Come on, Grandpa Mac! Enough already!"

Eventually, we began to move on and looked into domestic adoption. It was a tough decision in many ways, and I think we grew up a lot as we weighed the decision. After much discussion, we knew we wanted to share the life we'd built together with a child who needed a loving home. It all made sense, and it was so aligned with our values that we were surprised we hadn't landed on this option much sooner.

During the period of waiting for our birthmother match, attending adoption classes, completing paperwork, raising money, and preparing for the adoption process, Grandpa Mac's "gift" faded from our minds. But we hadn't forgotten about him. We even made plans to name our soon-to-be-arriving baby boy after Grandpa's last name: McIntyre.

The evening we got the call that our son's birthmother, Amanda, was in labor, we rushed to be there for our son's arrival. We visited with Amanda, who was incredibly generous to have us there with her in the room.

As Amanda's labor progressed, a nurse came in to tell us that the birth was imminent, and the doctor on call would be delivering our son soon.

In the minutes before we met the doctor, we all discussed naming the baby McIntyre. We also told Amanda the story of Grandpa Mac waiting to bestow a baby upon us. We chuckled together at the idea.

Then, the attending doctor walked into Amanda's room and offered her hand for us all to shake. I glanced at her hospital nametag, caught my breath, and reached for my husband's arm next to me.

"Hello, I'm Dr. McIntyre," she said. The name was even spelled exactly the same.

We all stared at her like she was a ghost. Amanda and I exchanged wide-eyed looks that silently screamed, "Did that really just happen?"

Things became a busy blur after that. Our son was born less than fifteen minutes later. Amanda held him first, and then Dr. McIntyre handed my husband and me our sweet baby, his fingers curling around ours.

We'd waited a long time for this gift.

~Kathy Lynn Harris

Chapter 2

Miracles and More

Messages from Heaven

11

The Love Bugs

Faith is to believe what you do not see; the reward
of this faith is to see what you believe.
~Saint Augustine

My husband Joey and I were newly minted empty nesters. Our son Joshua had recently moved into an apartment fifty miles away. And while I was proud that my son was spreading his wings and becoming independent, I couldn't help feeling sad.

My empty-nest syndrome was compounded by the fact that we had lost Joshua's only sibling, his sister Kyley, in a car accident. As Joshua's mother, I felt it was my job to protect him from any unforeseen danger. How could I possibly do that with him living an hour away? When Joshua admitted to being homesick, it further fueled the anxiety I was experiencing.

Sensing I needed to get out of the house, Joey suggested we go out to dinner. Spending more alone time with my husband was the upside to being an empty nester, and I eagerly accepted his invitation.

As we got to the car, Joey said, "Melissa, look!" There was a ladybug on the driver's door handle. I smiled. We had nicknamed our daughter Kyley-Bug, and ladybugs now provided us a sweet reminder of our girl.

All of a sudden, the ladybug took flight and landed right in the middle of my chest. She stayed for a few seconds before flying over to Joey and landing in the exact same spot on him. And then she was gone.

"Oh, my gosh! That was cool!" I squealed.

"Yeah, it's like that ladybug went straight to both of our hearts," Joey added as he cleared his throat, trying to rid his voice of emotion.

As we ate dinner, the conversation inevitably turned to our little red visitor. We'd had several ladybug encounters in the years since Kyley died, but this one felt special, like it had been divinely orchestrated — a sign perhaps? Joey agreed.

"All right, you two love bugs, here's your check." Our waitress set our bill on the table and promised to be right back. I grabbed my phone, fervently typing away.

"What are you doing?" Joey asked.

"I'm looking for something." I answered without looking up. Finding what I was searching for, I turned my attention back to my husband.

"Did you hear what the waitress called us?" I asked Joey. "Don't you find it a little strange that she would refer to us as love bugs? I mean, we're more than twice her age, and it's not like we're acting particularly lovey-dovey," I finished, before reaching across the table to hand my husband my phone.

A picture of a ladybug sitting on a woman's finger filled the screen. It accompanied an essay I had written that had been shared on the Internet. The story documented a time, years earlier, when I desperately needed a sign that my daughter was still with us. We had walked outside our house one Thanksgiving day and were overwhelmed by hundreds, if not thousands, of ladybugs blanketing our home and cars. The title of my ladybug essay: "The Love Bugs."

"It can't be a coincidence," I told Joey.

"No, it's definitely no coincidence," my husband said thoughtfully. "I wish a ladybug would visit Joshua, too. Maybe it would help him feel less homesick."

I was giddy on the drive home. I had gone months without seeing a single ladybug, and it had been years since I'd received what I would consider a sign that our daughter was near.

Joey stopped for gas, and just as he was about to get out of the car, my phone dinged. I clicked on the screen, and a message from my son appeared, accompanied by a picture.

"You've got to be kidding me," I gasped.

"What's the matter?" Joey asked.

Nothing was wrong… everything was just fine. There on the screen was a picture of a ladybug camped out on my son's jeans. Joshua's accompanying message revealed that he had spent the afternoon in his apartment watching television. He happened to look down and was surprised to find he had a visitor.

I breathed a sigh of relief. My son may have moved fifty miles away, but I needn't worry about him. It would seem he wasn't alone after all, and neither were his dad and I.

~Melissa Wootan

My Dream of Mom

12

*Love as powerful as your mother's for you leaves its
own mark... To have been loved so deeply... will
give us some protection forever.*
~J.K. Rowling

I had just sent a group text to my siblings, and my older sister, Bernie, was the first to respond. "Tell me everything. Don't leave anything out!" she demanded. My younger sister, Francie, called then, and both of my sisters reminded me that I was next in the queue — it was my turn to have my own dream of Mom.

"Mom's going in order," Bernie said. She had already had her dream, and my three older brothers had theirs too. These dreams had been arriving in birth order, from oldest on down. After anxiously waiting since my mother's passing eighteen months earlier, my turn had finally arrived!

My dream took place in a bright, sunny room that closely resembled my bedroom. My two sisters and my grown daughter, Christina, were there, too. I was sitting up in my bed, propped up against my pillows. Mom and Bernie were sitting on opposite sides of my bed facing me, and Christina and Francie were standing right behind them.

All five of us were laughing out loud — feel-good, rolling belly laughs. I remember covering my mouth as I laughed because I knew I had not brushed my teeth yet. I was still wearing my retainers.

Mom was not sickly and frail like she was in the hospital at the end.

In my dream, cancer wasn't even on the radar. She was twenty-five years younger — a vibrant, beautiful, and strong woman. She was the mom who walked me down the aisle at my wedding and played the organ at Sunday mass.

No words were spoken in the dream, only the outbursts of laughter.

That was all I could remember. I wanted there to be something more, something I could sink my teeth into and make sense of.

At the time my dream occurred, my husband's job was in limbo. The company where he had worked for twenty-five years had thrown him a curve ball, and it was unclear what the outcome would be. The way the company was dealing with my husband was hurtful, not to mention stressful. It threatened our marriage, health, home and family. Many times, I wanted to call Mom because she always had a way of making everything all better. Her rock-like faith never wavered. I was feeling very insecure, so it felt great to laugh in the dream.

Francie's words put my dream in perspective. "Mom is helping you with all your problems." I knew she was right.

That is why this dream was a lifeline for me, an essential medicine for my soul. Hearing Mom laugh again refreshed my mind, body, and spirit. Sharing it with my sisters and daughter injected me with strength.

These mysterious communications from Mom to each of her children are things I cannot explain. For each of us to have our own dream of Mom, starting with the oldest on down, can only be described as truly divine.

Mom knew that laughter was exactly the thing I needed at the time. It was such a simple, intimate act that boosted me with endorphins, as if I had literally been laughing. The message was loud and clear from Mom: Laugh!

Francie, the youngest, finally had her dream of Mom nearly a year later, completing the cycle for all of Mom's children. Mom managed to be there when we needed her. Nothing could stop her.

~Elizabeth Anne Kennedy

13

The Teddy Bear

Sons are the anchors of a mother's life.
~Sophocles

I had saved several voicemail messages from my son on my cell phone. I don't know why I never deleted them, but I was so glad that I hadn't. I loved to play them from time to time so I could hear his voice.

I had often thought that I would like to go to Build-A-Bear and create a camouflage bear. I would dress him in boots, a beret, and a dog tag. I also wanted to copy the voicemail message that my son had left me on Mother's Day 2009 and have it inserted into the bear, so I could squeeze its paw and hear my son's voice.

Hey, Mom, it's your son. I was just calling you to tell you Happy Mother's Day and that I love you and I miss you and I can't wait to come and see you whenever I get leave. So, um, call me back I guess whenever you get this message. Um, I am on my way back to Ft. Bragg right now so I will probably be driving, so if I don't pick up the phone, then I am probably on the road. But I will call you back just as soon as I can. I love you and I miss you, and I will talk to you later. Okay, bye.

Although I had been crying a lot since the death of my son, it wasn't really my personality to cry this much. And I definitely didn't like to cry in public. It was the main reason I had put off building a bear for over a year, but now I had a coupon for twenty dollars off at Build-A-Bear and I had to go right by the store to get some printing done at Staples. Also, I figured, since it was Valentine's Day and I didn't have a guy in my life, it would be a present to myself.

I dropped off the items I needed to print at Staples and then made my way to the Build-A-Bear store, where I walked around to view all the options. A sales clerk approached me. "Can I help you with anything?" she asked.

"Yes," I said. "I have a voice recording on my cell phone that I would like to put inside a bear. Is there some way we can do that?"

"Usually we have you make the recording in person," she replied.

I explained the situation and why I was hoping to be able to use the recording on my phone.

"Just a moment," she said and walked into the back room. A few moments later, she returned and asked me to follow her. She introduced me to her manager and said that they wanted to hear the phone message so they could determine the best way to go about making the recording.

After playing the voicemail message, the manager informed me that it was too long to get it all onto one of their recording devices.

"That's okay," I said. "I would just like to get as much as we can and leave it at that."

The manager asked the sales clerk to get one of the recorders. Then she turned to me and said, "We will record it back here so there won't be any background noise."

I positioned the phone right next to the recorder and played the message.

Once the message ended, the clerk said, "Do you want to hear it? I'm not sure how much of the message it captured."

"No," I said, choking back tears. "It will be okay. Let's just put it into a bear before I lose it."

The sales clerk gave me a hug and then a tissue. After I dried my eyes, we walked back out into the store to build my bear. Thirty minutes later, I was back in my car with my new bear. I carefully removed it from the box and pressed its paw.

Hey, Mom, it's your son. I was just calling you to tell you HAVE
A GOOD DAY and I love you and I miss you.

What? Had I heard that correctly? How could "Happy Mother's Day" become "Have a good day"?

I played it again; it was as clear as could be. I knew that a glitch had changed the verbiage, but for it to have manipulated the wording as it had and to end at the perfect spot was overwhelming.

I hugged the bear and cried, thanking my son and God for the perfect Valentine's Day present.

~Kelly Kowall

14

Neverland

A mother's love for her child is like nothing else in the world. It knows no law, no pity. It dares all things and crushes down remorselessly all that stands in its path.
~Agatha Christie

I stood in the ICU in a hospital in Washington, D.C., pulling my mother's lipstick, comb and perfume from her make-up bag. She never went anywhere without make-up. And she insisted on looking good no matter where she was.

She gestured with her hand for me to come toward her. She needed to tell me something. But she couldn't speak. And although our handwriting was practically identical, I couldn't decipher a single word that she wrote.

Mom had fallen and broken her neck. She was in excruciating pain. And my husband had just left another hospital, in New York, and I needed to go home and help him. It was one of the most difficult times of my life. I was torn between staying with my mom or going back to help my husband at home.

Finally, I told my mom I would be back in a few days and rushed out of the room. I refused to say goodbye, because I couldn't imagine I would never see her again.

***

Soon after my mom's passing, my cousins went to a medium to try to learn about their side of the family. My cousins called me after their session, shocked yet excited. The person who came through their reading loud and clear was my mom, which was not a surprise to me as she was a pretty forceful woman. Keeping quiet was not her forte.

Without any clues, the medium conveyed she saw a woman in a bed with something wrong with her neck. She saw a young man, blond, with struggles (my son), and he had to go on his own journey before he found his way home. At the time, we had thought we might lose our connection with him forever. The message the medium received from my mom was that he would come back to us, and he would be okay. My mother also said she hated that I felt so guilty about her hospital experience. She said I couldn't have changed what happened. She didn't like me thinking about it, and I had to let it go.

My cynical self listened as they gave me these messages from the "beyond," and I thought, *Well, this could all just be a coincidence. So, Mom, if you're really watching over me, and these messages are from you, I need a sign.*

I had a good cry and went back to working on my young-adult novel. In the story, the protagonist was a fairy, and one of her character "quirks" was messing with electronics.

When I write, I only use the word-processing application on my computer. Every other application stays closed so that I'm not distracted. I don't turn on the Internet or any music, including iTunes.

But as I worked on my novel, typing away, a song burst from my computer. The song was "Never Never Land" from *Peter Pan* — a song about magic and dreams.

That seemed weird. Why should music be playing from my computer when I hadn't turned on any music? I checked my iTunes application. And, just as I suspected, it wasn't open. I clicked on iTunes and searched my music library, thinking there had to be a glitch. Did I ever download any songs from *Peter Pan*? I didn't think so. Of course, how can we remember every song we download, right? But "Never Never Land" was not in my personal musical library. I searched through my whole computer but I couldn't find the song in any folder anywhere.

"Never Never Land" played all the way through and then stopped. *I'm writing about a fairy that messes with computers, and she actually messes with my computer?* That was impossible. And particularly singing a song about magic and dreams. I admit I was a little spooked, but I chalked it up to coincidence.

A week later, I was to meet my cousins for dinner. Before I entered the restaurant, I thought about Mom and what the medium had told my cousins. I began to sob in the car. I missed her so much, but I still refused to believe that the song on my computer came from her. I said out loud, "Okay, Mom, if you're really here, then when I turn on the radio, *The Sound of Music* will be playing."

I turned on the radio. "Edelweiss," a song from *The Sound of Music*, was playing.

I was a singer and actress, and my mom was truly my biggest supporter — the one person in the world who believed in me and all that I could achieve, even when I didn't believe in myself. Singing was important to us, so it made perfect sense. My mother sang to me from heaven. First, through my computer via that little fairy who liked to mess with electronics, and then through my car radio. She communicated to me the best possible way that her spirit could, and in a way that she knew I loved.

~Vicki Van Grack

15

Ever Present

*Grandma, you have always believed in me, you
have always listened to me, and you have
always encouraged me.*
~Catherine Pulsifer

I t was Friday night when they called to tell me that Grandma had died. Somehow, I already knew. I had already sensed that her spirit was free; I was just waiting for the confirmation. "I'll get on a plane tomorrow. Can you pick me up at the airport?" I asked my uncle.

"Sure, I can. You're free to stay with us, too. We were wondering if you might want to offer the eulogy at her funeral. The priest told us that a family member could say a few words at the end of the service. So, we all thought of you, since you two were so close."

"Yes, I'd be honored."

The next day, my small plane bumped along the runway of the rural airport in northern Minnesota where my grandparents lived. This was home, where the red-stained earth gaped with open wounds from years of stripmining iron ore. Grandpa had been a superintendent at one of those mines and Grandma was a teacher. She was a strict teacher — the kind whom kids either loved or hated, but never forgot.

I had already lost Grandma to dementia three years earlier. This followed almost twenty years of Sunday afternoon phone calls. We talked about my college courses, roommates and dates. Later, we talked about my wedding, career and pregnancies. She was so much more than my grandma. She was my best friend and my cheerleader, too. She gave me the confidence to keep going even when things got tough.

Now I was called to write a speech to honor her legacy. As her only granddaughter, I was *her* legacy.

My thoughts traveled back to our last face-to-face visit. We were sitting on her bed as one of my toddlers crawled at our feet. Grandma said to me, "Thank you for coming to see me while I still know you." She knew that her most dreaded reality was coming true. She was so proud of her astounding intellectual gifts. She had graduated from high school at sixteen. She was one of the few women who went to college in the 1930s. She also said to me that day, "When I die, if I can, I will come back to you. I promise."

Now, I needed to come up with a eulogy that would do her justice. After settling into my uncle and aunt's spare bedroom, I told my aunt, "I'm going to take a walk to think about what I'm going to say tomorrow."

"Oh, honey, you know you don't have to speak if you don't want to."

"Yes, I know, but I want to. I'm going to walk down past Grandma's old house and think about what I want to say."

The snow crunched beneath my winter boots, and the wind whipped at my face while the bright, sunny sky offered the possibility of something greater than what the eye can see. My thoughts were somber and serious as I contemplated the structure of my speech. I paused for a moment, looking at the house where Grandma used to live. A strange truck was parked in the driveway. Grandma's fancy curtains had been replaced with ordinary blinds. Then I heard a giddy, giggling voice say, "I'm not there anymore!" My spine went rigid with shock. I turned in circles, looking around for the voice, but no one was in sight. The cheerful voice continued, "I'm right here! Now, I can be with you always! I've missed you so much."

"Grandma?"

"Yes, I am here with you always. Your life will be just beautiful, just beautiful. You have nothing to fear. It's real."

"What's real, Grandma?" But there was no response, just a feeling of unconditional love surrounding me.

This presence not only accompanied me to Grandma's eulogy the next morning, but it stayed with me through my graduate-school studies in pastoral theology, and onto a career in hospital chaplaincy. From that day forward, I have never been without hope in the reality of eternal life. In all I do, I seek to share this manifestation of unconditional love with others when they are most in need.

~Maya DeBruyne

16

Jimmie

Our brothers and sisters are there with us from the
dawn of our personal stories to the inevitable dusk.
~Susan Scarf Merrell

When my dad passed away, I was saddened of course, but I felt a sense of peace. I knew in my heart we had spent quality time together. I couldn't think of anything I had forgotten to say to him. He knew I loved him, and I knew he loved me. However, when my brother, Jimmie, passed away unexpectedly in May 2000, I felt an emptiness and guilt I had never experienced before.

My brother and I were close growing up. When I received a doll carriage from Santa, Jimmie asked Mom for a doll, too, so he could play with me as I pushed that carriage up and down the sidewalk. He named his doll Billy Boy. And we spent many mornings back then chattering as much as a five-and-a-half-year-old and a three-year-old could, while our dolls lay side by side.

One Christmas, when we were in grade school, my dad took us ice-skating. I would always show off my skills, skating backwards and doing figure eights, while my brothers would play hockey with their new sticks. That day, the ice was clear and smooth except near the edges. Jimmie stopped knocking his puck long enough to dare me to skate by a hole, seemingly about eight feet from the edge. It almost had a mirage-like appearance. I gave him a dismissive hand gesture as if it were a simple request and started gliding toward it. But as I approached, the ice cracked, and I fell through waist-deep. Jimmie's chuckles quickly turned to screams for help. My dad was able to pull me out from the other side of the hole, but Jimmie felt bad. He never again dared me to do anything dangerous.

After I got my license, we started Christmas shopping in Boston the day after Thanksgiving. It became our tradition all the way through college. We'd get lunch and then we'd laugh and talk as we hustled from one store to the next.

When my children were young, my husband's job took us away from our hometown. I missed that face-to-face contact with my brother. We saw each other at family gatherings, but it was always busy, especially at Christmas.

My brother and I would try to connect every week by phone, but then we'd get caught up with our jobs and our kids and we'd forget to talk. So when I got the call that he had died, at fifty-one, I felt guilty and stunned. It had been six weeks since we had last spoken on the phone, and I kept asking myself why I hadn't called him.

As the days went by, and the seasons transitioned from one to another, the Christmas holiday crept upon us again. I was not looking forward to going home that year. I wanted Mom to come to my house, to get away from all that was familiar, but she didn't want to travel, and my brother Eddie was in the area, too. Mom missed her youngest son fiercely, and I had to think of her, not myself. I didn't want a tree that year, but I was glad to see Mom had put up her small one on a table near the familiar manger scene that Jimmie and I set up each Christmas. I so wanted to hear his voice right then.

I remember sitting in my mom's kitchen. We were waiting for my son, also named Jimmy, to arrive. He walked in loaded with presents and gave me mine right away. He then turned around and walked out of the room. Nothing said.

I opened my gift. It was a framed letter. I thought it was from my son, but as I read it, I realized it was from my brother Jimmie. He apologized for leaving so quickly. He wanted me to know that he loved and admired me, and was so proud of me. He wanted me to comfort our mom, but he wanted me to comfort myself as well. He said he could see me when I cried. He assured me he was in no pain and that he was with our dad. He also recalled all the fun we used to have Christmas shopping when we were younger.

I found my son sitting on the couch in the living room in tears, and I quietly asked him how he got the letter. At first, he couldn't explain what had happened, but then he told me he was watching a football game the Sunday before when, all of a sudden, he was drawn to his computer. He said it felt like his favorite uncle was standing behind him, dictating one word after another with no break. He couldn't see my brother, but he could hear him loud and clear. And he didn't stop tapping the keyboard until his uncle stopped talking. My son wrote things in that letter that he never knew about my brother and me.

The letter ended with, "Even though Christmas will be a little different this year, I want you to have fun because I plan on celebrating, too, and I need to know that you are comforted by the joy I plan on delivering to you over this holiday season... You are so special to me and I love you." And he told my son to sign it... "Your brother, Jimmie."

To this day, I have the letter hanging on my writing room wall. I didn't think anything could cheer me up that Christmas, but my brother's message from heaven certainly did.

~Elaine D'Alessandro

17

Grandpa's Last Visit

My grandfather was a wonderful role model. Through
him I got to know the gentle side of men.
~Sarah Long

I had always been extremely close to my grandfather. My family had moved from Chicago to Los Angeles when I was four, but we drove back every summer to visit my mother's parents and all the assorted aunts, uncles, and cousins who still lived in Illinois.

As I got older, I was often sent back by train — the El Capitan, which I loved — to visit over the holidays or for my birthday. While I did visit with all the various relatives, my home base was always Grandma and Grandpa's two-story brownstone. I can close my eyes and still see every single detail of the place — particularly the large kitchen where Grandpa and I would sit at the big, old wooden table and dip Grandma's homemade bread into his giant coffee cup while he told me stories.

My mother had told me all about his past, but all he told me were magical stories about talking rabbits, elves, fairies and the angels that watched over kids like me. His stories always made me feel safe. At night, I would often slip out of my bed in the guest room, creep into Grandma and Grandpa's bedroom, and make a pallet with my blanket and pillow so I could sleep next to Grandpa on the floor beside their bed. In the morning, I would either awaken on the living room sofa or on the guest bed. I never asked about it. I just accepted it.

As I grew older, my visits became fewer and farther between, but Grandpa always called me at least once a month. We'd spend far too long on the phone. I'd tell him what I was doing in school, if I'd had a recent crush or a broken heart, and what I was learning or dreaming about. He always listened and gave sage advice — with a twinkle of mischief in everything he said.

I had an ancient tintype that Grandpa had given me of when he was in the cavalry. It was very old and faded, but I cherished it. In the shot, he was very young, in full uniform. He sported a handlebar moustache and was standing in front of his horse.

Grandma and Grandpa came to visit us in California twice, but they didn't like it much. While we took them to all the normal tourist sites, they preferred to stay at our house, cook and talk. Mom and Grandma owned the kitchen; Grandpa, Dad and I owned the back yard. The two men told stories while I listened, soaking up all the history and magic of bygone times.

By the time I was married and my children started to arrive, my grandparents were too old to travel. My mother went back east a few times to visit, but I was too busy with my own young family to travel, plus we really couldn't afford it. I kept in touch with Grandpa by phone and made sure that he spoke regularly with my three girls. Of course, I told them about him, and repeated the stories that he'd told me. But, somewhere along the way, the old tintype of Grandpa was lost. My girls never got to see it.

By the late 1960s, Grandpa was well into his nineties and had suffered several strokes. One night in the 1970s, I woke to my youngest daughter gently pulling at my arm in the middle of the night. I rubbed the sleep out of my eyes and asked her what was wrong. She said, "Mommy, there's a nice man in the back yard. He wants to see you."

"Honey, you're just having a dream. There's nobody in the back yard. The dogs would be barking," I replied. "Just go back to bed. There's nothing to be afraid of."

"I'm not afraid. He's nice. He's wearing funny clothes and tall boots. He has red hair and a big, curly moustache." She motioned the image of a handlebar moustache on her own face. "He called me Dolly," she added.

That got my attention. "Dolly" was the pet name my grandfather used for me. I slipped out of bed and went to the back door. I looked out and saw the Collies lying on the patio, looking at something near the garden. I could just make out a tall shadow.

I should have been afraid. I should have called for my husband. But suddenly I was enveloped in a warm, safe feeling. I stepped out into the back yard, and I saw him. He was in his full cavalry uniform, young and vibrant with his huge moustache. He smiled at me, and I walked over to him. But as I approached, he seemed to just evaporate. However, I remember feeling the warm touch of a hand on my face and soft words that seemed to be whispers on the night breeze: "I love you, Dolly."

Then the vision was gone, and I went back into the house. I woke my husband and told him what had happened, but he just laughed and mumbled something about my vivid imagination, and said it was just a dream.

At that moment, our phone rang. It was my mother crying, telling me that my aunt had just called and told her that Grandpa had passed away from a stroke. Our dogs started to howl.

I might write it off as a dream, too, except for the fact that my daughter had never seen the tintype. She'd never seen her great-grandfather at all, let alone in a cavalry uniform with a handlebar moustache. And how did she know he had red hair when he was a young man? Even I never saw that. I had to ask my mother, who confirmed it. He had gray hair all of my life, and the tintype was black and white.

This happened over four decades ago, but it's still as vivid a memory as if it happened last night. I know Grandpa came to say goodbye to me. I know he loved me as much as I loved him. And that's the way I will always remember this strange and "other-worldly" event.

~Joyce Laird

18

The Heaven We Know

I guess that's what saying goodbye is always like — like jumping off an edge. The worst part is making the choice to do it. Once you're in the air, there's nothing you can do but let go.
~Lauren Oliver

My brothers and I, along with our families, had gathered to hang out at the acreage where my father, diagnosed with Stage IV cancer, had chosen to spend his last days. It had been ten years since the last time we'd all been together in the house where we grew up, the house that Dad built.

Friends and relatives had dropped off casseroles and baked goods. The smell of comfort food filled the house. As families do, even in times of sorrow, we told stories and shared jokes. We also took turns talking to Dad as he lay in a hospital bed in front of a wall of windows looking out over the rolling plains of Nebraska. He was mostly coherent; he recognized us and could still talk, albeit weakly, but as the evening progressed, Dad started slipping in and out of consciousness.

Later, as I headed home, I figured we'd all said our goodbyes. I knew I had. I suspected Dad had, too. I braced myself for "the call" to come sometime in the night.

But it was late morning when my cell phone chirped. My aunt, who adored my dad, her big brother, told me his breathing had stopped and started. Her voice trembled as she said, "You'd better come."

I rushed back out to the farm for what I thought would be Dad's last moments. When I got there, I found him quietly lying in front of a window Mom had cracked open, saying it would allow Dad's soul to leave. The other brothers were on their way.

Once everyone had arrived, we took turns talking to Dad, holding his hand, telling him we loved him. The day wore on, and before we knew it, we once again were laughing, telling stories, and sharing humor around the hospital bed of my father, who by then was no longer responsive. Around evening, the wives and grandchildren started showing up. We could hear the kids playing in the basement, the sound of pool balls clinking together over the background of their voices. Casseroles were again popped in the oven and warmed the house with delicious smells. Still, we all had one eye on Dad. It felt like he could be gone at any moment.

But he held on. His breathing was rhythmic and shallow but steady and unfailing. As night fell, we all went home and went to bed.

The next day, my youngest brother had to fly home. My wife went to the farm to check on everyone. A couple of work issues needed my attention, but I wrapped things up in time to see my brother off. He took a few moments to say an emotional goodbye to our dad for the last time.

Suddenly, distinctly, someone said, "Don't go!" I looked around to see who had spoken. My brother still sat by the hospital bed, head hanging. The voice sounded again, anguished. "Don't go!" It was my father's voice I heard, but as I looked at him, lying lifeless but for the rapid rise and fall of his chest, I knew he couldn't have spoken. My father had crossed into a realm where communication doesn't happen with audible words.

Tears sprang to my eyes. Dad's plea reminded me of a time when I was young, and my parents invited a couple for dinner. They had a little boy who was my age. He and I had so much fun playing together that when the night was over and it was time for him to go home, I cried because I didn't want it to end. Not having experienced much life, I didn't know I would have fun times like that again.

But Dad knew there wouldn't be any more times. He knew he'd never again be in a room filled with family. His wife, his boys and their wives were laughing and talking, and the voices of the grandchildren were drifting up from the basement. That's when I realized what sheer bliss the last forty-eight hours had been for my father. No wonder he hadn't left us yet. He was in heaven on earth.

After hearing my dad's telepathic outcry, and then saying goodbye to my youngest brother, I felt drained. I needed rest. I drove home and had just lain down to stare at the ceiling when I got the next phone call. It was my wife, who'd stayed behind at the house. "I don't think he's going to make it much longer," she said. "Hurry."

I rushed back to the farm and went again into the living room where my father lay. The window was still open, and the sounds of the windy spring night sobbed in the background as I held my dad's hand. It was still hard and strong from many years of work, but so cool to the touch now. I told him I loved him, and he breathed his last breath. He left the heaven he knew for a heaven unknown.

That night, my father came into my dreams. He showed me the things we see when we die. Hundreds of thousands of lights floated, fell and moved. They were like snowflakes, constantly changing shapes. Each time they flickered, a pulse of love showered over me, shimmering with light, bouncing and flowing, filling my empty places. Dad said, "I thought I was going to miss you, but I don't. Now I'm with you all the time. I'm with everyone all the time." He told me there was no pain, no fear, and no hate. I could tell those concepts were already fading from his memory. As he left my dream, he said, "This is great!" And then I was awake, and he was gone.

The father I saw in that dream wasn't the old man who died in the home he'd built with his own hands, the man I'd come to regard as a friend, or the man who'd lived a whole life of trials, tribulations, triumphs, and joys. It was the father I knew when I was a little boy — young, vibrant, and full of exuberance and hope for the life in front of us.

The night my father died, he gave me a gift — a little peek into what awaits us when we move on from this plane. I have a good idea of the peace he felt, surrounded by his family in the last days of his life. I can't fully explain what he showed me or how it made me feel, but I will always remember those last simple words: "This is great!"

~J.P. McMuff

19

The Request

More and more, when I single out the person who
inspired me most, I go back to my grandfather.
~James Earl Jones

I woke up when I felt someone sit on the side of the bed. I pushed my pregnant body up on my elbows, expecting to see my five-year-old daughter in need of comfort or refuge from a nightmare. Instead, I was surprised to see my Italian grandfather sitting there looking at me.

"Pop! What are you doing here?" I said.

He smiled and patted my leg. "I come to tell you something and to ask a favor."

"Oh, okay," I said, still groggy from sleep. He put his hand on my rounded stomach and smiled at me.

"You will have a boy coming soon," he said.

My jaw dropped. "How do you know?" He nodded, tapped his finger against the side of his head, and smiled—a gesture he always made to assure me of his wisdom.

"Now I ask a favor since I never had a son. For you to give him my name as part of his," he said.

I could never refuse my "Pop" any favor he asked of me. "I will be happy to give him your name," I said. He nodded and smiled, then stood up. He waved goodbye and walked out of the room.

I let my head sink back onto the pillow and lay there thinking about what had just happened. It must have been a dream, I reasoned, because my grandparents and other relatives lived three thousand miles away. But I was awake, and he was there. He touched me and talked to me.

Dawn was surrendering to daylight when the telephone started ringing. I wondered who would be calling me this early as I stumbled out of bed. My aunt's voice greeted me when I answered the phone.

"I have bad news," she said. I sucked in my breath and listened.

"Pop had a heart attack in his sleep and passed away," she said. I could feel the goose bumps rising on my arms as I slid onto the chair.

"I know," I said.

My aunt gasped. "How did you know? Did someone else call you?"

I wanted to tell her about Pop's visit, but I knew it would be impossible for her to understand because I was still struggling to put what happened in perspective. "Yes, yes, the call woke me up, so I don't remember who called," I said, knowing that was plausible since my relatives usually forgot about the three-hour time difference between the east and west coast.

We talked for a few minutes and agreed it would be unwise for me to travel during the last trimester of my pregnancy, so I wouldn't attend the funeral. She said she would send me a copy of the obituary and one of the funeral cards.

I rested my head on the table, feeling a mixture of sadness at his passing and joy from his visit. Memories of my grandfather played through my mind for the next few days along with the reality of his visit to me. I knew it wasn't a dream. It was too real. I felt his presence.

When the copy of the obituary and the funeral card came in the mail, I read the brief chronicle of my grandfather's life. He was born in Sicily, immigrated to America, married, and fathered two daughters. He was a self-taught mandolin player, having learned to play by ear at an early age. His work history, retirement date and church affiliation were included.

The funeral card showed the cause and time of his death. I blinked and read the time listed once again. Pop's time of death was only minutes before I awoke to find him sitting on the side of my bed.

I did give birth to a boy two months later. His middle name is

Sebastian to honor my grandfather. And like his great-grandfather, he is a self-taught musician of a similar stringed instrument — the guitar — which he learned to play by ear at an early age.

My loving memories of "Pop" live on.

~L.A. Kennedy

20

Friends Forever

A single rose can be my garden…
a single friend, my world.
~Leo Buscaglia

How lucky I was to know Sylvia! We taught together in Los Angeles and became great friends in spite of our twenty-three-year age difference. I was in my late twenties and Sylvia her young fifties. During my divorce, Sylvia became my best friend, cheerleader, and travel partner. Sylvia's husband, Cliff, became my dear friend and partner in crime. I became the daughter they never had.

A year later, I moved to Colorado, but my relationship with Sylvia became stronger than ever. Several times a year, we traveled together or spent extended time at each other's homes. Saying our goodbyes at the airport always resulted in tears and immediate plans for our next opportunity to get together. Somehow, having something on the calendar took the sting out of the physical distance between us. My mantra was "Friends Are Chosen Family," and Sylvia and Cliff felt closer than the family I was born into.

Over the years, our relationship deepened. Sylvia and Cliff joined me for holidays and important family functions. Sylvia and I cooked Thanksgiving dinner together for approximately twenty-five friends and family members. I was the cook, and she was my sous chef. We enjoyed this tradition for many years, and we guarded our holiday time together jealously.

In December 2009, Cliff died from a heart attack. Having been married for forty-five years, Sylvia was not prepared for life without him. We spent even more time together.

In November 2012, Sylvia called to say that she needed to stay in Los Angeles for Thanksgiving. I was crushed but understood. That Thanksgiving morning, I had the worst dream ever. In my dream, her sister Charlotte called and told me that Sylvia was dying in the hospital. Throughout Thanksgiving Day, I couldn't shake the dread and sadness of the dream. I phoned Sylvia a few times, but was unable to reach her.

The next morning, my dream became my real-life nightmare. The phone rang. It was Charlotte telling me that Sylvia had a stroke at the Thanksgiving dinner table. My dear friend was in a hospital in Los Angeles. I flew to be by her side and realized that the stroke had taken a massive toll. My beautiful, vibrant, seventy-five-year-old friend was completely incapacitated. Within a few days, Sylvia was transferred to a nursing home with complete paralysis of the left side of her body.

As she tried to recover from the stroke, we were all saddened that Sylvia wasn't getting better. In fact, her health declined and she was moved to the hospital when the nursing home could no longer care for her. Then, after three long months of paralysis and illness, Sylvia was diagnosed with stomach cancer. She would not be getting any better.

The days leading up to Sylvia's passing were excruciating. While nurses tried their best to keep her physical discomfort to a minimum, she was clearly uncomfortable and in pain. One day, I sat by Sylvia's hospital bed while she floated in and out of consciousness and I gazed down the hallway, not focusing on anything. Suddenly, I saw an older Asian gentleman walking down the hallway toward me. I burst into tears as I recognized Sylvia's husband, Cliff, who had passed away three years before in the same hospital. There he was in his favorite jeans and Hawaiian print shirt, looking larger than life. I did not want to take my eyes off him because I knew he would go as easily as he came. When I finally blinked, Cliff was no longer visible. Tears fell, partly because I missed Cliff terribly, but also because his visit was a sure sign that Sylvia's time was limited.

Later that evening as I sat with Sylvia, I sensed the spirits of her mother and father outside her hospital room, looking in. Selfishly, I said out loud, "You can't have her yet."

On Sylvia's final day, it felt as if her spirit was coming and going from her struggling body. I held her hand that evening as she took her last breath. She was finally free to be with Cliff and her family members on the other side.

The next morning, I headed to the airport, sobbing as I drove. I started talking out loud, even though no one was there to hear it. I told Sylvia how bad I felt about her last few months, and how I was terrified of living life without her. I sobbed my disappointment that she would not see my girls grow up and that she would not be moving to Colorado after my retirement as we had planned. I yelled my apologies that I had been unable to save her, unable to provide the miracle that she had been counting on. I struggled to see the road through my tears and I hoped the drivers in the next lane were not watching my complete breakdown.

Then I felt a presence in the back seat as if someone were riding with me. I stopped talking. I might have stopped breathing as well. If there was someone in the back seat, what should I do? My mind raced. Should I pull off the busy freeway? Keep driving to a police station? I didn't know my way around Los Angeles, and I could tell this wasn't going to end well. I was terrified. I looked in the rearview mirror, afraid of who I might see.

Instead of a dangerous stranger, I saw the most beautiful gift anyone could have ever given me. In the back seat, sitting close together, were Sylvia and Cliff in spirit. They looked younger than when they died. Sylvia looked a little dazed and tired, but Cliff looked so content. I laughed through my tears. I knew it was preposterous, but I didn't care. I soaked up every minute of it. I thought of the movie "Driving Miss Daisy" and laughed at the oddity of my chauffeuring the spirits of my two dearest friends around Los Angeles.

Seeing Sylvia and Cliff together — both having transcended the trauma of illness and death — helped to heal the raw pain I had been carrying. They were both fine and were together in a good place. They showed me that they would always be there with me, whenever

I needed them. I felt such love and healing. I would not have to wait to be reunited with them; instead, I felt they were never leaving me.

~Ruth Anderson

Miracles
and More

Answered Prayers

21

The Cell Phone

What matters most, God was there
for me, when I needed him.
~Lailah Gifty Akita

I was coming back from a boat outing with a few veterans, part of my nonprofit that works with wounded warriors. We were motoring through the canals heading back to my dock when I received a call and answered my cell phone. Ending the call, I slipped the phone in my Army jacket's breast pocket.

We said our goodbyes, and I got busy cleaning the boat, getting it ready to be hoisted out of the water. And then it happened. I leaned over to attach a line to one of the boat cleats, and my cell phone slid out of my pocket and right into the water.

I stood frozen on the bow of the boat, watching in horror as my phone slowly sank into the murky depths until it was no longer visible. I thought about jumping in to save it, but I knew the water would be cold, I wouldn't be able to see the phone due to poor visibility, and I didn't relish raking my hands through the muck trying to feel for it. I knew that the phone must have sunk at least four to five feet before it hit bottom, and then it would have settled into a foot or more of mucky silt.

I decided I should just continue to put my boat up on the lift and then visit the Verizon store to get a new phone. After all, I'd been told that my data was being backed up, so I should be able to retrieve all the info that was on my now waterlogged phone.

When I got to the store, I was told that getting a new phone would not be a problem because I had insurance, but that the only data they backed up was my contacts and voicemail. My photos and videos were lost forever, as they resided on the SIM card that was in the sunken phone. Unless I had backed them up on my computer, they were gone.

I hadn't backed them up, and when the reality sank in, I burst out crying. There were pictures and videos on my phone of my son going through basic training and of other visits I had had with him at Ft. Bragg before he had been deployed to Afghanistan. These were pictures and videos that could never be replaced. It felt as if I were losing my son all over again.

I know the salesman felt horrible, and I could see that he was not sure what to do with this hysterical woman who was having a total meltdown. He knew that I had, just a few months ago, buried my son.

"I am so sorry," he said. "I really don't know of anyone who has ever been able to recover their phone once it went into the water. But if you can somehow retrieve it, I may be able to save the pictures and videos on the SIM card. The card can be in the water for about two hours before the images start to deteriorate."

I left the store determined to rescue my phone, even though the odds were against me. I jumped in my car and drove to see a friend who had a swimming pool. Karen would have a net, and I was definitely going to need a net if I had any hope of retrieving the phone.

I got the net and went home to lower my boat back into the water. Then I maneuvered it to where I thought it was when my phone slipped out of my pocket. My mother was standing at the top of the dock watching.

I turned to her and said, "Mom, please pray like you have never prayed before."

After saying a quick prayer myself, I dipped the net into the water until I felt it hit bottom. Then I pushed it down into the silt, scooped it through the muck and lifted up the net. I watched as about twelve inches of the brown mucky substance began draining out through the netting. The net had a few holes in it, so I was worried that I might just drop the phone right back in, even if I was lucky enough to scoop it up.

After about three-quarters of the muck had leaked out, I thought I saw the corner of a bright blue phone case. It was a miracle. With just one scoop, I had my phone. Unbelievable. I quickly swung the net around to my mother, who was also standing there in shock. She grabbed the phone from the net and started to dry it off with a towel.

I threw down the net and bounded up the dock stairs. Grabbing the phone from my mother's hands, I thanked her and told her I would be back as soon as I could. I jumped into my car and sped off to the phone store.

I ran into the store holding up the phone for the salesman to see.

"Look... can you believe it? I was able to retrieve my phone. Please tell me that you can save my pictures!"

The salesman took the phone from my hands and pulled out the SIM card. He reached for a bottle of clear solution, rinsed the SIM card and then dried it off with a cloth.

"I won't know for sure until I put the SIM card into a phone. Give me your new phone," he said.

I handed him my phone, and he put the SIM card inside and then lifted the phone to his ear. "I can hear that it's trying to load. That's a good sign."

Then he looked at the screen. I was holding my breath and trying to read his face. I couldn't tell if he saw anything or not. Then he turned the face of the phone slowly around to me, and I saw it: a picture of my son. I exhaled, and once more broke down and cried as I sank to my knees, thanking God for his blessings.

~Kelly Kowall

22

Ask the Universe for Help...

Be careful what you wish for; you may get it.
~W.W. Jacobs

Money was painfully tight. My husband had been unemployed for months, my meager salary had been frozen for years, and our rent had just gone up. I'd applied for dozens of part-time retail positions for the holiday season, hoping I could somehow fit one in around my full-time job as a magazine editor, but I hadn't received any responses.

In addition to my day job, I'm also an author. I write picture books for children, but it had been years since I'd sold a new book. One of my publishers had gone out of business, another was teetering on the verge of bankruptcy, and a third told me bluntly that they weren't accepting new submissions. Meanwhile, I had a stack of finished manuscripts that was growing in tandem with a pile of rejection letters. I had to sell more books to get more money flowing in.

Around that time, I read an article about how one man improved his life by changing his password to a mantra — something that he wanted to remind himself about multiple times per day; something that would make his life better; something that he was asking the universe for help in achieving. It seemed like it was worth a try.

I changed my password to SellMoreBook$. Several times each

day, I typed SellMoreBook$ into my computer. I hoped the universe was listening.

The universe, it seems, has a sense of humour. Within a week of changing my password, I got a part-time job for the holiday season — as a salesperson in a busy bookstore.

~Sheri Radford

23

The Eyes of an Angel

We should pray to the angels, for they
are given to us as guardians.
~Saint Ambrose

I was lost and terrified in the middle of the bustling Munich train station. An overconfident twenty-two-year-old, I was traveling in Germany without knowing the language. I fully expected to make my way through the country with a combination of grit and determination. So it came as a shock when I found myself in this dire situation.

The year was 1989, and I was traveling from Munich to Düsseldorf to meet my brother. We had organized our timing prior to my trip and confirmed our plans the night before. Now, I had no way of contacting him, because this was long before cell phones. When something like this went wrong, there was no quick fix, no simple communication. My brother would be worried sick when I didn't arrive in Düsseldorf on my train.

I tried desperately to make sense of the German signs. Speaking in English, I asked several people for help, but was met with blank stares. What was I going to do? Could I get myself out of this situation? How would I contact my brother?

I began to pray. Since childhood, I had felt a strong connection to my guardian angel, so in the midst of the frenzied train station, I focused my attention on prayer.

"Please, dear guardian angel, help me! I'm alone, scared and in way over my head. Please help me find my train. It doesn't seem anyone else here can help me but you."

Within minutes, an elderly man emerged from the dense crowd. He walked toward me with a tender expression on his face, carrying a hot dog and a soda. When he reached me, he gently extended his arms and, in German, seemed to be offering me the food and drink. I listened to him and then replied, "*Ich spreche kein Deutsch.*" ("I don't speak German.") This was one of the very few German phrases I had learned. He nodded and then offered me the food again.

Then I noticed the man's eyes. They were my grandfather's eyes! Although he had died two years before, my grandfather's eyes were emblazoned in my memory: crystal blue and shimmering with glee, kindness and the deepest love. I'd never forget my grandfather's eyes.

I should have been terrified but those eyes reassured me. I was safe, and this man was taking care of me.

I suddenly realized how hungry I was. Where did this man come from and how did he know I needed food? I gratefully accepted the hot dog and soda from him and choked out my best, "*Danke schön.*" ("Thank you very much.")

Suddenly, I felt guided to ask him this one-word question: "Düsseldorf?"

With my grandfather's smile and the shimmering blue eyes to match, this German angel waved for me to follow him. I obliged, and after rounding several corners and traveling down a few ramps, he led me to a train platform. His mesmerizing eyes guided mine to a sign that read "Düsseldorf."

With a heart full of gratitude, I repeated several times, "*Danke schön!*"

The familiar smile filled the gentleman's face again, and he leaned down and gently kissed my hand. As he drew his face upward, my grandfather's beautiful blue eyes met mine and shone with great affection. Then, with no further words, he drifted back into the crowd and seemed to evaporate.

Soon afterward, I was comfortably situated on the correct train traveling northwest across Germany to meet my brother, marveling at what had just occurred. With my belly full and my senses calmed, I drew a deep breath and said another prayer. This time, my prayer was one of thanksgiving. I prayed to my guardian angel *and* to my grandfather, thanking them for providing their love and protection when I needed it most.

~Jen Flick

Medics and a Rifle Sight

Prayer is not asking. Prayer is putting oneself in the hands of God, at His disposition, and listening to His voice in the depth of our hearts.
~Mother Teresa, Saint Teresa of Calcutta

There was an announcement in church. One of our congregation, Rob, had followed in his father's footsteps and joined the military. Now his platoon was being deployed to Iraq. Rob would be at a table in the foyer, with a list of the men in his platoon for those who were interested in "adopting" a soldier to pray for during their deployment. You could also write letters and send care packages to your adopted soldier if you liked.

After the service, people swarmed the table, eager to sign up for a soldier. When it was my turn, I asked Rob if there was a soldier who was married and had children. He looked at the list to see who was still available and said, "Matt is married and has two children."

Over the months that followed, I prayed for Matt, his wife, and children—a boy and a girl. I sent some letters and care packages based on what his wife told me he could use. I had a picture of him and his wife on a bulletin board in the kitchen, so I saw it often and was reminded to pray for him.

One day, I was passing through the kitchen. Suddenly, I heard

Pray for Rob right now! The intensity with which it was said stopped me in my tracks.

Rob? I was looking at Matt's picture on the bulletin board, not Rob's.

Yes, Rob. Pray for Rob right now!

I asked God what I was supposed to pray for, and suddenly the words came into my mind: "Lord, please protect Rob, and Matt and the others, too, but please especially protect Rob. Please keep him safe. Don't let him get hurt. Please keep them from getting ambushed. If they are ambushed, please don't let him be hurt. Don't let him or anyone in his platoon get killed. Father, if they are ambushed and are wounded, please let medics be there immediately to take care of the wounded. Let them appear out of nowhere. Let them be there, even if that isn't where they were supposed to be at that time. Provide medics for them — even if they are angels dressed like humans. Just have medics be there as soon as they are needed, even if the soldiers are shocked to see them there."

My thoughts were directed to a new line of praying. "Lord, please don't let Rob be killed." The urgency of the need for prayer was startling.

Suddenly, an image of a rifle and its sight came into my mind. *Pray that a bullet aimed at Rob's head will be deflected by his rifle sight and not kill him.*

Well, that didn't make sense. A rifle sight is so small. It would take a miracle for a bullet to hit a rifle sight and be deflected. But that voice in my head said, *Pray it anyway.*

So I did. "Please don't let a bullet aimed at Rob's head hit him like the shooter intended. Please let the bullet deflect off his rifle sight. Don't let it kill him. Please protect his life!"

I continued to pray until the inner urgency left, and my spirit was peaceful once again.

During a Sunday morning church service, we learned that Rob and members of his platoon were ambushed when they were checking out a house. We didn't have much information at first, but what we had didn't sound good. Rob had been shot multiple times.

He was taken to Germany, and then flown back to the United States where he spent many months in the hospital until he was well enough to be discharged to continue his recovery at home.

Over time, I learned what had happened in the ambush, and I knew why God had urged me to pray so specifically that day in the kitchen. It turned out that a bullet *had* deflected off Rob's rifle sight, saving him from even worse injuries. And there *had* been medics on site immediately, including one with advanced medical training that was needed to save Rob's life.

~Maureen Longnecker

25

Purim Power

*There is no surprise more magical than the surprise of
being loved. It is God's finger on man's shoulder.*
~Charles Morgan

s much as I loved single life, watching all my friends get
married, settle down, and start having babies was making me lonely. I grew up in a marriage-minded community, where we dated solely for marriage and tended
to marry young. It was time for me to find the right man.

And so I prayed. I prayed that I would find my soul mate soon,
and that I would be blessed with love, harmony and fulfillment.

On March 10, 2008, I prayed like I had never prayed before. It
was the Jewish holiday of Purim, the most joyous day in the Jewish
calendar, marked by festive celebration and partying. It's also known
as an opportune time for prayer because those who pray on that day,
taking time away from all the merriment, tend to see increased blessings
as a result. I spent hours throughout that night pouring out my heart
to G-d, asking Him for the one thing I wanted more than anything
else — to find love.

Two weeks later, I met my future husband. We were married in
September of that year, and have enjoyed nine blissful, meaningful
and beautiful years together. While one never knows the reasons for
what happens in life, I always gave a lot of the credit to my prayers
on that day.

But I didn't realize just how important those prayers were until several years after our marriage.

One day, I shared my story with my students to encourage them to find some time for prayer on the holiday of Purim. They were visibly moved.

When I came home, I told my husband what I had taught that day, and I realized I had never actually shared with him how hard I had prayed that day and how soon after he had come into my life.

He looked at me and smiled.

"You don't even *know* how quickly your prayers were answered!" he told me. "Before we met, I was inundated with offers from matchmakers who wanted to set me up. I brushed everyone off, telling them I wasn't ready for marriage. I told my parents and my mentors the same thing. I needed some more time before I started dating, and they were very understanding. Then, one morning, I woke up and decided I was ready. It was inexplicable. Nothing had changed; there was no revolutionary incident. I just decided I was ready and started the ball rolling. And out of all the girls who had been suggested to me, I chose you to meet first."

Can you guess the date this "wake-up" occurred?

It was March 11, 2008.

~Devora Adams

26

Angels Unaware

Home, the blessed word which opens to the human
heart the most perfect glimpse of Heaven, and helps
to carry it thither, as on an angel's wings.
~Lydia M. Child

Our family has lived all over the world. We've moved from Tennessee to Africa, Indiana to Australia, and it was in New South Wales, Australia, where a miracle took place that changed my house-hunting strategy forever.

It started one morning with a knock on my front door. It was our landlord announcing that we needed to move out in two weeks. He wanted the house back for himself. That evening, we gathered our children around the table and told them, "Tomorrow morning, Mommy will start looking for a new home for us."

It was a job I hated—hours of driving around in the heat, up and down streets, talking to real estate agents, inspecting one home after another, and dealing with disappointments. Two weeks? How could we find a new home and make a move that quickly? I felt it was time to pray.

I once heard a religious leader advocate that when you desperately want something from God, you must be specific in your prayers. I wondered if it would actually work. So on the eve before I started looking for yet another home, I knelt in front of my sofa and started to write.

Number One on the list, I wrote, "Granny Flat." We were expecting our grandma and poppa to arrive soon for an extended visit. We could certainly use the extra room.

Number Two on the list was a workshop. My husband was Chief Woodworker Extraordinaire. We desperately needed space to stockpile his collection of tools, random stacks of wood, and current projects.

Number Three on the list was for me. I had recently returned from a weeklong visit to the beautiful Blue Mountains. I came home wishing it were possible to walk outside any time of day and lift my eyes to the mountains in the distance.

Number Four on my prayer list was just one word: LIGHT. Our current house was spacious, but the rooms were dark and gloomy, and the windows were covered with blinds and heavy drapes. I found myself praying for a new home where light would come streaming into every room.

And then I paused. I knew I could go on and on with a more specific list, but aiming to sum things up, I very simply made one last petition. "And please, please," I prayed, "give us a home where the angels are encamped around us."

The real estate agent arrived early the following day. He drove me through two neighborhoods, showing me houses that were too big, too small, or too costly. The third stop was at Number 10 William Street, near the top of a hill in the heart of beautiful St. Mary's. As soon as we pulled into the driveway and turned off the engine, the agent realized he had left the key to the front door back in his office. So he walked around the back to see if the laundry might be open, and he motioned for me to come that way.

Walking past the garage, I noticed there was an attached extension in the rear.

"That's a Granny Flat," he told me. "Self-contained kitchenette, living room, and one small bedroom."

Beyond the Granny Flat, in the corner of the property, was yet another small building. "That's a workroom… tool shed… whatever," he mumbled.

Turning to enter through the back door, we passed a revolving clothesline in the center of the back yard. And standing just underneath where one might peg laundry in the breeze, I could see the misty, familiar haze of the stunning Blue Mountains in the distance.

Yes, the back door was open. We tiptoed through the small laundry in the rear and entered into a long, bright hallway. There were windows from one end to the other. Sunshine seemed to be pouring in from everywhere, and with it came a peace that perhaps, just perhaps, this was going to be our new home.

After viewing the rooms and the small but adequate kitchen, we left through the front door and headed back to the car. A neighbor was watering her garden on the other side of the fence; her daughter was dancing in the grass nearby. She gave a nod of hello to the agent, and he led me in their direction.

"Just bringing a lady to look through the house," he called out. And with no further introduction, he made a gesture toward the next-door neighbors and whispered to me, "Those are the Angels."

And indeed they were — Mrs. Bubs Angel and her dancing daughter, Debbie. And throughout the years that we lived at 10 William Street, they were nannies to our children, friends at tea time, gardeners in time of need, and a constant source of music, both through our kitchen window and, more importantly, in our hearts.

~Charlotte A. Lanham

27

Pray for James

For He will command His angels concerning
you to guard you in all your ways.
~Psalm 91:11

I'll never forget the day I received a message from God to pray for my cousin James. It wasn't unusual for me to get a sudden urge to pray for someone — a co-worker, a family member, or a friend. Sometimes the urge was to call that person after work, too, but this time felt different.

The first time I heard that still, small voice inside me, it was a simple command: *Pray for James.* I mentally said a quick prayer for him, and asked God to help him have a good day and take care of any needs he might have. I thought that was that.

A few minutes later, the feeling came again with much more urgency. *PRAY for James!* This time, I got a very uneasy feeling. This had only happened to me a few times — once when a friend in high school was attempting suicide across town; another time while a different friend was being rushed to the hospital with a severe case of food poisoning; and a third time when a cousin had broken her ankle and almost drowned when she fell in a pool. This time, I prayed with more fervency, and I made a note to call James after work.

Twenty minutes later, I got the urge again. But this time, it was like a voice was yelling at me. *NO! STOP WHAT YOU ARE DOING! GO OUTSIDE AND PRAY FOR JAMES!*

I mumbled, "I'm taking my break early," and rushed outside. I prayed for James as long as I could and continued praying in my head when I went inside to attend a mandatory meeting.

The meeting included my eight co-workers, plus several managers. We never interrupted these meetings with senior management, but when my phone rang I did the unthinkable — I answered it. There was no caller ID, but I knew this had to be about my cousin, so I picked up the phone and said, "What happened to James?"

I wasn't prepared for the chilling response. I heard my brother's voice grimly saying, "Don't you want to know about the rest of them?" Tears started streaming down my face. By now, the room was in complete silence as everyone stared at me. No one could believe I had the audacity not only to answer the phone, but to do it in such an unprofessional manner. I'm sure they were also shocked by my look of total horror as my brother told me that five of my family members (grandma, and cousins Jonathan, James, Josh, and Cheri) had been in a bad rollover accident, and my cousin Josh had been the only one who made it out of the car. In my mind, that meant everyone else was dead.

I ran outside in tears, frantic to get home and do something to help. My supervisor followed me out and drove me himself. I arrived home to find that all five of them were alive and had been sent to two separate hospitals. While Josh, Jonathan, and Cheri had survived with minor injuries, James had injured his back, broken a few bones, and shattered the growth plate in one of his feet. Grandma was in intensive care with multiple serious injuries and not expected to live through the week.

My grandmother is a very strong and stubborn woman who ended up proving everyone wrong. She is still alive today, twenty years later. But for several years, I questioned God. Many times, I asked him, "Why did you have me pray only for James, whose injuries weren't even life-threatening? Why didn't you have me pray for Grandma, who almost died and still doesn't have full use of all her limbs?"

A few years after the accident, I got the answer. I was finally telling James about God having me pray for him that day. His eyes got huge, and he got the biggest goose bumps I've ever seen.

"Connie!" he interrupted. "You don't know? You still haven't heard all the details of that day?" He then told me that the SUV he and the rest of the family were in that day blew a tire and went off the road, rolling seven-and-a-half times on its way down the hill next to the freeway. I had heard this before. Then he told me something new. He told me the car suddenly stopped rolling on the middle of the slope and that the witness statements said it stopped "as if it had hit a wall," but there was nothing there to stop it. At that moment James's seat belt malfunctioned and he was thrown from the vehicle that surely would have crushed him if it had finished the eighth roll. Thank God for sending his angels to stop the SUV from completing the eighth revolution! I still get goose bumps recounting this years later. At the time, I couldn't see the whole picture, but, as always, God knew exactly what he was doing.

~Connie Brown

28

Never Above a Whisper

The loveliest masterpiece of the heart of
God is the heart of a mother.
~Saint Thérèse of Lisieux

My daughter Patty writhed on the rumpled sheets. Her sweat-matted blond hair and pale face revealed the pain she endured silently. I held back my tears and faked a calm demeanor.

Patty's story reflected that of many young women. Meet a man. Fall in love. Love turns sour. Patty's courtship had spiraled down into an abusive nightmare. She decided to end the dangerous relationship rather than subject her yet-unborn baby to it.

It had led her to this maternity ward in this teaching hospital. She had arrived early that morning to have her labor induced. So far, many hours had passed with no progress.

The worst labor nurse in the history of the world attended my daughter. I privately dubbed her NurseZilla the Hun.

To each of Patty's requests to walk or turn on her side, NurseZilla the Hun would respond brusquely, "No. We have monitor lines on the baby. Just lie still."

To our great relief, after hours of NurseZilla's "no, no, nos," Super Nurse took her place. She smiled at Patty and said, "Let's make you more comfortable." She commenced doing everything NurseZilla had nixed.

Patty was checked throughout the day by the obstetrics team.

One doctor examined her and frowned. "You're not dilating as fast as we'd like. We'll hold off on the epidural for now."

Patty grimaced. "The pain's pretty bad."

"We'll keep checking you," he said, and walked out of the room.

Patty groaned and drew her knees toward her chest. I held out my hand. "Squeeze it," I urged. "Squeeze as hard as you need."

She shook her head. "No, Mom, I'd crush your hand. I don't want to hurt you." Patty gripped the bed's side rails in a white-knuckled hold instead.

Time slowed to a crawl. Shadows shifted across the walls as darkness fell. Footsteps echoed past our quiet room. The monitors tracked the vital signs for mother and baby. I wiped away the sweat trickling down Patty's face and longed to ease her suffering.

More pain-filled hours passed. Finally, a doctor examined her and pronounced, "Good news. You're dilating. You can have that epidural now."

The anesthesiologist arrived and prepped Patty's back for the spinal injection. "Sit up and hold still," the young man cautioned. He worked carefully while Patty fought to stay motionless. After what seemed an eternity, the man said, "Done. It'll take effect soon."

A relieved smile spread across Patty's face. "Wow, I feel so much better. Thank…" She slumped to the side in mid-sentence. The man caught her and laid her back on the bed. Her head lolled on the pillow.

The monitor showed Patty's blood pressure dropping steadily. I pointed to it. "Is that normal?"

Her vital signs became erratic, and the anesthesiologist called for help. A nurse appeared, checked the monitor, and made another call. The next person came in and requested more back-up. Super Nurse hurried in and laid a comforting hand on my arm. "It would be best if you stepped out. You can wait in the family lounge."

Instead, I slipped back into the corner of the room. More staff members rushed in. They ignored me as they entered "save-the-patient mode."

Every motherly instinct screamed, "Go to your daughter!" The rational part of my mind warned, "Stay out of their way so they can help her."

There was only one thing I could do for my precious daughter. I clasped my shaking hands together and prayed: "Lord Jesus, please save Patty and her child." Softly, quietly, I sent my whispered prayer past the confines of the chaotic hospital room.

The unnerving racket of clattering instruments and beeping monitors filled the air. The fast-moving medical professionals called out instructions.

I remained in the corner, whispering prayers.

After what seemed an eternity, Patty's blood pressure stabilized. Faint color tinged her cheeks. She opened her eyes blearily, and the medical team visibly relaxed.

After that, the labor and delivery progressed normally. I experienced the incredible joy of witnessing my grandson Asher's birth.

Patty looked like she'd been through a battle. But with her newborn son cuddled to her chest, she radiated absolute joy.

When the nurse took baby Asher out so Patty could rest, I smoothed the tangled hair from her forehead and thanked God that she and her new child were alive and healthy.

Patty reached out. "It's safe to hold hands now," she joked. Our fingers intertwined, and she drifted toward sleep.

"I love you, Mom. And I know you're going to stand there and pray," she murmured. "But please pray quieter this time."

"What do you mean?" I asked.

"After the epidural, I just wanted to sleep, but I couldn't. You were praying too loudly."

"Honey, things got pretty hectic when you collapsed."

Patty looked at me, uncomprehending. "Mom, what are you talking about?"

"You passed out. The staff worked frantically to save you and the baby. It got really noisy in here."

Patty's eyes widened. "I don't remember any of that. I only heard you praying super loud."

Astonished, I asked, "The beeping, the clattering, the staff yelling instructions to each other? You didn't hear that?"

Patty shook her head. "No. I only heard you praying. It sounded like you were shouting."

Realization jolted through me. God had used my prayers to get Patty's attention and tether her to life when she was drifting toward death.

And those prayers she perceived as being so loud? I'd never lifted my voice above a whisper.

~Jeanie Jacobson

Covered

*If you have a mom, there is nowhere you are likely
to go where a prayer has not already been.*
~Robert Brault

My middle son, Sam, had joined the Marines, something he had wanted since age nine. We knew there was a high probability of him serving a tour of duty in Afghanistan, yet nothing prepares a family for deployment, no matter how much information and communication they get from the Family Readiness Officer (FRO).

His deployment occurred while his father and I were getting a divorce, so emotions were already high. I felt as if I couldn't breathe, moving numbly through work and daily activities. Sam told me not to worry about him, that God is with every Marine at all times.

I believed that, but still, one of the hardest things for military families is the waiting time between each phone call, waiting to hear again the magical words, "I'm okay." All I could do was pray every day, for Sam and for all our service members.

We weren't told the exact day of deployment, but one day we received an e-mail from the FRO letting us know that Sam was already on his way to Afghanistan. We were told that each of our Marines would contact us as soon as he or she was able, but the FRO would keep us updated as possible in consideration of operational security (OPSEC). We all understand OPSEC's importance in keeping our loved ones safe.

As the days passed without word, new reports grimly announced the lost lives. I forced myself to stay focused on what I knew — that each of my children is a precious gift from God and always in His hands. These thoughts, prayers, and the supportive people around me helped me get through the days of not hearing.

Around 10:30 p.m. one night I was awakened with an urgent need to pray for my son. My heart was racing as I got down on my knees and prayed earnestly for Sam. Again and again, I petitioned the Lord to cover him and every Marine with him. Throughout the night, I prayed with fervor, asking God to move these boys into safety, to hide them from the enemies. By 3:00 a.m., I was exhausted and fell into a deep sleep, surrendering to the Lord for whatever was next.

It was several days before Sam called, and I wept in gratitude upon hearing his voice say, "Mom." Then I heard the words, "I'm okay." I asked him what had happened during that night I had felt the strong urge to pray.

Sam asked quietly, "Was it on the news?"

My heart skipped a beat. "Nothing on the news, but I was awakened to pray. Can you tell me what happened?"

He gave a soft laugh. "I knew you were praying, Mom. I felt it. I can't tell you now, but when I get back, I will. But I knew you were praying."

Months later, at work, I was again overcome with an urgent need to pray. I was attending a meeting at the time, but excused myself and went to my office to pray for the safety of Sam and his unit.

The next time Sam called, I asked him about that date and time. He laughed. "I'll tell you when I get back. I knew you were praying, Mom. I felt it."

Months later, Sam returned. I sat in the back seat with him as we drove home, wanting to hold, touch, and look closely at the young warrior who had been returned to us. He was changed — always amazing, he was now an amazing man. At a quiet moment, I asked him about those times when I'd been prompted to pray.

He faced me, inwardly seeing things that were horrible to convey.

"The first time, we were on the helicopter just coming into Kandahar province. There was a sudden firefight, and a helicopter was shot down in front of us." He paused, his eyes distant. "Our pilot pulled some pretty fast maneuvers and got us out of there.

"The other time, we were meeting up with another unit. We had a map that our guide, an Afghan, was helping us follow, but the map led us to the wrong place. Somehow, we wound up in a place where there was a dead end surrounded by the Taliban. Every one of us could feel the tension, like we had walked into a trap. But then an old man with a beard, in robes, came out of nowhere and said he could help, that he knew where we needed to be."

Sam shook his head and grinned. "Mom, this man was ancient looking! A little old man! Our guide told us not to listen to him, but the man insisted he was there to help us and could lead us to where we were supposed to be. Against the advice of our guide, we all decided to follow this man. He really insisted he had come to help us, but we didn't know how."

His eyes sparkled. "This little man started leading us out of the city, into the desert in the darkest of night. We were thinking we were really being led into an ambush now, but suddenly there was the unit we were meeting up with! We all turned to thank the old man, but he wasn't there. He just disappeared." He got an incredulous look on his face. "I knew you were praying, Mom. I know God got us out of there. I think that man was an angel."

I wiped away my tears, thankful to God for sending that man, or angel, in answer to this mother's urgent prayer — and for giving me my miracle yet again.

~Patti Wade

Pink Cupcakes

*Love and kindness are never wasted. They always
make a difference. They bless the one who receives
them, and they bless you, the giver.*
~Barbara de Angelis

I was hugely pregnant and feeling stir-crazy in our 500-square-foot apartment. I had finished my last college final the day before, and I suddenly felt lost. I had spent every day for four years studying engineering, but now all I could do was twiddle my thumbs and wait for my little boy to be born.

I needed to channel my energy into something. I decided to cook an elaborate dinner to make up for all the nights my husband and I ate pizza on the floor surrounded by textbooks.

I grabbed my keys and headed to the grocery store. I quickly found the spinach and tomatoes I needed but continued wandering the aisles. Dinner was still hours away, so I was in no hurry to go back to our little apartment. Then I thought of my younger sister, who was finishing the last exam of her freshman year. She had struggled with the transition from high school to college and was worried about her grades this semester. I wondered if I should do something nice for her.

Pink cupcakes, I heard a voice say. Startled, I jumped and looked around. The words sounded like they were spoken directly into my ear, but no one else was in the aisle.

Pink cupcakes, I thought, and suddenly I felt peaceful. I thought my sister would appreciate a treat to celebrate her last exam, and pink cupcakes seemed as good a reward as any. But why did they have to be pink? And why cupcakes? Cupcakes weren't her favorite dessert, and pink wasn't a color that she favored. But I bought all the ingredients anyway and went home to bake.

As I frosted the cupcakes and arranged five of them on a plate for my sister, I heard that voice again: *Take some to your neighbor.*

I thought of our new next-door neighbors. They were a young couple with two kids, and they had just moved in that weekend. We were planning to move out soon, so I hadn't made any effort to meet them. But we couldn't eat all those cupcakes by ourselves, so I made another plate of five cupcakes and knocked on my neighbors' door.

There was no response, and I started to feel silly. I had half expected something important to happen, what with the voice giving me those weird instructions. I shrugged and put the plate down outside their door.

Just then, the door opened. A woman with tangled hair, stained clothes, and a tired face stood there, with a baby on her hip and a nervous preschooler hugging her leg. When she saw the cupcakes, tears filled her eyes.

Her daughter's fear turned to elation as she eagerly grabbed a cupcake. "Pink cupcakes!" she exclaimed with pure joy and pranced into the other room.

The exhausted mother looked at me with deep gratitude as she told me about their move across the country after her husband lost his job. They hoped to make a fresh start after he finished his degree, but as soon as they arrived, they wondered if it was a mistake. The space was cramped, the kids were restless, and they had no friends. She told me of crying into half-unpacked boxes and worrying in bed late at night.

On this particular day, her biggest issue was pink cupcakes. They were her daughter's favorite, and she had promised that they could get some soon. Early that morning, the young girl reminded her mom of the promise. Yet the baby was fussy, and the house was a mess. The cake pan hadn't been unpacked from the boxes yet, and there was barely enough money to buy the ingredients. My neighbor was devastated that she had to ask her daughter to wait yet another day.

Then she overheard the girl praying for pink cupcakes. This broke her heart even deeper. She was completely overwhelmed with life and felt like a failure as a mom. She lacked the energy to provide the simplest treat to her sweet and patient child.

And then I knocked on the door and delivered the pink cupcakes.

I had no idea why I was making them, or whether this family would even want them. But I didn't have anything else to do, so I made pink cupcakes. My sister was grateful for the sentiment, but I quickly realized that the treat was never meant for her. The pink cupcakes were for my frazzled neighbor and her beautiful daughter, but they were also to teach me a lesson about love and helping others. I discovered that everyone around me is fighting battles that I know nothing about. I learned that I should be kind to all, even if they will only be in my life for a moment. Those pink cupcakes taught me that no matter how hard life gets, we are never alone, and we are never forgotten.

~Julieann Selden

Chapter

4

Miracles
and More

Divine Guidance

31

Trust Your Intuition

Intuition is a spiritual faculty and does
not explain, but simply points the way.
~Florence Scovel Shinn

M y wife had just left to go grocery shopping, but now she was calling. "Can you check on Michael?"

"You just left. He's fine!"

"I feel like something's wrong, honey. Just go check on him, please."

Our son has high-functioning autism. He likes to wander.

I looked in the house and around the yard — no Michael. I called his name — no response.

When our son gets upset, he'll run down the path that leads to a cove by the bay. I decided to check.

"Michael! Michael! Where are you?"

I arrived at the shore as I called out.

No answer.

"Michael, where are you?"

"I'm over here, Daddy." I could barely hear his voice.

I couldn't see him anywhere, so I called out again.

Then I saw him a few hundred feet up the shoreline.

"Michael, come here now!"

He ran farther away and then stopped.

I saw the swiftly rising tide out of the corner of my eye.

My heart raced. My son did not know the danger he was in. He needed to come back now, or we would have to swim.

"Get over here now!" I called out.

"I can't," Michael said.

"What do you mean you can't?"

"I'm stuck."

I almost didn't believe him, but as I hurried toward him, I saw that he certainly was stuck. He had decided to walk through the eelgrass and stepped into the loose, black, muddy area of the cove. He was waist deep in the muck and couldn't get himself out.

I grabbed his hands and began to pull, but he was really stuck. My footing gave way, and I slipped into the muddy water.

Now we were both stuck!

Then I realized that being next to him gave me more leverage. I could push him up and out.

I heard the sucking sound as the mud relinquished him. Success; my boy was free.

Once he was out and on semi-firm land, I told him to stay right there and not take off again. My arms ached, but somehow I managed to get myself out. My daily weightlifting had paid off.

We were covered from chest to feet with thick, black, smelly saltwater cove mud.

As we walked the shoreline toward the path, I scolded him. My voice echoed throughout the cove and woods. I looked back at the spot where we had been stuck. The eelgrass was already under two feet of water.

We walked home, rinsed off with the garden hose and went in the house. I hugged him tight as I helped him pull a clean, dry shirt over his wet head.

It horrifies me to this day to think that if my wife Cherrilynn had not obeyed her impulse to call and check on Michael, I would never have known that our son was down there alone.

~Michael Bisbano

32

The Fall

One thing you can say for guardian angels: they guard.
They give warning when danger approaches.
~Emily Hahn

My friend and I sat bareback on our horses in the middle of the arena, having just enjoyed a ride. The musky scent of the animals lingered in the breeze, which smelled delicious on a Friday evening after a long work week. We were chatting — the easy, relaxed, sometimes meaningless talk that two old friends can have.

"Do you want to try to meet up again this weekend to ride?" Melissa asked.

"That sounds good," I said and prepared to dismount. Just then, both of our horses bolted forward at top speed. I was tossed forward on Star's neck. I grabbed onto his mane and held tight. The two horses reached the end of the arena and made a sudden turn. I lost my balance, flew over Star's shoulder, and slammed into the ground. I tried to stand up quickly to tell Melissa I was okay and to see how she was. But, strangely, I couldn't stand.

I heard a man's voice in my right ear. *Get down and cover your head with your hands.* I turned to see who was there, but instead saw the two horses galloping straight toward me. In their blind panic, I knew they wouldn't see me. I simply did what I was instructed to do. I bent over my legs and covered the back of my head with my arms and hands, just like we practiced for tornadoes in grade school.

I could hear the thunder of hooves, and then felt them pound into my back. The air in my lungs was forcibly expelled like a bellows with each foot contact. I stayed that way until Melissa's voice drifted over. She was talking to the horses, trying to calm them. I sat up and observed that she had caught both of them. My fingers touched my forehead and, much to my surprise, they felt warm and sticky. I looked at them in disbelief.

Melissa was suddenly beside me.

"Are you okay?" she asked.

"My hip hurts, and I'm bleeding," I said. "Are you okay?"

"I fell off right behind you," Melissa said. "I'm fine. Let's go in the house and get you cleaned up."

Melissa helped me walk across the arena into John's house. He was the owner of the barn and lived in an apartment attached to the stable. My hip hurt when I walked, and my back felt like it was on fire. John and Melissa helped me clean up my face.

"You'll need stitches in your forehead," John said.

He sat me in a chair in his kitchen. He called my husband to let him know that I should go to the ER. As we waited for my husband Ken to arrive, we talked about what happened. Neither Melissa nor I knew what had startled the horses so badly.

"John, if you hadn't told me to get down and cover my head, I'm sure I wouldn't be sitting here in your kitchen," I said.

John and Melissa looked at me, puzzled, and Melissa corrected me. "It was just us in the arena, Amy. John was inside the whole time."

"Then who told me that?" I asked. They both looked at me worriedly, thinking I must have really hit my head.

Ken arrived at that moment. He and John carried me to the car because I had stiffened up and wasn't able to walk on my own. We were in the ER the entire night and didn't get out until it was just turning light. The X-rays showed I had a fractured pelvis. The MRI revealed a hairline fracture in my cheekbone. There were several bruises, clear as tattoos of hooves on my back, and I got stitches to close the wound in my forehead. Amazingly, I did not have a concussion.

"It would have been a lot worse," said the doctor, "if you hadn't had the sense to duck and cover. Those hoof prints would have been on your head, and it could have caused permanent damage or even a fatal injury."

I knew he was right. I had received guidance from someone outside the earthly plane.

"Thank you," I whispered to my angel.

As soon as I was healed enough to be able to get out of the house on my own, I bought a riding helmet.

"This is so you won't have to worry so much when I ride," I told my guardian angel with a smile.

Now before every ride, I invite my angel to come along. I feel blessed to be able to still climb into the saddle. My scar and the stiffness in my hip remind me always of the help I received from above.

~Amy Rovtar Payne

All in the Timing

The true adventurer goes forth aimless
and uncalculating to meet and
greet unknown fate.
~O. Henry

"I t's small but airy up here. Take your key. You can start moving your things in whenever you're ready."

With that, I handed the lady my deposit money, took a deep breath, and slipped the key into my pocket. Finally, after six years of living in a noisy, crowded, impersonal city near Boston, I was getting out. The New Hampshire seacoast offered the space, beauty, and quiet I was more accustomed to, having grown up on a small New England farm. In fact, this place looked like a big old farmhouse, and the elderly landlady who lived downstairs was as friendly, chatty, and outgoing as most folks back in the city were not. While by no stretch oceanfront property, the house was only minutes away from the water by car or bike.

This move would be a better fit, and what was there to stop me? I was living alone, between jobs, with no romantic ties to hold me. I could almost smell the crisp ocean breeze and feel the soft sand between my toes.

Back in the city, I started sorting through my things, deciding what to pack and what to toss. I collected cardboard boxes and crates from the supermarket and filled them with the things that add up to thirty years of living: books, letters, pictures, photo albums, favorite shoes, and such. I was a model of efficiency, driven by my single-minded purpose.

And then something peculiar happened. One morning, I woke up to the sight of all those packed boxes, and a sinking feeling came over me. I was getting cold feet, but I couldn't figure out why. I ascribed it to the usual last-minute doubts and fear of the unknown — normal feelings that can easily be put to rest. But instead, those feelings kept growing into a mass of qualms and misgivings. They were telling me not to move, but I couldn't understand what was happening. Finally, those powerful feelings forced me to drive back to the house in New Hampshire.

I knocked on the front door, and the little lady greeted me with a big, welcoming smile. I pulled out the key and told her I couldn't take the apartment. She looked puzzled but shrugged and said it was all right. She even returned my deposit — the same envelope of cash I had handed her two weeks earlier. She wished me well. I gave her a hug. Then I reluctantly headed back to the city without a clue as to what had torpedoed my big plan.

Back in my apartment, I stacked my neatly packed boxes in an out-of-the-way corner. I was in a strange place — following my instincts without any idea why. It was back to life as usual, only now minus the prospect of getting out of the city. I tried not to think about it — what was done was done. I kept busy and found pleasure in small things: the sparrows gathering on my porch rail; the Angora cat secretly eying them from below; the sounds of laughter from the neighbor's young children playing outside. These were small consolation, but helped to make my sudden change of plans more bearable.

The month passed uneventfully, and then I was unexpectedly offered a six-week temporary position editing a small weekly newspaper in town. I accepted the job and dug into the work, and the seacoast apartment began to recede in my thoughts.

Then, one day I heard the click-clack of heels in the hallway outside my office. Was someone stomping around in cowboy boots? The imagined boots turned out to be the leather-heeled shoes of someone working in layout. That someone was a bearded young man, about my own age, with a rather serious demeanor. He chose to wait until my last day on the job before speaking to me. With almost no preliminary small talk, he invited me out for coffee. Being unattached and with nothing to lose, I nonchalantly accepted.

We spent the evening at an atmospheric coffeehouse in Harvard Square, talking for hours as if we had always known each other. By the time we left, I had the feeling we would be friends forever. He claims he knew we were going to marry. Before long, both of these things came to be.

At last, the unexplainable reason for my not moving away was revealed. Fate or some other mysterious power had meant for us to meet. I was just supposed to wait a few weeks longer. It was clearly all in the timing.

We were married a few months later and moved outside the city, closer to the seacoast. We have spent countless hours enjoying the stunning natural beauty of the majestic New England coastline. His love of this area has only grown over the years, even exceeding my own. That old house I almost moved into has since been replaced by an imposing brick mansion. Still, whenever we drive by the place, I am reminded of how close I came to missing out on what fate had in store for me. I give my husband's hand a squeeze, ever grateful for the way it all turned out.

~Lisa Loosigian

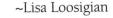

Saving Jack

Brothers and sisters are as close as hands and feet.
~Vietnamese Proverb

I was an only child until I was seven. Then my baby brother arrived, and I loved helping Mom with diapers and looking out for him when the need arose. We were great pals.

Then, I hit the teenage years. I became moody and difficult, and everything annoyed me — especially my little brother Jack.

We fought and yelled. If there was any dialogue between us, we were usually scrapping. I'd just started high school in a new neighbourhood, feeling alienated and alone. One Saturday morning, I was particularly cranky as Jack and I fought over the television. We were both sent to our rooms and ignored each other for a while.

Then, when I was walking to the bathroom, I heard a whisper. Barely audible, a croaky, little hoarse sound called my name.

"Sylvia…"

It was Jack. I usually ignored him. He was annoying. What did he want?

Then I felt something come over me.

A voice in my head spoke calmly, *Go to your brother.*

I heard myself say, "Jack?"

I re-routed toward his bedroom. It was as if someone had grabbed my hand and pulled me to his door. I don't know who it was, this invisible influence, but it took over.

When I pushed the door open, I saw Jack sitting on the bed. He

Divine Guidance | 109

held a toy guitar on his chest, but in his attempts to flip it like a rock star, the strap had gotten twisted and tight around his neck. He was being strangled and could barely croak out, "Help…"

I didn't panic or flinch. The force that overcame me drew me to my brother. The strap was so twisted and tight against his larynx that I didn't know which way to attempt untwisting it. But somehow my arms reached out, and with a few manoeuvres, I had removed the guitar.

Jack and I hugged, realizing how close to danger, to death, he had come.

We held each other.

Thinking back, I see the thick strap, so entwined and knotted around my brother's throat, and I marvel at the miracle that came to us that day.

I tried not to take my baby brother for granted after that, and I thank God every day for the divine intervention that spared him. It was a reminder that, even when we are at our worst, miracles can happen.

~Sylvia Diodati

35

Whispering Angel

*The guardian angels of life sometimes fly so
high as to be beyond our sight, but they
are always looking down upon us.*
~Jean-Paul Richter

I was twelve years old and sitting at the dinner table on a balmy, summer evening with my mother, father, and two younger brothers. There were dinnertime rules at my house when I was growing up. I was supposed to eat everything on my plate and then ask to be excused from the table.

As I took a bite of meat from my pork chop, a tiny voice seemed to whisper into my ear: *Take that pork-chop bone to Reds.*

Reds was a large Irish Setter mix who had become the neighborhood dog. He didn't seem to belong to anyone, but he lumbered into many of our yards and porches on a daily basis for love and handouts. I had no way of knowing whether or not Reds was in our yard at the time. Yet the voice was insistent.

Take the bone to Reds... NOW, the voice whispered.

There was instant conflict inside my young head as to whether or not I should risk the consequences of getting up from the table before my plate was empty.

Yet the voice continued, urging me to get up at that instant and go out the back door to the porch and look for Reds.

Pushing back my chair despite my parents' surprised expressions, I walked through the kitchen and out the back door. I did not see

Reds on the porch — but what I did see was fire! Our garage, which was about twenty feet away, was ablaze.

"Mom! Dad!" I yelled as I rushed back into the kitchen, pork chop in hand. "Call the fire department NOW — the garage is on fire!"

It seems that one of my brothers had engaged in an altercation with some older boys in the neighborhood that day, and they had threatened to "get even." Although the boys never admitted to it despite a police investigation, we believe they poured kerosene around the walls of the garage and set it on fire.

My father's car that was parked inside was not damaged because we were lucky enough to live two blocks from the fire station, and the fire was extinguished in time.

What was the whispering voice that told me to get up from the table and go outside? I will never know for sure, but I will always believe it was my guardian angel. I felt such a strong push to leave the table and risk my parents' reprimands, and that was very unusual for me.

That blaze could have spread, my father's car could have exploded, and our house could have been next. But that did not happen... all because of a whispering angel.

~Beverly F. Walker

36

The Quiet Voice

Don't go against your inner knowing.
Just don't. Trust yourself.
~Maria Erving

I was walking to my car in the parking lot when I heard a soft voice over my left shoulder: *Don't drive away.*

I spun around. Nobody stood there. I shrugged and reached for the car door. Again, the voice whispered, *Don't drive away.*

Was someone playing a trick on me? I glanced into my car — nothing strange there. My store coupons were still on the dashboard; the folded army blanket was still on the back seat. Everything seemed to be in order. Yet somehow I felt I must obey this strange and soft voice.

I walked around to the back of the car. Again, things appeared normal. The only sound I heard was the buzz of summer bugs. Down the block, I could hear several children playing hide-and-seek. All was well. I shook my head and turned to enter my car. But the voice came again: *Don't drive away.*

The hair on my arms stood up although it was a sweltering day.

I walked around the car again, looking in the windows. Then I glanced down at the ground. And that's when my knees buckled. I had to grab the car door to avoid falling. For there, under the car, I saw a child's arm — a skinny, little arm sticking out of a red T-shirt.

I must have made a sound — a gasp or something — for the child who had been hiding under my car pushed his way out. He stood in front of me, brushing the gravel from his shirt. While I stood there in complete shock, he grinned, said "Hi," and then ran across the parking lot to his friends.

If I had ignored that quiet voice, that innocent child would have been directly under the wheels of my car.

Somehow I stumbled into my car. And then I had to sit there for a long time before I could drive away.

Listen to that voice if you hear it. Listen to that wise and quiet voice.

~Pat Lay Wilson

37

The Bus

*The tie which links mother and child is of such pure
and immaculate strength as to be never violated.*
~Washington Irving

A s I glanced up from my housework to check on my two youngest children, I noticed with a start that two-year-old Sammy was missing. Minutes ago, he had been playing quietly next to his baby sister, Rose, who was sleeping in her stroller. I quickly checked the other upstairs rooms and then ran down the steps to the main floor of the house.

My husband and I and our three children had only just arrived in this large South American city the previous week to work with a group of youth counselors. The youth home where we lived was a large cement house — part of a row of houses with front doors that opened directly onto a busy city sidewalk in a somewhat rough part of town. As I ran down the stairs to the living room, I saw that the front door was open just a crack. I decided I'd better check outside first, before searching the downstairs rooms.

I quickly scanned the area for my missing boy, but he was nowhere in sight. Then I noticed a large city bus parked almost directly in front of me, and a thought came to me that he was on that bus. "That's crazy," I reasoned. "There's no way that a two-year-old could climb up on that bus, and why would he even want to?" But something inside me insisted that I must get onto that bus and look for him there.

So I climbed up into the bus and began walking down the center

Divine Guidance | 115

aisle, calling his name while the people crowded in the seats stared at me curiously. I looked thoroughly from seat to seat until I reached the back of the bus and then went out the back door. He definitely wasn't there, I thought, so he must have been in one of the back rooms of our house with some of our co-workers. I was about to re-enter the house and search for him there when again I was hit with the feeling that he was on that bus. I had to get back on that bus and look again.

This time, it was getting harder to see, as the sun was almost setting, and the light inside the bus was much dimmer. I peered anxiously into the crowded seats as I repeatedly called for him. I was again in the process of stepping out the back door when I suddenly heard his little voice behind me calling, "Mommy."

I swung around and there he was, sitting on the lap of a strange woman who was seated in the dim back corner of the bus. I reached over the crowd and grabbed him from her. I raced off that bus and into our house in a stunned daze. As I stood shaking with emotion, I glanced out the window — the bus was already gone!

I learned afterward that it was not uncommon for children — especially blond, blue-eyed children like Sammy — to be stolen and sold. We were told that we would never have found him if he had been taken.

Sometimes, I remember and I shudder with horror for what could have happened. But mostly, I am filled with a sense of awe when I think about that unseen presence that so gently but persistently pushed me to that bus and then insisted that I look again, miraculously leading me to my child in the nick of time.

~Larraine Paquette

38

Turn Around

Miracles come in moments. Be ready and willing.
~Dr. Wayne Dyer

I had just gone through the drive-through and pulled onto Sunset Road. The car was beginning to smell like fried chicken as I made my way to I-77 to head back to work. I really wasn't paying much attention to anything. Then I heard a voice say, *Turn around.*

I looked in the rearview mirror to confirm I was alone in the car. I reached down and turned on the radio to make sure it hadn't been playing, then turned it off again. I looked in my mirrors some more, but there was no traffic behind me.

When I got to the bridge, I heard the voice again: *Turn around.* It startled me and I looked at the two cars on the other side of the bridge for answers. That's when I saw the pedestrian on the other side, and realized a second later that he was standing on the wrong side of the railing.

As soon as I crossed that bridge, I turned around and went back.

I pulled up beside the man and got out, leaving my car parked in the lane. He was looking at the traffic below as I leaned on the rail next to him and started a conversation. I asked him if he was thinking what I thought he was thinking. He said he was sure jumping on the freeway wouldn't hurt for long. I asked him if he had given any thought to the driver who would hit him.

That led to talking about his battle with crack and the hold it had on his life. I told him I knew a little about that, but what was important is you can only beat it if you're here to fight it. The tools he needed for the fight were inside him.

As we were talking, two squad cars of Charlotte's Finest pulled up. The police officers quietly got out and grabbed the man as we were talking. They handcuffed him and took him away. I got back in my car and drove to work.

I have no idea what happened to that man after that. I just know he did not kill himself that day. I don't know if what we talked about meant much, but talking was better than jumping.

If I ever hear that voice again, you better believe I will pay attention.

~K. Drew Fuller

39

Miracles Happen

Miracles are instantaneous; they cannot be summoned,
but come of themselves, usually at unlikely moments
and to those who least expect them.
~Katherine Porter

I was supposed to be on vacation, but a little voice told me that I had left a chore undone at work. I couldn't figure out what it was, and it nagged at me until I gave up and decided to check in at the office on the way to visit my mother.

I was working for a small accounting firm in a strip mall. My boss shared the space with his wife Karen's software company, and quite often she brought their young daughter with her while she was working. Sure enough, when I pulled into the parking lot, little Lisa was sitting outside on the pavement, her hair shining in the sun, quite content with her coloring book and a box of crayons.

This was three decades ago, back when parents felt secure letting their children play alone outside. It was a different world — a safer world. But that day, something made me uneasy.

After greeting Lisa, I stepped into the bakery next door and purchased a rye bread for Mom and a brownie for myself. As an afterthought, I bought a black-and-white cookie for the child and took her inside the office with me to ask Karen if she could have it. She said yes, so the little girl sat down at one of the desks and started eating her treat.

Moments later, Karen and I heard a loud crash and the sound of glass breaking. We ran to the front window to see what had happened.

A driver had lost control of his car and ran up on the sidewalk, swerving into the door of the bakery—right over the spot where Lisa had been sitting. Eyes wide, we stared at each other and then looked back at Lisa, still eating her cookie.

I never did remember what chore I had forgotten.

~Bonnie Campbell

40

The Unforgotten Keys

Everyone entrusted with a mission is an angel.
~Moses Maimonides

I love going to garage sales, and on a recent Saturday morning I came upon a massive one right on the main street of my hometown. It was early, but the vast array of toys, clothing, furniture and assorted housewares on the front lawn had already drawn a small crowd. One woman was picking through a box of coffee mugs; another perused a row of neatly folded blouses laid out on a blue tarp. Nearby, a little boy played with a huge plush rabbit as his father eyed a pair of tennis rackets. I parked my car and waited for a break in the traffic to safely get out, and then began climbing the home's long, steep driveway in hopes of finding a few gems of my own.

I had gotten a little more than halfway up when a sudden, overwhelming feeling came over me, telling me to head back to my vehicle. The word "keys" flashed into my mind, and I thought perhaps in my haste to get to the bargains, I had left my keys in the ignition. Instinctively, I patted my jeans' front pocket, but the familiar bulge of jingling metal wasn't there. The word "KEYS!" resounded again in my head — this time louder and more insistent — so I stopped and turned around, fishing through my purse as I shuffled back down the driveway.

Traffic was steadily whizzing by when I reached the edge of the busy road, forcing me to pause once again at the curb. Just as I thought it was safe to dash around to the driver's door, my right hand (which was still making swirling loops in my bag) snagged something that could only be one thing—my keys! Sure enough, I pulled them out and examined the key ring as if it was some odd, unexpected curiosity, wondering what had brought on that weird and misguided bout of key-panic.

I was about to begin my second trek up the driveway when the little boy who had been admiring the stuffed rabbit came barreling toward me. His father was still on the lawn facing away from us, waiting to pay for his yard-sale purchases. The child wasn't watching where he was going and was focused instead on something in his hands. Whatever it was had him totally captivated; he kept alternately bringing it to his mouth and then pulling it away so he could peek at it, giggling. The little guy was picking up speed as he scurried down the sharp incline, headed directly into the street.

I stepped into his path, blocking his descent just as he reached the end of the drive. Startled, he stopped abruptly and looked up at me, his hands clasped tight around his treasure.

I felt the rush of air sweep against my back as a big delivery truck rumbled by, passing over the exact spot where the toddler would have been at that moment if his mad dash had not been interrupted.

"Jacob!" his father shouted just then, now also descending the driveway. He was holding the tennis rackets in one hand and waving with the other. "Wait up, buddy!"

The child turned around and spotted his dad, then smiled and ran into his arms. The man scooped up his son and carried him off. As they passed me on the driveway, the little boy held out his right hand, revealing what had so mesmerized him that he almost ran out into the bustling street.

It was a set of toy keys.

~Miriam Van Scott

Chapter 5

Miracles and More

Miraculous Healing

41

Hand of God

*It is only in misery that we recognize the hand
of God leading good men to good.*
~Johann Wolfgang von Goethe

It was the phone call that nightmares are made of. My one-year-old son had fallen from our second story and fractured his skull. I needed to get to the hospital as soon as possible to say "goodbye."

I drove like a crazy woman, sobbing, screaming, and cursing God for this tragedy. We'd named our son "Matthew," meaning "gift from God," so why was God so hell-bent on taking him away? Hadn't we been through enough? I'd had a dozen surgeries to try and get pregnant. We'd done a year of infertility treatments only to be told it was hopeless. And then, when I did miraculously get pregnant, I began to bleed and spent the next thirteen weeks in bed before delivering our son eight weeks prematurely. It felt like the only "hand of God" I knew was a hand to take away.

Matthew suffered respiratory distress syndrome, sleep apnea, croup, and bronchitis during his first year. It was only in the last few weeks before his first birthday that we'd finally believed that he would live.

And now this.

I was unprepared for the sight of my son at the hospital. His head had swollen so much that he looked like a little alien. Both eyes were completely black and blue — or, at least, the part we could see. The pressure in his brain had swollen both eyes shut and folded his little ears in half so that they muffled Matthew's hearing. The brain scans told a horrific story — nearly a third of Matthew's left hemisphere was destroyed, and with it his large and small motor skills, spatial skills, emotional centers and speech centers. If he survived — and that still was an "if" — he would probably never walk, talk or function normally.

But that didn't matter at that moment. What mattered then was my child's suffering. His writhing. And thrashing. And the screaming. I'll remember that sound until the day I die — the piercing, animal-like sound of raw, unbearable pain.

In the beginning, the only thing that stopped the awful sound was to nurse my child. Yet, within hours, they wouldn't let me. Matthew's temperature had spiked, and they feared milk in his stomach would trigger a seizure or stroke — and kill him. So, instead, I held my baby as he screamed, and I died inside. Oh, it was true sometimes I couldn't help it and gave in to nurse him. Our situation was bleak, and if my child had to die, I wanted him to have experienced some final comfort in my arms.

But he didn't die. In fact, a week later, he got down out of my husband's arms, looked up with a smile... and ran across the floor! We were astounded.

Yet that joy was not to last. Even though we'd been allowed to bring our child home, something wasn't right. A bubble like a balloon began to form over his fracture and pulse. As it grew, his movements stopped. First Matthew's right foot began to drag, then he lost the use of his right hand, and then his face drooped and stopped moving.

We took him back to the neurologist only to learn that the fracture was growing and, with each heartbeat, was destroying more of his tiny brain. He would need surgery immediately to remove the dead brain cells and close the fracture.

But this was 1991, and that kind of surgery was still rare and new. We reached out to every medical professional we knew and found a brilliant doctor who'd come from South Africa and was practicing at the local teaching hospital. Because of apartheid, he'd done many surgeries like this on people beaten during that terrible time. And, as fate would have it, when we called for an appointment, someone had just canceled. We were able to see him the next day rather than wait the usual three months.

When Matthew saw this doctor, he waddled up to him and snorted. The doctor squatted down and snorted back, and a bond was formed. Within days, we were at the hospital preparing for surgery.

It was supposed to take two hours.

Five and a half hours later, the doctor came out to reassure us. "You have to be frantic," he began. "It's okay, but it was much more involved than we thought."

The plastic surgeon was still working to puzzle Matthew's skull back together again and would take another hour or so, but the doctor wanted to share something with us.

"I don't know what your belief system is," he began. "People say that I create miracles all the time. I'm in the business of miracle-making. But they're not really miracles — just good luck and technical knowledge. But I need to tell you that a real miracle happened in there just now.

"The surgery was hard, but I wasn't alone. Something — someone — was guiding my hands to do things I never dreamed I could do. It was incredible. It was as if I wasn't even doing the surgery — that the hand of God, or whatever you want to call it, was doing it through me. I've never felt anything like it. But it was strong, and we all felt it. I don't know who your son is or what pull you might have, but I would call what happened in that operating room a real miracle."

That was twenty-six years ago.

Today, Matthew is still a miracle, and definitely a gift from God. Despite learning disabilities, horrific headaches and ongoing anxiety attacks — the legacies of his fall — Matthew is a behavioral specialist for developmentally disabled young men, dealing with the most severe behaviors and non-verbal young people because he "really understands them." He's working two jobs to pay his way through college as he moves toward a master's degree so he can continue his work with these special kids. He also volunteers at an animal sanctuary and has helped to settle new immigrants from Africa. And he hosts his own video-blog promoting veganism and animal rights. His life is about service, compassion, justice, and love.

Twenty-six years ago, I thought all was lost. Today, I realize that my son's life is a constant string of miracles, grace and heaven-guided experiences. I have a faith and certainty about my son... and about all our lives in general. For I've felt the hand of God.

~Susan Traugh

Something Powerful Happened

*It is reasonable to expect the doctor to recognize
that science may not have all the answers
to problems of health and healing.*
~Norman Cousins

My sister had undergone a hip replacement, and I had returned to our hometown to help her during her first few days of recovery. We sisters reminisced and laughed that first night, sharing childhood memories. As we talked, I noticed that Dorothy was continually rubbing her leg. When I asked her about it, she replied, "I'm worried about the circulation."

I felt her leg and gasped. The leg was so swollen that it felt as hard as wood. Now we were both concerned.

Later, as I got ready for bed, I knelt to pray for Dorothy. "Please, Heavenly Father, if there is anything I can do for my sister, please show me."

Earlier, when I had spotted a *Chicken Soup for the Soul* book, I set it at my bedside to read. I read randomly, and as I read through the fourth story—a story about healing—I was overcome with a warm sensation in my chest. And then God used the story to show me how to help my sister.

I felt apprehension the next morning. What if Dorothy thought I was just being weird and wouldn't let me help her? Tentatively, I told her about reading the story and God's directions to me. I stumbled and stammered through my explanation, telling her, "I don't have a clue what I'm doing."

She didn't ridicule me, nor look at me as though I'd soon be admitted to a psych ward. She merely smiled and said, "Let's try, Ellie."

I'd never been so grateful for my sister's easygoing attitude as I was at that moment. She trusted me and appeared to have more confidence about where we were going than I did. I was filled with a mixture of exhilaration and trepidation.

I rubbed my hands together vigorously for some fifteen seconds, and then held them an inch above my sister's injured leg. Slowly, I moved my hands back and forth, barely above her leg. Suddenly, I opened my mouth in shock, wanting to describe what I felt — yet I was momentarily speechless. Then, with a half-laugh, yet in absolute awe, I asked, "Oh Dorothy, can you feel that?"

By now, a magnificent energy was pulsing back and forth between my hands and her leg.

I looked up at my sister, wanting her to feel the same thing. At first, she indicated she could feel nothing. But within seconds her eyes lit up, and she said, "Ellie, it is so powerful, I expect to see sparks!"

We were both experiencing the same phenomenon. I was in awe! I continued to move my hands up and down the swollen leg while experiencing the incredible, pulsing energy.

Strangely, we didn't discuss what had taken place when I was finished. Perhaps it was because we were both so astounded by the entire event.

Later that evening, a friend of Dorothy's arrived at her house. The woman was in pain, having just had a biopsy done on her neck. Dorothy said, "Oh, let Ellie do this hand thing on you!"

I experienced mixed feelings about this. Was this all right with God? Would the energy still be there? Was I supposed to do this for others? I said a silent prayer and repeated what I had done for my sister, moving my hands over her friend's neck, yet not touching it. She later told my sister the amazing result: The pain disappeared!

Eighteen months later, I decided to write an account of the event that had taken place that day at my sister's. I wondered if the energy had really taken away her pain. As I wrote, I realized I needed my sister's feelings and impressions of that day, so I phoned her.

"Dorothy, please tell me what you felt that day."

She was quiet, yet I felt her reverence even over the phone. Her voice changed as she relived the moments. "Oh, Ellie, it seemed like there was something over the top of me, above me. It was very powerful, and I experienced such a feeling of love. The pain just seemed to dissolve."

~Ellie Braun-Haley

I'd Rather Die

It is during the worst times of your life that
you will get to see the true colors of the
people who say they care for you.
~Ritu Ghatourey

"**I**f I have to live like this, I'd rather die."

Dale, my husband, leaned closer over my hospital bed.

"What did you say?"

I didn't think I had spoken aloud and declined to repeat my death wish. Trips to the emergency room had become routine ever since a doctor had discovered Crohn's disease a few years earlier.

I recalled the diagnosis with complete clarity. Dr. Matthews' words had been chilling: "Crohn's disease makes your intestines die. Most people experience repeated episodes of intense pain during flare-ups, which require medical intervention. Many people undergo surgeries to remove diseased sections of bowel tissue, and some people don't survive."

You mean they die, I thought.

The doctor presented the colonoscopy pictures and used his pen as a pointer. "There can be no question about the diagnosis. It's clear from these photos you have Crohn's." The small, circular images showed inflamed, angry tissue covered with red ulcers.

Two more words from Dr. Matthews caused my hands to shake. "It's incurable."

The shock numbed my brain. His description of treatment options sounded as unintelligible as the adults on a Charlie Brown cartoon. What I did comprehend though was that the rest of my life, however long it lasted, would be miserable.

I needed to leave his office. Immediately. "One more thing," the doctor called before the door closed. "Try to avoid stress. It can be a trigger."

A bitter laugh bubbled up from my diseased belly. I muttered, "I'll be sure not to stress, Doc. Right after I cry my eyes out."

Dr. Matthews' prognosis proved accurate, and for the next several years my regimen included anti-inflammatory drugs, steroids, and dietary changes. Nothing prevented the diarrhea, cramps, and emergency-room visits. Every twinge of stomach pain spurred a frantic rush to the medicine cabinet. I gulped drugs before I knew for certain I needed them.

Three years after the diagnosis, I attended a church women's retreat. While unpacking before the meetings began, I discovered I had forgotten my Crohn's cocktail of drugs.

I perched on the edge of the bed and practiced relaxation breathing. *Stay calm*, I told myself. *Stressing out won't help*. My fingers trembled, and tears welled. Fear alone could trigger an attack.

The first day of the retreat passed uneventfully. I avoided foods that could upset my system and told the curious ladies I was dieting. The half-truth helped avoid embarrassing questions.

Toward the end of the second day, I led a small group discussion. I fought to ignore my rising panic and increasing discomfort, and focused instead on listening to the discussion. Perspiration trickled down my neck even though it was cool enough that most of the ladies were wearing sweaters.

"Rhonda, are you okay?"

The woman's question crumbled my defenses, and I admitted to not feeling well. I excused myself to lie down. In moments, the pain grew intense. I thrashed and groaned, grasped my belly, and attempted to muffle screams. I sprinted to the hall bathroom past the woman who had expressed concern, and her eyes widened at my distress.

On wobbly legs, I returned to my room, changed into a nightgown, and got in bed. Before long, a parade of ladies marched in, including Pastor Carolyn, my best friend. She sat beside me and clasped my hand, asking, "Where is the pain?"

I forgot about modesty, pulled down the sheet, and gestured frantically over my entire abdomen.

"We are not tolerating this, sister." The firm set of Carolyn's jaw showed her determination. "Ladies — let's pray."

Seeing my flushed face, one woman opened the window and let the cold, autumn air rush in. Some women quoted Bible verses, and everyone prayed while I writhed.

More than an hour passed with no change in symptoms.

"Does it hurt any less?" Carolyn's gentle question sparked guilt.

I lied. "A little."

Encouraged by my deceptive answer, all the ladies prayed aloud at the same time. The volume rose and fell like waves crashing on the seashore. A sensation originated in my stomach, traveled up my throat, and left my lips with a sigh. My spasms ceased, and overwhelming peace wrapped me in a cocoon. My moans subsided. The ladies' prayers hushed to whispers, then stopped. No one moved.

Carolyn's calm voice broke the silence. "Are you in pain? Even a little bit?"

"No," I murmured. I was so tired I couldn't keep my eyes open, and I could barely muster up the energy to express my thanks.

Carolyn smoothed my gown, straightened the sheet, and added a light blanket for good measure. "Good work, girls," she whispered. "Let's leave her to rest."

I slept through dinner and the evening meeting, not waking until the next morning. Startlingly refreshed, I felt light and peaceful. I was even hungry. When the ladies inquired about my condition, all I could do was grin through tears of joy.

I never experienced symptoms of Crohn's disease again. Not ever.

Three years passed, and I missed my one year follow-up with Dr. Matthews. I was certain I had been supernaturally healed, and I didn't want to face physical evidence that the disease might merely be dormant. Common sense eventually overcame my reluctance, and I scheduled the colonoscopy.

Before the procedure, Dr. Matthews chided me. "Where have you been? You were supposed to be here two years ago. Didn't my staff call you for an appointment?"

"I've been feeling great," I responded. I didn't have the courage to announce I was healed.

"Let's take a look," he directed. "We'll decide what to do after we know how the disease has progressed." And then I heard nothing more, as the anesthesiologist put me under.

Dale held my hand in the recovery room, giving it a comforting squeeze as I climbed back to consciousness.

Dr. Matthews appeared, shaking his head. He spoke only two sentences. "I can't explain it, but I don't see any signs of Crohn's. Come back for another colonoscopy in ten years." He exited in a flash of white.

I giggled uncontrollably, drunk with anesthesia and joy, cackling so loudly I snorted. The nurse entered and arched an eyebrow as I gasped for air between peals of laughter. She glanced back and forth between Dale and me and asked, "Is she okay?"

Dale beamed. Raising his voice to be heard over my mirth, he replied, "Yes, I think she'll live."

~Rhonda J. Dragomir

44

Caught Between Life and Death

Prayer is man's greatest power.
~W. Clement Stone

On Sunday evening, April 24th, the phone rang. I was sitting in my den reading a novel, and the sound of the phone startled me. Who would be calling me late on a Sunday night?

It was my brother James, and he didn't sound very good. I could feel my stomach tighten.

"I'm in the hospital." He took a breath. "I drove myself over here because I could feel my heart rate go really high."

"How high?"

"Around 200. But there's more. My heart has serious arrhythmia. My heartbeat is highly irregular, and it skips beats."

I could feel my stomach tightening further as a cold fear crept across my chest. "Can they do anything about it?" I asked.

"They're trying some medications, but so far my heart rate and arrhythmia haven't changed."

"Do you want me to come over?" James lived in Oshawa, an hour away from us.

"No, I don't think so. They've got me lying down hooked up to all these machines. Look, I've got to go; they want to do some more tests."

I hung up and began to think. My older brother had died at

age fifty-eight just nine months before, and it was unthinkable that something could happen to my only other brother. I sat back in my wing chair, closed my novel and shook my head. My hands gripped the arms of my chair tightly as I shook my head in disbelief.

I tried not to think about my brother and his heart problems, but to no avail. On Monday night, the phone call came that I had been dreading. My brother called me from the hospital for a second time in twenty-four hours. I wasn't looking forward to the news James would give me.

"Well, my heart rate is still really high, and the arrhythmia is just as bad. They've tried all the medications they have."

"Can't they bring your heart rate down some other way?"

He paused for a moment. "There is no other way. The doctors are concerned. If they can't stabilize my arrhythmia, it won't be very good."

"What does that mean?"

"My heart will just wear out, and that will be it."

I didn't know what to say. My skin suddenly became clammy all over, and I felt tightness in my throat. "How long can this go on if things don't change?"

"Days at most."

We both sat in silence as I contemplated what might happen.

"There's not much you can do except pray," James added. "I'm hooked up to all these heart monitors, and they're following my condition closely. But my heart rate isn't coming down, and they can't get rid of the arrhythmia no matter what they try." James sighed and lowered his voice. "To be honest, they're not optimistic."

I paused as I tried to put aside my sense of dread. "I wish I could do something practical. Should I contact Milly?" Milly was his wife, but she was a thousand miles away in Mississippi with her father who was dying.

"Don't worry. I called her. The nurse just came in, so I'll let you go."

I sat in my den staring straight ahead. I felt numb. I had this creeping fear that my brother was going to die. In nine months, I would have lost both my brothers, and I would be the only one of five in my family still alive. My mind took me back over the years to one scene after another of spending time with James — our trip to the Rockies, our summers at camp, and his wedding in North Carolina on the hottest day in history.

Then I said out loud, "God, I don't think I can handle this." At that moment, I did something I had rarely done before. I got down on my knees and began to pray. I prayed from deep inside me — from a place I didn't even know existed.

"Oh, God, save my brother. Oh, God, please hear me because I have no one else to turn to. PLEASE!" I saw a vision of my brother in a dark place with life on one side of him and death on the other. He was walking a razor's edge.

At that point, the tears began to flow. I don't know why I began to weep, but I did. I felt my whole body convulse as I knelt there. Waves of emotion swept over me like I had never known. Every part of me was focused on one thing: asking God to save my brother's life.

I don't know how long I was like that, but it seemed like hours. Then, all of a sudden, a deep peace slid over me. It was amazing. I felt I could stop praying. The tears stopped and so did the shaking. I felt a lightness come over me as if something had been lifted off my shoulders. I opened my eyes and stood up slowly.

As I dried my eyes, I glanced at the miniature grandfather clock on my desk. The time was 9:42 p.m. The number stuck in my mind for some reason, and I headed upstairs to bed. I was very tired.

The next morning, the phone rang again around 10:00. I saw the long-distance number and recognized it as my brother's hospital. My body went tense again.

"Hello." I held the phone tightly in my hand. I expected the voice of a nurse giving me bad news.

"Morning." James sounded so much better than last night.

"How are you feeling?"

"Good. You won't believe this, but the strangest thing happened last night. Just after I talked to you, the nurse came into my room with a printout tape showing my heart rate. Suddenly, on its own, it dropped from 200 to 74, which is normal. And the arrhythmia just stopped. They couldn't figure out how it happened, but my heart returned to normal all by itself. She was so excited she just had to show me."

I sat in silence for a few moments. "What time was printed on the tape she brought in to show you?"

"9:42 p.m. Why are you asking?"

"James," I could feel my hands shaking, "last night I prayed for you like I have never prayed before. When I stopped praying, I looked at the clock. It was 9:42."

~Rob Harshman

45

The Lost Heartbeat

I believe that prayer is our powerful contact
with the greatest force in the universe.
~Loretta Young

"I don't know of anything to do except prepare you for a stillbirth." Our pediatrician spoke softly with genuine compassion. "We haven't found a heartbeat for a month. We have to assume now that your baby will be stillborn." We left his office in shock.

A month earlier, my wife Sandi had been returning from lunch to her job at Baylor College of Dentistry in Dallas when a pickup truck ran a red light and broadsided her car. The impact crushed the driver's door into the seat. It knocked her across the console of our brand-new Toyota Celica and smashed her head through the passenger-door window, embedding hundreds of pieces of glass in her face and skull.

She kept telling the ambulance drivers that she was pregnant. "Yes, ma'am, we know," they kept reassuring her. They were much more anxious about what they could see. They had carefully put her in a neck brace, and had removed only the pieces of glass and debris that threatened her eyes as they sped to the hospital.

"But I'm pregnant!" she continued to wail. Perhaps she knew. Perhaps in that motherly, instinctive way, she knew that something was wrong with the baby.

It was our first. For almost five months, we had planned, dreamed, painted and bought furniture. We argued and laughed over boy and girl names. We put our hands on her tummy and rejoiced at every kick and turn. Everything was so new and wonderful. We were going to have a baby!

Then, in the blink of an eye, everything came to a screeching halt. The hospital phoned me at my job, and by the time I got to the hospital, they had realized that something might be wrong with the baby.

They continued to dig glass out of Sandi's head for a few hours, and by the time I got to see her, the pediatrician had already arrived and was one of the first to sit down with us.

"It's natural," he said, matter-of-factly, "for us to lose a baby's heartbeat after a traumatic injury like you've sustained. It should just be a matter of a day or two, and the baby should be kicking up a storm."

Oh, thank God! We were relieved. But Sandi was not to return to work. "A few weeks of bed rest," the doctor ordered. "Come see me every Monday, and…" he paused, "if anything should happen, any hour of the day or night, call me."

We expected on our first Monday visit to hear that everything was fine. But it wasn't. Still no heartbeat. The next Monday, same news.

We spent four weeks carefully doing everything right. No straining. No bending. Just resting. Sandi ignored her own pains, and quite often I caught a glimpse of her laying her hand on her tummy and whispering a prayer. I had quit laying my own hand on her tummy, quit hoping to feel the kicks that had once been so much fun.

Finally, after a month, the pediatrician delivered the bad news.

"What do you do with a stillborn baby?" I asked a co-worker. "Do you have a funeral?" He didn't feel comfortable talking about it.

"Should I buy a burial plot?" I asked my boss. He didn't know. I couldn't have those conversations with my wife. I simply didn't know what to do when my baby was stillborn.

We did nothing but wait. "Keep a suitcase ready," he had suggested, "so you can leave the house instantly. Call an ambulance if you have any excessive bleeding or pain."

A week after his final word, I was weary with our despair. I came in from work and told my wife we had to do something. We had to get up and go outside, go to the mall, go anywhere, but just go! We had spent over a month in anguish. The depression was too much. But she didn't want to go out. She couldn't fix her hair well because of the head injuries. She still had tiny scars all over one side of her head from the glass pieces.

I saw that a group of churches was having a rally on the following Saturday at a hotel conference center. "We could slip in and sit at the back. No one would pay attention to us," I assured her. "And we need the spiritual uplift. Let's go."

She agreed, and on Saturday we deliberately arrived a little late, found a place to sit without being seen, and enjoyed some good singing and a warm, spiritual environment. When the final prayer was over, we slipped out quickly.

Hurrying through the hotel foyer, a voice called out, "Danny boy!" I turned to see my childhood pastor, Paul Hosch, walking toward me. My wife didn't really know him, and I knew she was anxious to get out, so I tried to rush our meeting.

Paul was always a gentle and thoughtful soul, and I'm sure he could sense the tension in us. So he just hugged me and said the usual stuff about being glad to see us after so long a time.

Then he turned to Sandi. His smile was disarming. "Baby girl," he whispered. "I always like to pray for the girls in my church who are pregnant. Do you mind if I pray for you right here? I might not get to see you again before this baby is born."

Sandi started to cry. The pastor didn't know that our baby was going to be stillborn and we didn't tell him. We just let him pray.

He put her hand on her tummy, then put his hand on top of hers and quietly offered a sweet prayer. "Let this baby be born in perfect health," he whispered while we cried.

We thanked him and left. The drive home was quiet. We undressed and lay down, almost without a word. Our sadness was overwhelming.

In the middle of the night, Sandi woke up screaming. I lunged out of bed, grabbing the trousers I kept on the chair, aware of the suitcase waiting on the floor. I fumbled for buttons on my shirt while she kept crying, "No! No! No!"

Finally, she called, "Stop!" I flipped on the lamp. She was sitting up in bed, bawling, with one hand on her tummy. "Come!" she called. "Come here!"

I went. She took my hand and placed it on her tummy. The baby was kicking up a storm. Allison would be her name, and she was born in perfect health!

~Danny Carpenter

46

The Gift of Tears

There is a sacredness in tears... They speak more
eloquently than ten thousand tongues. They
are the messengers of overwhelming
grief, of deep contrition, and
of unspeakable love.
~Washington Irving

I remember nothing of the ride to Boston. I don't remember leaving Worcester. I don't remember arriving at the hospital. I don't know how I found it or where I parked. I don't remember walking inside. I can only surmise that I followed signs to where I thought I needed to be. I did not know where to go. No one was expecting me.

A nurse noticed my lost and shaken demeanor and asked if she could help. Words would not come out. I tried to speak, but could only cry. Despite all that I cannot recall, I will never forget that shattering feeling. My eyes welled and blurred my vision, and no words would form. She held my shoulders as if to keep me from toppling over. With extraordinary effort, I managed to say finally, "My boy." After I collected myself, I muttered that my son should be there, somewhere. After placing some calls, she looked at me soberly, placed her arm around me and escorted me to the ICU.

Eight days prior, my son Jacob had been ill for more than a week with pneumonia. Though concerned, we thought it was simply the latest ailment among our children. A teenager on the couch, moaning and groaning about going to school, is not uncharted territory for any parent.

I told Jacob to toughen up, get up and get ready, assuring him that he'd likely feel better once he got moving. His mom saw something different, though, and decided to take him to the doctor. Not long after, my wife telephoned me from an ambulance. She said when they had arrived at the doctor's office, Jacob was staggering, and his oxygen saturation level was alarmingly low. He couldn't breathe.

He wasn't just sick. He was dying. He was whisked from the office to UMass Memorial Medical Center.

Jacob's lungs had shut down and he was in critical condition. He would need to be intubated and vented in order to be oxygenated. As medical staff hastily prepared, I re-assured him that they just wanted to make him better. His fearful eyes tore my heart apart. I stroked his hair, and when he went under, I fell apart, sobbing.

The efforts to restore his lung function failed. The frustration of the doctors was palpable. As a result of Jake's particular pneumonia, blister-like areas known as blebs ruptured all over the surface of his lungs, rendering them useless. The situation was bleak. The whispered medical voices were not hopeful. I felt in my heart that Jake would die.

One evening, wearily driving home to shower and change clothes, the reality dawned on me that there would be a funeral for my son. I felt that no one knew Jacob like I did. I decided that no one was going to speak about my son except me. So I did what no parent should ever have to do. Through swollen eyes, I penned his eulogy — on my birthday.

The next morning, Jacob's doctor, with a grave look, said simply, "He needs to go to Boston. He needs to go now."

So there I stood in Boston Children's Hospital on December 13, 2014, having raced ahead of Jacob's ambulance. As he arrived, the team went to work in a whirlwind of activity. A normally calm and collected type, I was reduced to wringing my hands.

My state must have been obvious. The team leader turned from the commotion that surrounded Jacob and sat me down. He could see I was barely holding on. He put his hand on my knee and told me confidently, "*You* can only get nervous when *I* get nervous. And I don't get nervous." It was exactly what I needed to hear. Sometimes, men can communicate eloquently using precious few words.

Jacob's prognosis was poor. He grew more critical by the day. I struggled mightily. I didn't know why Jacob dying would be part of God's plan.

As days passed, though, things began to appear clearer. I experienced the deepest sense of faith, love, peace and community that I ever had. I had been thrust from my usual, comfortable role as a giver to that of a receiver. Our friends, families, co-workers and community rose together. People brought meals and gas cards. They visited, talked and prayed. They came with piles of gifts for the kids, recognizing it would be a dreary holiday. A school fundraiser was organized. Hundreds of people attended to lift our family up in time of great need and sorrow. It was overwhelming. I had come to feel as if somehow God was using Jacob's illness as a vessel for love and compassion.

Four days before Christmas, I was contacted by a fellow named Joel. Prayer requests from our church had reached him in Texas. He said he felt compelled to reach out to me, as he was blessed with what he referred to as the Gift of Tears. He explained this spiritual phenomenon as an uncontrollable weeping experienced during times of deep prayer and communion with the Lord. The flowing tears were not due to sadness or joy, but to the love of Christ manifesting itself in the Believer. He shared with me that, some years prior, his own son had been given just days to live. When he prayed over his son for those days, he experienced the Gift, which he said rarely occurs. He described it as being in the very presence of the Holy Spirit. His son recovered fully. Doctors called it a miracle. His son's name was Jacob.

Joel had my attention.

He told me that when he prayed for my Jacob, he experienced the Gift again. A man I had never met, halfway across the country, told me with joy and confidence that the hand of God was unequivocally on my son.

Then came the dramatic change. Where previous efforts had failed, there was suddenly success. The machines and medications started working, and Jacob's body was responding. Doctors used words like "incredible," "remarkable" and "miraculous." Their astonishment was genuine. From a medical standpoint, the restoration of Jake's lungs was astounding. One doctor told me plainly, "Someone is watching over your son. People don't get any sicker than he was and live." The healing had begun.

On Christmas Day, Jacob's doctors announced it was time for him to breathe on his own. They would wean him from his sedatives and attempt to wake him. Two days later, he was woken and extubated. His lungs worked. Jacob breathed.

A long and arduous recovery would follow. The sinister illness stole much from him. He had to learn to speak, eat and walk again. In late March, Jacob was discharged. A walking miracle, he arrived home to a still-lit Christmas tree and a mountain of gifts.

The greatest gift we all received that year was decidedly the Gift of Tears.

~Keith Nano

47

Traveling Angel

*Be not forgetful to entertain strangers: for thereby
some have entertained angels unawares.*
~Hebrews 13:2 KJV

It was a five-hour drive to Reno via Donner Pass from my home in Fresno, so I temporarily relocated to the neighborhood adjacent to the hospital to care for Mom. After three months in the hospital, she had already suffered a long list of life-threatening illnesses, infections and several injuries, with many transfers in and out of the ICU.

It was two in the morning and there was a new face on the ICU floor that night — a traveling nurse. I was exhausted but I made small talk about my job at a nurse staffing agency. She graciously listened as I rambled, but quickly returned to asking questions about my mom's condition.

"It's funny," I said. "I can tell when Mom gets an infection without you guys doing lab tests or taking her temperature. Sitting in her room for hours, I can see when she becomes restless and talks in her sleep, and then she starts ghost knitting."

"Ghost knitting?" the nurse asked.

"Yeah, it looks like she is knitting. Repetitive movements with her hands, twisting phantom yarn around, back and forth, over and over. Sometimes, she lifts up the bedsheet and works it into her 'knitting.' She isn't even a knitter," I chuckled. "So I call the nurses in and let them know something is going on. They call the doctor, tests are run, and before long, Mom has a new bag of antibiotics in her IV." We shared a nod of acknowledgement, two women who know the idiosyncrasies of the people they love. "After the third or fourth bout of pneumonia," I continued, "they told us they put Mom on IV steroids to keep her lungs healthy."

I stood to hold Mom's hand. After that long in the hospital, Mom sometimes lost track of time. She became forgetful after days of lying in a bed. She didn't want to hear about what was going on outside because she couldn't get out there herself. Conversation was rough during these times.

Then, things got even worse. Mom stopped talking and she began staring through me as I sat next to her hospital bed. The nights became longer as she thrashed for hours on end. After a week of that, she deteriorated further, and began crying and drooling. The worst was when the wailing started — and never stopped.

Even with antibiotics she didn't improve, and the doctors told me she was suffering from "unspecified encephalopathy." Basically, her brain was broken, and they didn't know why. There wasn't a treatment for the unspecified broken brain except to wait — indefinitely. I was left to watch over my mom as the torment continued night after night, day after day, for three weeks. They sedated her and put her on a breathing machine, which was a devastating blow.

We watched Mom's eyes flutter, her hands twitch, and her feet pull against the soft restraints they put on her so she didn't break another toe by ramming it up against the bed railing. As I stood over her, I confessed to the temporary nurse, "I've been praying over her."

"I know you have," she said with reassuring confidence. She made her way around the bed, and I moved so as not to be in her way. "You're fine. Stay right where you belong," she instructed gently.

I confessed, "I can't bring myself to pray for her to survive if this is the state she'll stay in. I certainly can't pray for the alternative. I know I have to pray, but I struggle for what that prayer should be. I just don't know what to pray anymore, not that I'll stop. I haven't lost my faith."

Mercy. In the dim light of the medical equipment, I heard that one word. It wasn't the nurse's soft voice. It wasn't voiced out loud at all. It was a supernatural voice of authority, filled with compassion. One word. I began praying over my mother, out loud yet whispered, tears streaming down my face. "Heavenly Father, I pray for your mercy. Please have mercy on her body."

Just as she wrapped up her tasks, the nurse looked at me. "I've seen this before," she said. "It's called steroid psychosis. They have your mom on a high dose of steroids. When you see the neurologist, ask him about it." She left the room.

I left the hospital shortly thereafter. I would sleep a few hours and then return to try to catch the neurologist on rounds. Deep in thought, I realized I forgot to get the nurse's name. That was unusual for me, but I was tired.

As I made my way back to the hospital early in the morning, the sun was coming up, but the light was still gray, much like my mood. Trying to track down one of her many doctors was usually close to impossible, even when "urgent." But I had to try.

I headed up the elevator, called through to the nurses' station for permission to enter the ICU, and walked through the automatic double doors. As I rounded the corner, I saw a man examining her chart. I introduced myself. He identified himself as the neurologist. Dumbfounded and stammering, careful not to reveal my source, I asked if he felt there was any merit to "something I heard" about steroid psychosis.

"Your mom isn't on any steroids," he replied flatly. I pleaded with him to double check since I had been told they put her on them weeks ago for her recurring pneumonia. He searched through the two long pages of medications and found it. There was unmistakable shock on his face. "That's a long time to be on a high dose of steroids. We will begin tapering down her dosage today."

Within a week, they took her off the sedatives and pulled out the breathing tube. The following week she improved more. Five weeks after my conversation with that neurologist, my mom looked up from her bed and finally saw me.

To my knowledge, that nurse never again worked in the ICU after that one night.

I inquired about her, but no one seemed to know who I was describing. Not surprising. In their minds, she was just a traveling nurse. In my heart, though, I knew she was a traveling angel.

~LJ Weyant

48

It Happened One New Year's Eve

Miracles happen to those who believe in them.
~Bernard Berenson

My eighteen-year-old daughter Olivia and I were dining at a local restaurant for the first time all year, courtesy of a gift card I'd received from work for a performance achievement. We were seated in the corner with only one table as a neighbour. A couple in their sixties came in and were seated there when we were about halfway through our meal.

When we rose to leave, the lady, observing that Olivia was likely a cancer patient, said, "Hello, how are you, dear? How are things coming along for you?"

"I'm doing okay," said Olivia.

"I've been where you are," said the lady.

"Oh?" I asked. Olivia told her that she had osteosarcoma and would have an operation the next week to have a bone in her arm replaced with a metal rod.

The lady tapped her arm. "This one here," she said. "I have two metal rods. Osteosarcoma for me, too."

We had not met anyone with osteosarcoma since we began this journey in September, and here we were on New Year's Eve in a restaurant we hardly ever went to, meeting this beautiful person who was so willing to share.

"Can I ask when you were diagnosed?" I said.

She replied, "Fourteen years ago, and I'm still cancer-free." Olivia's face lit up like a Christmas tree.

We exchanged names, and the lady shared more of her story and wished Olivia much success with her surgery the following week.

"God bless you for taking the time to speak to us and for sharing," I said with a lump in my throat.

"You're so welcome," she replied. "Have a wonderful year."

Olivia and I walked toward the car, both of us in a state of disbelief.

"I will remember this moment for the rest of my life," I said to her.

"Me, too." She said with a smile. "Me, too."

My daughter had surgery on January 6th. The tumour was removed in its entirety. When the pathology was done, it was determined that it was 100% necrosis, meaning it was 100% dead cancer cells. The surgeon and my daughter's oncologist said it was the first time in both their careers that they had ever experienced this in an osteosarcoma patient. Her surgeon proclaimed it a miracle.

~Nancy Barter-Billard

Miracles
and More

Divine Timing

The Call

Let gratitude be the pillow upon which you kneel to say your nightly prayer. And let faith be the bridge you build to overcome evil and welcome good.
~Maya Angelou

My mother was waiting for me at the bus stop. I was a freshman and she hadn't picked me up in years, so I knew something was wrong. She hugged me tightly, told me to get in the car, and told one of my classmates, who was also my neighbor, to get in as well. My mom drove us the four short blocks home, but those four blocks seemed to last a lifetime. She told us something had happened, and from the way she choked up on the words, I could feel her fright and sorrow.

"The World Trade Center has been hit by a plane," she managed to say. I thought something had suddenly forced all of the air out of the car. I couldn't breathe. She dropped off our neighbor and pulled into the driveway. Inside the house, the TV was still on, and images of the smoke billowing from the North Tower showed on the screen. We were stationed in Germany, where my dad was a soldier in the Army, so it was already mid-afternoon for us. I remember feeling helpless as we watched the second plane approach the Tower on television. I watched it hit, and I felt the strike as if the weight of it would pull me down through the floor.

Being so far away from my homeland when it was hurt was strangely isolating. Suddenly, I was much more aware of the foreign land surrounding us. My mom was on the phone trying to call friends in New York. I'd been born in New York, and my mom had visited the city frequently when she was growing up. When the second plane struck, my mom cried. Not quiet tears; she fell to her knees and cried out loud. She knew seventeen people whom we would later learn had died in the Towers.

The military base was put on lockdown, which meant my dad couldn't come home. I was sitting on the floor, holding our German Shepherd, Hobbes, while my sister toddled around in her walker, blissfully oblivious. Suddenly, I felt an overwhelming need to call my grandfather, Pa, who lived in Virginia. I needed to know he was safe.

Mom told me we would call him later when he got home; the phone lines would be very busy due to the attacks and rescue efforts. But I didn't listen, which was hugely out of character for me. I knew I *had* to call him right that minute. It couldn't wait for him to get home from work.

I went and picked up the phone. To dial out of the house, we had to dial 9, then 0-0 to make an international call. Then we had to dial the country code for the United States — 1 — and then the phone number. I could never remember the number for the house I lived in, much less dialing to the States to Pa's cell phone. We always called him at home. He didn't like the charges on his cell phone from an international call. I knew he'd be annoyed because of the cost, but I didn't care. I had to call him. I had never had such an intense feeling in my life.

Somehow, I dialed the right numbers, including Pa's cell phone. He answered and said I caught him just as he was about to go through security at the Pentagon, which meant turning in his phone because he couldn't take it into his office. If I had called more than a minute later, his phone would have already been turned off.

My voice was shaking when I told him I just needed to know he was safe. He could tell I was upset, so he walked away from the security line toward the parking lot so his signal would be better. He told me he was just fine, perfectly safe, and the guards at the Pentagon were protecting everyone so I didn't need to worry. That is when Flight 77 crashed into the Pentagon, destroying Pa's office.

He told me he would call me back — that he had to go. I didn't know what had happened until it came on the news a moment later. Mom cried again later that day when Pa called back. He was home safe because my earlier phone call had kept him from going into his office. I will be forever grateful for whatever grace allowed me to remember his cell phone number in that moment I needed it.

That urge to call my grandfather was the most miraculous mercy I've experienced in my life. It gave me fourteen more years to share with the most wonderful grandfather anyone could have.

~C. Solomon

50

A Christmas Miracle

*Our prime purpose in this life is to help others. And if
you can't help them, at least don't hurt them.*
~Dalai Lama

During World War II, my father served as a gunner and then as a copilot on a B-17 Flying Fortress, based out of England. On what was to become his last mission as a copilot, he and his crew were to drop several huge bales of anti-Hitler leaflets over Stuttgart, Germany, and then return to base.

Unfortunately, after dropping the bales on the city, my dad's plane was hit by anti-aircraft guns and so badly damaged it was unable to continue flying. The captain and my dad were able to make an emergency landing in the forest. While the plane was totaled, the crew survived the crash, although the engineer and the gunner had been badly hurt and were unable to walk. The captain decided his first priority was the health and safety of his men, and stated that they would try and make it to Switzerland where they could get medical help for the two wounded men.

It was winter, and in addition to being cold, a lot of snow was on the ground. The captain and my father had the men strip the plane for anything remotely useful and then make a sled for the injured men from the hatch door. The crew would take turns pulling the sled. When not pulling, they would be on the lookout for German patrols.

After two days of sneaking through the German countryside, the injured men were in a bad way. The Captain and crew decided that allowing themselves to be captured and sent to a POW camp was the only way they could get help for the injured men.

The next day, the crew came across a German patrol. My dad and the captain ordered their men to drop their weapons and surrender to the Germans, and that's when the unexpected happened: The German patrol simultaneously tried to surrender to them. My dad said it was amusing and scary at the same time, as they and the Germans were all standing there with their hands in the air trying to surrender to each other.

The captain, the navigator and my dad all spoke a little French and a few words of German. The commander of the German unit — there were five German soliders — also spoke a little French. Using French and some German, the German commander (named Fritz), the captain, the navigator and my dad worked out a truce and a plan.

It was about five days until Christmas, and they were still probably a hundred miles from the Swiss border. The Germans had not been supplied with food, warm clothes or even ammo in a very long time. They were cold, hungry and sick. Having been forced to fight for a cause they didn't believe in (two were originally from Austria), they had decided it was time to desert. Fritz, wanting to save his men from freezing and starving to death, had decided they would surrender to the first Americans they saw and sit out the rest of the war in a British POW camp.

The men worked out a plan. If they came upon more Germans, Fritz would pretend that the crew from the B-17 were his prisoners, and that he was on his way to turn them in. If the group came upon an Allied patrol, the captain and my dad would ensure that Fritz and his men weren't harmed, and that they made it safely to an Allied POW camp.

The group of men spent the next five days walking together through the countryside. As the days passed, the B-17 crew and the Germans ended up becoming friends and helping each other survive.

Thanks to the navigator's skill, they made it across the border into Switzerland on Christmas Day. The captain and my dad escorted Fritz and his men to a British unit, and saw that they were safely turned in and given food and medical help. The captain and my dad later vouched for Fritz and his men, who were sent to a British POW camp. My dad was permanently grounded after suffering a back injury in the crash, and he and the other members of the B-17 crew maintained their friendship with Fritz and the others, visiting them whenever possible in the POW camp.

After the war, my dad, Fritz, and several of the men on both sides maintained a lifelong friendship, often visiting each other. When my dad told his preacher father what had happened, he said it was a Christmas miracle. The B-17 crew had survived being shot at and then a plane crash. Somehow, they had not been tracked or followed by the Germans, and had run into Fritz and his unit who were hoping to meet some Americans. They had not shot each other, and as a group they all made it alive into Switzerland. And all of them survived a German winter with almost no food, medicine, or clothes. Perhaps it was a miracle after all.

~Leslee Kahler

51

January 26th

We can only be said to be alive in those moments
when our hearts are conscious of our treasures.
~Thornton Wilder

I wiped the tears from my eyes and willed the day to be over as soon as possible. It was only 10:00 a.m., and I already felt emotionally exhausted. I had been feeling the dread grow inside me as the small square on the calendar inched closer and closer. Now, it was here: January 26th.

A year ago on this day, one of my best friends — beautiful, vibrant, inimitable Celine — had been killed in a car accident. It was undoubtedly the worst day of my life.

I made plans for the first anniversary of her death as best as I could, trying to keep busy. I taught a writing class for kids, and their innocent laughter helped raise my spirits a bit. I met a friend for lunch. I went to a salon and donated eight inches of my hair to Locks of Love in honor of Celine, but I barely made it to my car before breaking down in sobs. It seemed impossible that she was gone forever. I wanted something to blame, so I blamed the numbers on the calendar.

"January 26th is a terrible day," I told my boyfriend Allyn that night. He had sweetly made my favorite comfort foods for dinner, plus double-chocolate brownies for dessert.

"I know," Allyn said, patting my hand gently. "It's almost over." He had never gotten a chance to meet Celine. She lived in Paris, and we had planned to visit her that summer. We had already bought plane tickets. It made me so upset that they would never get to meet each other.

"Seriously," I continued my rant, "this day should be purged from the calendar. Did you know that January 26th was also the day of my dad's car accident?"

Allyn's eyes widened. "I never knew that."

When I was in high school, my dad, a sports columnist, was rear-ended by a drunk driver on his way home from covering the Super Bowl. It was January 26, 2003. His car was totaled, and Dad suffered a major neck injury that required disc fusion surgery. He had to leave the job he loved because his body could no longer handle the long commute to games and the late nights of furious typing on deadline. Even all these years later, he still deals with neck pain and nerve damage in his fingers.

"Dad never complains about it," I told Allyn, "but that night changed his life forever. January 26th is a cursed day."

Allyn didn't say anything. He just looked down at our intertwined fingers and squeezed my hand.

Eventually, the awful anniversary drew to a close. We went to bed and woke up to sunshine, birdsong, and a new day.

A few days later, Allyn surprised me with a weekend getaway to Russian River Valley in the wine country. My eyes filled with tears when he got down on one knee. "Yes!" I exclaimed. January 26th was the worst day of my life, but January 30th was now the best day of my life.

We began to plan our wedding. During such a joyful season of life, the one sore spot was knowing that Celine would not be there to celebrate with us.

One evening, Allyn and I logged back onto our long-disabled online dating accounts—where we had originally met more than two years before. Allyn's best friend, who was to be a groomsman in our wedding, had requested our online dating profiles for a gift he was creating for us. I also thought it would be fun to print out our profiles for a scrapbook and save our first messages back and forth to each other, the ones we sent before we switched over to texting and talking on the phone. It was fun to read the essays we had written about ourselves when we first signed up for the online dating website. Rereading them, I was struck by how genuine and honest Allyn's profile was. His writing voice captured the man I had grown to love so deeply.

I remembered the thrill in my heart when I first stumbled across Allyn's profile and glimpsed the photo of his warm smile. I had reached out immediately with a cheerful message. Allyn later told me it was obvious I was new to online dating because the tone of my message was so chipper and bright. I had only been on the website for a week when Allyn and I went out for ice cream. Soon after, we disabled our online dating accounts.

We clicked onto our messages to reread our first conversation. When I saw the date recorded at the top of that first cheerful message I had sent, reaching out to him, a shiver passed through me.

There it was, in stark blue lettering: January 26, 2014.

My relationship with the man who would become my husband began exactly one year to the day before my dear friend died.

Some miracles are big: an accident avoided, a disease cured, a life saved. Other miracles are small. As small as the date on a calendar.

I now see January 26th as a microcosm of life itself: the lows and the highs, the worst and the best, the curses and the blessings. I no longer let Celine's death define her memory; I miss her and celebrate her every single day of the year. Instead of viewing my dad's car accident as a stroke of bad luck, I choose to focus on the miracle of his survival — he walked away from that car accident when he very likely should have died that night. When January 26th comes around, I mourn the loss of one of my best friends — a dazzling star who was extinguished much too soon — and I also thank the universe for bringing my amazing husband into my life.

I still cry each year on January 26th, but they are no longer tears of pure sadness and anger. They are tears of grief and joy, regret and gratitude — and they are tears of hope. Each year, when Allyn and I celebrate the anniversary of the day our relationship began, I smile to imagine Celine is celebrating with us, too.

~Dallas Woodburn

52

CPR 101

*We are not put on earth for ourselves, but are placed
here for each other. If you are there always for others,
then in time of need, someone will be there for you.*
~Jeff Warner

"Please help me!" someone shouted while pounding on the front door of our apartment. The voice didn't sound familiar, but the "knocking" got stronger, and the words turned into frantic screaming.

"I'll be right there," I said, as I grabbed the first thing out of the closet — one of my husband's old sweatshirts. I had just arrived home from work — an hour later than my usual time — as I had attended a refresher course on CPR that day. Although I worked as a medical secretary — for a surgeon's office across from Deaconess Hospital in Spokane, Washington — the course was still required of all employees.

My husband Mark and I both worked part-time and went to Spokane Bible College (now Moody Bible Institute) full-time. It was Friday evening, and I was exhausted.

The pounding on the door started to scare me, and I almost called 911 because it sounded as if someone was dying. I could feel my heart in my throat as I opened the door.

Nothing could prepare me for what I saw.

The young mother from the adjacent apartment, Heather, was dripping wet, and tears streamed down her cheeks. She had lost her voice from screaming so loudly and could only point weakly to her apartment door before she collapsed in my arms. I knew she had two children — Tommy and Crystal — but they weren't with her.

As I ran toward the apartment, I saw she had left the door wide open. The wet footprints on the beige carpet led to the bathroom. I couldn't believe what I found there. Four-year-old Tommy was sitting in the bathtub with his eighteen-month-old sister, Crystal, who was floating on top of the water — face down.

I pulled Crystal out of the water. Her eyes were closed, her face and lips were bluish in color, and she had no breath sounds. I laid her down on the white tile floor and immediately started chest compressions, pinched her nose and covered her mouth with mine — breathing soft puffs of air into her lungs. I continued with CPR until a gush of water released from her mouth.

I did what I was trained to do by turning her head to the side and letting the rest of the water flow out, checking her mouth for any choking hazard before continuing with resuscitation breathing and compressions. Having just finished CPR 101, everything was fresh in my mind — except I was working on a precious baby girl and not the dummy figure that we used in class.

At one point, I wondered if I was doing more harm than good. I didn't know how long she had been in the water, and maybe she was already gone. If she lived, would she remain in a vegetative state?

Crystal's eyes remained closed while I checked for breath sounds. There were none. Panic set in, so I prayed, "God, please let her live!" As soon as I uttered those words out loud, Crystal vomited water and started to cry.

It was the most beautiful sound I had ever heard. Crystal choked and sputtered, but finally caught her breath. She was breathing on her own! Her face and lips were still a bluish-purple, but she was alive.

I grabbed a towel, wrapped it around Crystal tightly and held her close to me. I shouted to her mother to call 911. Heather was shaking so badly she couldn't press the numbers on the phone.

While still holding the baby, I hit the numbers, and the operator answered, "You've reached 911. What's your emergency?"

I explained that I needed an ambulance right away as I had an eighteen-month-old baby girl who had a near-drowning experience but was now breathing on her own. The dispatcher assured me that emergency vehicles were on their way and should be at the apartment in five to seven minutes.

As soon as I hung up the phone, I could hear the sirens. I wrapped Crystal in more towels and rocked her gently while sitting on the bathroom floor.

When the firemen arrived, they pulled Tommy out of the bathtub and asked me what happened. I handed Crystal over to one of the firemen and explained that she was floating on top of the water when I found her. I performed CPR until she started breathing on her own.

The police arrived and then the ambulance personnel, all of whom wanted statements. Heather explained that she had put her children in the tub and then answered the phone. "It was only a few seconds," she said in a quivering voice. "And then I heard Tommy screaming and saw my daughter floating on top of the water. I didn't know what to do, so I ran to Connie's apartment."

I confirmed her statement while the ambulance team arrived and checked Crystal's vitals. Her color was starting to come back, but they needed to take her to the hospital for observation and to run some tests.

The yard was filled with emergency vehicles and flashing red lights, a crowd of neighbors gawking. Heather, Tommy, and Crystal were all in the ambulance headed for Deaconess Hospital when my husband arrived home.

Mark jumped out of the car and ran to my side. "What happened? Are you okay?"

I nodded my head "yes" and blurted out, "It's a long story…."

Crystal returned home from the hospital a week later after a bout of pneumonia, which I feared might happen. I didn't get all the water out of her lungs. But, otherwise, she was normal and healthy and full of her usual spunk, her blond curls bouncing as she played with her brother in the front yard. Her mom never stopped thanking me. With tears in her eyes, she'd grab my hands — pressing them together — and say over and over again, "Thank you… God bless you!"

Not a day goes by when I don't think about Friday, October 8, 1976. At the time — as a busy college student working part-time as a medical secretary — the CPR class that I had to take on that Friday afternoon seemed like such an inconvenience and waste of time, but little did I know it would also be the day I helped save a little girl's life.

In over forty years, I've never had to use CPR again, and I hope I never have to. But I've also kept up with my training because we never know when we'll get that "knock" on the door!

~Connie K. Pombo

53

The Right Place at the Wrong Time

*A good holiday is one spent among people whose
notions of time are vaguer than yours.*
~John B. Priestly

I was so angry. My visit to Machu Picchu, the Incan mountain-top citadel in Peru's Andes — a bucket-list trip — was totally ruined because my hotel's night-desk attendant neglected to ring my room at 5:00 a.m. The plan was to meditate at the Temple of the Sun at sunrise to try and commune with the spirits said to still inhabit the sacred site. It was a once-in-a-lifetime opportunity, now lost due to someone's oversight. How could something like this have happened? Every single hotel guest had been awakened except me....

Finally up and dressed, bemoaning the fact there'd been no alarm clocks in the rooms, I dejectedly shuffled through empty halls to an empty reception area. The hotel was completely deserted. Everyone was up at the Temple. Staff didn't even arrive until breakfast time, which would be served when all the tourists except me returned from their sunrise experience.

And then I heard it — a long, drawn-out, anguished moan. I couldn't see where it emanated from — the lobby seating consisted of recessed banquettes, two steps down. I circled their perimeter and suddenly saw a young man, maybe twenty, lying prone, splayed out on his back, hiking paraphernalia dumped at his feet.

Another moan… I inched closer.

"Are you okay? Do you need help?" I asked.

The feeble response: "Dysentery."

"How many days have you been ill?"

"Three, four…" he whispered.

"Are you alone?"

"Friends, hiking Inca Trail. Left me here this morning. Too weak…"

He was sweating profusely and shivering, and he was so pale except for his flaming red cheeks. I touched his forehead gingerly. It was burning. Somehow I sensed the situation was truly dire. My adrenaline kicked in, and disappointment over my earlier missed opportunity dissipated in a flash — it seemed like this kid really needed aid.

I ran through the silent hotel yelling for help, but no one was about. I didn't see a soul until I burst through the double swinging doors of the hotel's kitchen and found a chef prepping breakfast for all the returning guests. Even though I was out of breath and almost incoherent, the chef finally got the gist of what I was saying. But by the time the two of us returned to the hiker, he was already foaming at the mouth.

There's a tiny town at the base of Machu Picchu, really just a terminus for the train that delivers tourists daily to the famous site high above the Urubamba River. A local doctor was in residence there in case visitors experienced health problems — usually altitude sickness due to the citadel's 8,000-foot height. The chef frantically searched for the phone number and called him. Twenty minutes later, the doctor arrived by car, but the hiker was already fading in and out of consciousness. An emergency medical helicopter was summoned to fly him to the nearest hospital. I waited with him until we knew the helicopter was on its way.

What would have happened to this young man had I received my wake-up call? I would have been outside with all the other guests while he lay alone, in dire need, in the hotel's empty lobby.

I returned to the dining room with the chef since I knew my tour group would soon gather there for breakfast. Guests slowly began trickling back from the coveted sunrise viewing at the Temple. Tour mates I'd been traveling with repeatedly asked where I'd been and mentioned seeing a helicopter flying toward the hotel. They thought perhaps a celebrity was arriving. When I explained what happened regarding my forgotten wake-up call, a fellow traveler confided, "You didn't miss a thing. It was so noisy and crowded up there, no way you could've meditated. People were laughing, yelling, and jostling each other for photo ops. Others were snacking 'cause they were hungry. Some were even complaining about the crush of people. And another tour group regaled everybody with 'Happy Birthday' while breaking out cake and champagne for a member's 50th."

Everyone finally settled down for breakfast. Since my group had been awakened so early, our itinerary allotted time for a two-hour nap before our planned departure. And so I asked our tour leader if I could hike up to the Temple to meditate a bit while everybody was sleeping. Aware of the hotel's oversight, he agreed. As I climbed up Machu Picchu's ancient, chipped stone steps, I saw the emergency helicopter land at the hotel. I said a prayer for the hiker's recovery and gave thanks for being able to help.

Up at the Temple, I was the one and only tourist. Blissful silence. Sacred space. Mystic murmurings. I was so grateful — it was a gift, heavenly. I positioned myself in a little niche, sitting on a ledge, and briefly meditated. I even saw a shimmering image of a man in traditional Incan dress in front of me, one of those promised spirits I had heard about.

I had the most spiritual, meaningful experience at Machu Picchu — being able to help someone in need — all because of a fortuitous mistake in timing.

~Marsha Warren Mittman

54

Friday the 13th

*There are only two ways to live your life. One is as
though nothing is a miracle. The other is as
though everything is a miracle.*
~Albert Einstein

When Ann phoned on Friday morning, January 13, 2017, to confirm our breakfast date later that morning, I was thrilled. Get togethers with my dear friend were rare enough. But outings that included our husbands as well only took place every few years. The fact that Ann and my husband Chuck had recently celebrated birthdays made this post-holiday outing even more special.

"Will Marjorie be joining us as well?" Ann asked. "I hope so!"

Just like that, my excitement plummeted, delight now tinged with guilt.

"I don't think so," I hedged. "Mom needs two hours to get up, get dressed, and be ready to roll, and she often doesn't fall asleep until three or four in the morning. I'd hate to call now and wake her up."

True enough, every word. But on another level, how could I tell someone who adored my upper-octogenarian mother that I'd really like a break from her? For months now, ever since preparing for and hosting her forty-first annual art show, my mother hadn't been herself. But Ann had asked me a week ago to invite Mom, so I felt bad for not conveying the message sooner. It was partly because I had forgotten, but I'm pretty sure I also delayed because, deep down, I really didn't want to include my mother. I just wanted to kick back and relax with friends for an hour without feeling any responsibility or worry.

Conflicted, I hung up. "It's too early to call Mom," I groused to my husband. "She needs her sleep. And I need a break!"

Still, with most of my mother's friends deceased or battling serious health issues, I knew the inherent value of an invitation. Whether she went or not, she'd appreciate being asked. And wasn't I always wishing more people would include Mom in their plans?

Being a good daughter — or parent, grandparent, partner, friend — is not always convenient, and we all need a therapeutic break now and then. But in this case, love and compassion won out. I knew I wouldn't fully enjoy my breakfast unless I made that call.

Mom answered the phone sounding groggy and marble-mouthed. I *had* woken her up. I berated myself for not extending the invitation earlier.

"I'm sorry I woke you, Mom," I sighed.

"That's okay. I have to get up anyway," she said, still oddly garbled. "I have a hair appointment this morning."

"Oh, what time is that?" I asked, wondering if the scheduling might work out.

She mumbled something I didn't catch.

"Sorry, Mom, what did you say?"

"It's at 16 17."

"What time is your hair appointment?" I asked again.

"I told you," she snapped. "16 17!"

My blood ran cold. "Okay, Mom," I soothed. "I'll let you go and get ready."

As I hung up, a word that a friend had mentioned to me twenty years earlier suddenly came to me: aphasia. The strange jumbling of speech. A possible symptom of stroke.

My heart hammered.

I immediately drove to my mother's house where I found her padding around the kitchen in her bathrobe trying to lay out her morning pills. Not wanting to alarm her, I casually asked a few simple questions. Once again, she seemed to have difficulty responding.

"I don't understand you, Wendy," she said irritably. "I don't have my pants on yet."

When she repeated her peculiar pants statement a minute later, this time pointing to her head, I suddenly grasped what she was trying to tell me. Her hearing aids were not in yet!

Turning, I hurried to my mother's bedroom, shut the door, and dialed her doctor. Then I called Chuck and asked him to call 911 for an ambulance. Sick with fear, I ran back to my mother, who by this time had given up on her pills.

"I don't feel right," she whispered, trembling. "I felt funny early this morning, too, so I went back to bed."

Afraid that Mom's already-high blood pressure might spike dangerously, I guided her back to her bedroom and calmly explained that we needed to go to the hospital and get her checked out. Chuck and I never made it to our breakfast that morning, but my mother did make it safely to the hospital, where tragedy was averted.

Later that day, sitting quietly beside her bed, I relived those terrifying first moments. Certain the morning's events were anything but random or coincidental, I was overcome with gratitude and humbled by God's great mercy. Had my friend, twenty years earlier, not described her own mom's experience with aphasia in such detail, I might not have recognized my mother's danger signs as quickly. Had I invited Mom to breakfast earlier in the week, only to have her decline, I would never have placed that last-minute call. And had Ann not unknowingly tugged at my conscience by calling to reiterate her hope that Marjorie would join us, I would have blithely gone about my morning and never visited Mom until later that day — or the next day, even! By then, who knows what kind of damage her brain might have sustained?

I believe God was watching over all of us that day. His divine timing ensured that I heard and interpreted Mom's bizarre "16 17" reply as an urgent cry for help. Eight months later, my mother still struggles at times to express herself accurately. But considering what could have happened that fateful Friday the 13th, she is without question one very lucky lady. And I am, without question, one very lucky daughter to still have my mom in my life.

~Wendy Hobday Haugh

55

Joy in a Bowl of Cereal

If we never experience the chill of a dark winter, it
is very unlikely that we will ever cherish the
warmth of a bright summer's day.
~Anthon St. Maarten, Divine Living

I became a widow at age twenty-eight. My first husband, Matt, collapsed one evening from what we later discovered was a ruptured brain aneurysm. We lived an hour away from a hospital that could treat him, so he was transported by helicopter to the hospital in the city. For eight excruciating days, I watched the effects of the ruptured aneurysm destroy his brain.

On the evening of that eighth day, his doctor took me into a dark room to show me brain scans and deliver the news that Matt had irreversible brain damage. His body was no longer capable of staying alive without the help of machines. Fortunately for me, Matt and I had a long conversation during the Terri Schiavo case about our final wishes. I was in support of sustaining life artificially and not giving up hope, but my husband argued that our faith tells us that our hope is not in doctors and medicine. He personally felt that it was an act against faith to sustain a life artificially. His wishes were to be allowed to pass peacefully when it was time.

I left the hospital in shock, and when I got on the highway to make the hour-long trip home that night, I rolled down the windows.

I cried, screamed and begged for the entire trip. I wanted to know why. I knew that in the coming hours I was going to experience more pain than I had ever felt in my life.

When I finally got home, I crawled into bed, though I knew that I would only sleep when I passed out from exhaustion, which happened to be around 4:00 a.m. I woke up at 6:00 a.m., sat straight up in bed, and had a thought. "Eddie needs a kidney." The thought grew louder and louder in my head until I realized that I was saying it out loud.

Eddie was one of my sister's childhood friends. We had just spent New Year's Eve with him, and while he was able to play board games and enjoy our conversation, he spoke of his disease and how dialysis had restricted his diet, among other things in his life.

Matt and I felt so bad for him. He was barely an adult at the age of nineteen, and he was facing death. But despite that, he had a kind and caring demeanor and was a joy to be around. Eddie did need a kidney... and now Matt was going to give him one.

I fumbled for my phone and called the ICU. When the nurse answered, I asked her if Matt could donate his organs. She was shocked. When husbands are still alive, even just barely, it is not common for wives to call and ask about organ donation. I explained to her that I was searching for purpose and felt that part of the purpose in Matt's life was to give Eddie a kidney. The nurse told me that she was going to call me later that morning to discuss meeting with LifeNet Health, the organ procurement organization that serves our area.

I was able to arrange for Matt to be a direct donor to Eddie. They would have to go through several tests to determine eligibility for the transplant, and I was warned that the odds of Matt's kidney going into Eddie's body were slim, but it would move Eddie up the list for one that did match if Matt's kidneys went to other people. I called Eddie to ask him if he wanted it, and he tearfully accepted.

The tests were run and Matt and Eddie were a perfect match. I was told that the odds were less than 1 in 700... but they were a match!

Matt died at the age of thirty. We had been married for six and a half years, and I fulfilled my wedding vows to be with him until death—he died in my embrace. After I said my final goodbyes, Matt was taken to an operating room, and his kidneys and other organs were removed. One kidney was put on a helicopter bound for Pittsburgh where Eddie was at the hospital getting prepped for surgery, and Matt's other organs were sent to other recipients.

My children and I traveled to Matt's and my hometown for the funeral, just outside of Pittsburgh, a few days later. With final arrangements for Matt set, I decided that we would drive to Pittsburgh to visit with Eddie. After making our way through the maze of corridors at the hospital, we finally arrived in Eddie's room. When I walked in, Eddie looked up from his bed and said, "I ate cereal today for the first time in two years." We both cried as we hugged each other. It was comforting for me to know that a piece of my husband lived on in him. We visited and talked about what a wonderful man Matt was, and Eddie gave my children a pillow shaped like a kidney on which he wrote: *Your dad is my hero.*

It wasn't until after I arrived back home that I really processed Eddie's comment about eating cereal. This young man had struggled with kidney failure for years, his life all but destroyed because of his disease. He had dropped out of college and could barely do anything beyond go for dialysis. The day that Matt gave his final gift, Eddie received many blessings and was rejoicing in all of them, including even the smallest, a bowl of cereal. Eddie taught me that joy can be found in everything.

~Heather A. Carlson-Jaquez

56

The Unexpected Miracle

The most incredible thing about
miracles is that they happen.
~G.K. Chesterton

I wake up each morning and take a few minutes to pray that my two sons will be safe, make the best choices, and have everything they need. My younger son, Jeremy, is a construction worker building bridges and is keenly aware of having what is needed at all times. He had taken his Boy Scout training to heart and learned well the motto of being prepared.

One frigid cold January evening that training proved very valuable, when a man in our town had a terrible accident. He was driving home after a twelve-hour shift at the plant and he took a shortcut on a back road that was not well traveled. The man's wife was off work, and she was preparing an evening meal. His two small children were playing and waiting for their daddy. The man looked forward to his warm house, a comforting dinner and some bedtime stories with his family.

The evening was already dark when a deer suddenly jumped onto the road and into the bright headlights of the man's truck. He tried to avoid hitting the animal, but his sudden jerk on the steering wheel sent his truck off the road and over an embankment where he crashed into a tree and slid into the lake. As the truck caught fire, the man struggled to pull himself out of the burning vehicle and then out of the freezing water. He lay on the bank and shivered uncontrollably as he watched his truck explode. As he tells it, this felt like his last day on earth.

At the same time, Jeremy went to pick up his daughter, who had spent the afternoon with a friend. At the last minute, he decided to drive his wife's SUV instead of his pickup, and he grabbed his overstuffed backpack from his truck. Because of his construction job and Boy Scout training, Jeremy is always prepared with that loaded backpack. He has been teased for toting that load around.

Jeremy and my granddaughter had never traveled this particular way at night. It was growing dark, but she wanted an empty road to practice her driving.

My granddaughter was behind the wheel when they saw a huge ball of flames burst orange above the trees. As she drove closer, they could smell the burning fumes. She stopped the car, and they got out. Looking over the embankment, they stared in shock at the remains of a burning vehicle.

"Help me!" a voice screamed. It was darker now and hard to see who was calling out.

"Please! Please help me!" A stranger climbed up the bank toward them. He shivered so violently it was nearly impossible to understand his words.

Jeremy helped the man into the heated seat of the SUV, helping him out of his frozen, wet clothing and giving him dry clothes from the backpack. Then he wrapped him in a blanket and called 911. Within a few long minutes, Fire Rescue arrived, and the stranger was transported to the hospital.

The stranger was a young man, exactly my son's age. And, like my son, his name was Jeremy. He was released later that night from the hospital with an injured shoulder and some bumps and bruises, but so grateful to go home to his family.

Two Jeremys, two families, and one deserted road at exactly the right time.

And now when I wake up each morning to pray for my sons, I think of all the events that occurred to make a miracle possible. My son and his daughter chose that deserted road, and the stranger's vehicle exploded after he had gotten out — just in time for the flames to serve as a signal for help. It truly was a miracle of timing and divine intervention.

~Linda J. Hawkins

57

In the Blink of an Eye

Good instincts usually tell you what to do
long before your head has figured it out.
~Michael Burke

idland, Texas. January 1982. I sat on Mrs. Everett's sofa and glanced at my watch. My last appointment for the day had rescheduled. If I could wrap this one up quickly, I could get home in time to play with the kids and cook a hot supper for my family.

My client decided on a lovely cream and rose–striped fabric to reupholster her sofa. I thought we were finished when she said, "I'd like to talk about the dining room now. I think I'd like new draperies."

I pasted a smile on my face as she talked about her ideas for the room. Then I reproved myself. As an interior designer, I owed this client my full attention, especially since she would be spending a substantial amount of money for my services. An hour and a half later, I packed up my samples and headed home, leaving a happy client behind.

It was Friday afternoon, and the week had been long. Looking forward to an early start on the weekend, I stopped by the grocery store and picked up ground beef to make lasagna, and a chocolate-cake mix. The kids couldn't yet tell the difference between a boxed or homemade cake. Besides, they loved to lick the batter bowl.

I smiled as I pulled into the driveway of our lovely, old home. Even though the inside was rundown, I loved the grand dame. Built in the 1920s in the Art Deco style, it was rambling and spacious. We had dedicated two large rooms for the design business. Four ladies did the office work there while I worked in the field. The rest was our family home.

As a bonus to the arrangement, one of the ladies, a grandmotherly type, loved Amy and Jonathan. Miss Wilma would make their snacks and see to their needs after school until one of us got home. The kids walked the two blocks to and from school with the gaggle of neighborhood children who lived around us.

Amy, our eight-year-old, sat at the kitchen table eating a peanut-butter-and-jelly sandwich and watching cartoons.

"Hi, sweetie. Where's Jonathan?" I asked as I refilled her glass of milk.

Talking around a mouthful of peanut butter, she said, "His teacher wanted to talk to him after school."

I groaned. With dark, curly hair and green, mischievous eyes, our six-year-old was precocious and funny. After the first six weeks of school, his teacher sent home a note with his report card: "If you ever want to get rid of Jonathan, I'll take him." I knew there was a reason I had liked her at first sight.

Unfortunately, he then developed a propensity for chatting too much in class. He just couldn't help it; there was so much energy in his small body. After the second six weeks, she sent another note home: "I changed my mind." If Jonathan was meeting with the teacher, we likely had another parent-teacher conference coming up.

I went to my office to write the orders for the last job before Jonathan and my husband Mical got home. I'd learned it was much better to complete the paperwork while the details were fresh in my mind. Putting off the task could lead to costly mistakes. Besides, it would only take fifteen or twenty minutes, and then I would be done for the weekend.

At my desk, I glanced out the window. Steel gray clouds were forming in the east, and I could already hear distant thunder. I thought about my sweet little boy. This morning, he had come down for breakfast in his robe. When he turned to go back upstairs, I noticed a hole near his bottom in the back of it. I asked what happened. He grinned, revealing his missing front teeth. "Musta' stood too close to the heater in the bathroom." Thank heavens for child-safe fabrics.

He was likely right now at the duck pond on his way home. Between the school and our house was a lovely small park with a pond in the middle — a rare treat in our arid desert climate and one of the reasons we had chosen the house.

Jonathan loved the ducks, and they loved him. More than once, he had come home with a fat duckling waddling behind him. We would have to walk back to the pond to reunite the feathered family. I could picture him tossing his left-over lunch crumbs to them, with his tongue stuck through the space where his two front teeth had been.

I spread the materials and drawings out on my desk and began to work. As I was transcribing the fabric numbers, a dark sense of foreboding dropped over me like a heavy mist. I tried to shake it off and told myself to stop being silly.

In the next moment, the premonition turned to cold fear. I grabbed my keys and ran out of the house.

Large drops of rain had begun to fall. At the end of the block, I turned left. The pond was on my right and just past it the elementary school. A ramshackle car had parked beside the pond. When I pulled in behind it, a man with a greasy shock of shoulder-length black hair jerked around in the driver's seat and stared at me. I scanned the area looking for Jonathan and caught sight of his bright red-and-blue jacket. Four or five feet in front of Jonathan, and obscuring my full view of him, a scrawny man with bushy, bleached-blond hair appeared to be talking to him. The man's clothes were tattered and hung on his frame like a scarecrow. I started to get out of the car and wave to Jonathan when he pointed toward me. The man wheeled around, and then sprinted to the old car and jumped inside. The car sped away.

Jonathan waved to me and headed to the car. When he climbed into the passenger seat, I asked, "Who were those men?"

Jonathan shrugged. "I dunno. They called me over, so I went to see what they wanted. One of 'em said, 'Your mama's looking for you.' You drove up right then, and I pointed to your car and said, 'Yep. There she is now.'"

My breath caught, and I started shaking. Another minute, even less, and he would have been gone. Possibly forever. What if I had not come home early? What if I had waited to finish the paperwork for the order?

It seems our precocious little boy had a destiny neither a bathroom heater nor nefarious men could thwart. Thirty-six years later, Jonathan has a beautiful wife and three children of his own. He is an active member in his community and a deacon at his church in West Monroe, Louisiana. I still tremble when I think about how different life could have been, in a matter of seconds.

~Carolyn Hill

58

Being There

Put your ear down close to your soul and listen hard.
~Anne Sexton

It was nearing Christmas, and we had already planned to fly to Chicago to visit my father-in-law, probably for the last time. I still had so much to do before our trip. But then the phone rang and I learned that Dad wouldn't make it to Christmas, or even through the week. My husband was already at his side, two thousand miles away.

I was paralyzed by shock. But then I sprang into action, running through the house, pulling suitcases from closets and clothes from drawers while calling the airline to change our flight. My two-year-old was asleep for the night while the other two kids took advantage of their later bedtime due to my distracted state.

Tears flowed down my face as I packed. My father-in-law meant so much to me. He was one of those true, gentle souls.

In the midst of my frenzied packing, I felt a warmth on my shoulder, as though someone had placed a hand on it. I felt an instant calm. I looked around for the source of the touch, but no one was around me. Normally, a physical contact of unknown origin would put me in a panic, but this was different.

"John, Julia. Want to pray the rosary with me?" I asked.

They were nine and seven at the time. Until this moment, I had never prayed the rosary before. As a convert to Catholicism in my early twenties, I had never learned how to do many of the rituals of the Catholic Church, but something pushed me to round up the kids and pray.

In seconds, John and Julia were in front of me. "Yes, Mommy, let's pray," John said. Julia nodded her head in agreement. They had no idea why I had asked them to pray. I can only guess that they felt the same pull I did, not only because of their quick response but also from their wide, understanding eyes.

"I don't know how to pray the rosary. Can you teach me?" I asked.

"Yeah, be right back." John sprinted from the room and returned with the large rosary his second-grade class had made two years earlier.

"Let's sit on your bed, Mommy," Julia said.

The three of us sat in a circle, the hefty rosary clasped in their small hands as though the weight of it were too heavy for one person to hold.

"Grandpa is very sick and needs our prayers," I said.

"Is Pop-Pop going to die?" John asked, on the verge of tears. Dad and John had always shared a special bond.

"I don't know, but I think God wants us to pray," I said.

Since my father-in-law's diagnosis six months earlier, my faith had weakened. I don't know how anyone's faith doesn't falter at least a little when they watch someone suffer the way he had. I prayed a lot during those six months, sometimes begging God to take him so he wouldn't be subjected to another day of pain, but somehow he remained.

We prayed aloud for twenty minutes. John and Julia were entranced, with their eyes closed and their fingers traveling over each walnut-sized bead at the end of every Hail Mary, Our Father, or Glory Be. There was a peaceful calm in our circle when we finished. I felt as if a heavy weight had been lifted from our hearts.

Julia broke the silence. "God, please be with Grandpa. We know he has to go to Heaven. Tell him we love him, and we'll miss him. Amen."

"We put him into your hands, God," John added.

Their faith was so much stronger than my own.

We continued to sit in silence, and then the phone rang.

Both John's and Julia's eyes met mine. A flash of understanding on their faces squeezed the breath from my lungs. I reached for the phone as they reached for each other's hand.

"He's gone," my husband said and sobbed.

I listened to him cry, desperate to hold him, while tears escaped my own eyes.

John ran into his room, grabbing the paper airplane kit that Pop-Pop had given him months before and clutching it to his chest as he cried.

"When did he pass?" I asked my husband.

"About ten minutes ago."

"We were there with him," I said.

"What do you mean?"

"One minute, I was frantically packing, and the next I was praying the rosary with the kids."

"I've never seen you pray the rosary."

"That's just it. I never have. I didn't even know how. You said he passed about ten minutes ago, the same time John asked God to take Dad into His hands," I said. I was filled with awe for this miracle that allowed me to be with my father-in-law, and my children to be with their grandfather, at the exact time of his passing.

A few months after my father-in-law's death, we were all in the car. My youngest, Jessica, was carrying on a conversation with herself as she gazed out the car window.

"What are you talking about?" I asked her.

"I'm talking to Grandpa," she said and pointed to the window. "He's right here."

No one laughed or told her she was silly because we all knew that what she saw was what we felt. He was still with us.

~Jan Steele

Miracles
and More

Everyday Miracles

59

The Force Was with Me

The Force will be with you. Always.
~Obi-Wan Kenobi

I was a senior in high school and graduation was approaching. "What would you like for your graduation present?" my mother asked.

"I'd like to meet Mark Hamill," I replied. Some of my classmates wanted money, cars, or expensive jewelry. Even if we'd had the finances for that, I wouldn't have been interested. I just wanted to meet a Jedi, or rather the actor who had played one in the movies.

Mum laughed. "I don't think we can really arrange that." I shrugged. She'd asked what I wanted.

Nobody who knew me would have thought my request — to meet the actor who had played Luke Skywalker in the original *Star Wars* trilogy of films — was at all out of character. As a child of the 1980s, I'd grown up with *Star Wars*, and it had been one of my favorite things. I drew countless pictures of the characters. When we lived in New England for a few years, the snowy fields became the frozen wastelands of Hoth, and I pretended I was Princess Leia, scouting for trouble on the snowbanks. My friends took on the roles of Luke Skywalker and Han Solo.

My favorite Christmas present one year was a toy *Star Wars* spacecraft. When I was seven, I made my own comic book starring Luke and

Yoda. I had a collection of *Star Wars* action figures and activity books.

While I loved most of the characters, I glommed on to Luke Skywalker in particular. I admired Luke's determination to follow his heart and do what he thought was right, even when nobody else agreed with him. He'd never have saved Darth Vader if he'd listened to anyone else, after all.

My *Star Wars* mania ebbed as I grew up, but it was always lurking in the background. By the time I hit high school, it had returned in full force. It confused people and made it even more difficult for them to figure me out. I was a bright bookworm who alternately dressed like a goth or wore tie-dye leggings, I did ballet *and* listened to hard rock, and I voluntarily spent weekends wandering through museums. There wasn't anything much happening with *Star Wars* in the mid 1990s… What did I see in it? Even I didn't totally know. It didn't matter. I named my cat Chewie, as in Chewbacca. I dressed up like a Dark Jedi for Halloween one year. I had a toy TIE Fighter in my room. I even chose a quote from Obi-Wan Kenobi to accompany my senior yearbook photo.

On my graduation day I was allowed to choose a fancy restaurant for lunch with my mother and aunt. I opted for the prix fixe lunch at The Russian Tea Room. After our glorious meal, we decided to amble down to Fifth Avenue to show my aunt some of the sights.

As we approached the Warner Bros. store on the corner of 57th and Fifth, I froze in my tracks. There was a huge poster in the window: *Meet Mark Hamill!*

The date on the poster was the next day.

At first, I wondered if it was some sort of joke. It wasn't. Hamill voiced the role of the Joker for Warner Bros.' animated *Batman* series and was doing some promotional work for it, including a meet-and-greet at the studio store. I didn't even need to buy anything to meet him; I just needed to show up and get in line. I had a ballet recital that day, but the meet-and-greet was early enough that it wouldn't conflict with my performance schedule.

The next morning, I stuffed my ballet costume and shoes into my backpack and went off to the store for the meet-and-greet. I brought a friend for moral support; we were two of the first people in the queue. I'd like to say that I was dignified and mature when I finally met Mark Hamill, but I'd be lying. I was as giddy as you'd expect a seventeen-year-old lifelong *Star Wars* fan to be. It was a wonder that I was able to say anything coherent at all. In the photo I took with Mr. Hamill, I had an ear-to-ear grin. Somehow, the Force — or an amazing amount of synchronicity — had been with me, and I received the graduation gift I'd dreamed of.

~Denise Reich

60

A Cookbook and a Prayer

I would maintain that thanks are the highest
form of thought, and that gratitude
is happiness doubled by wonder.
~G.K. Chesterton

"**M**om, can I borrow your bread cookbook?" My mother shot me an incredulous look. I knew exactly what she was thinking; she didn't even have to say it. The expression on her face said it all. "I don't think so, dear."

When it came to cooking and baking, my mother and I were of the same mind. We both clipped recipes from women's magazines and could spend hours perusing cookbooks and planning special dinners as though it were sport. Oh, we were both creative in the kitchen, all right, and frequently joked that our talent must have been an inherited gift. After all, my grandmother could craft anything from apple strudel complete with homemade phyllo dough, to barbecue with all the fixings. What I didn't inherit, however, was both ladies' meticulous style.

Since childhood, I'd watch in awe as my two mentors operated with nary a spill or so much as a grain of sugar dropped to the floor. On the other hand, I was a mess. I'd start off with the best of intentions, ingredients lined up like soldiers with measuring cups at the ready. But then I'd turn to grab the salt shaker and catch a cup of milk with my elbow, spilling it across the counter, or pour the flour a bit too fast from the container, dusting the floor. I tried to be neat, I really did. But despite it all, some unhappy little accident always seemed to happen.

My clumsiness didn't deter me, though, and I continued to increase my repertoire by mastering the art of baking with yeast. My mother made wonderful loaves of bread from recipes in this special cookbook. Walnut and oatmeal, raisin-cinnamon, or my favorite, a crusty French bread — her house smelled divine whenever she baked. I wanted to borrow that book. I needed to have it. "Mom, won't you reconsider?"

"Don't you remember what happened to the last book you borrowed?" she reminded. "You spilled buttermilk on the corner, and the pages stuck together."

"I won't do that again," I assured her. "Besides, that was an accident."

"It's always an accident with you."

I suppose I must have looked especially pitiful that day, or perhaps my mother was anticipating the extra loaf of bread she knew I would bake for her, but with a sudden change of heart, she reached into her cabinet and pulled out none other than *The Bread Book*. "Nothing better happen to this," she warned.

"Nothing," I parroted as I grabbed the book with one hand and crossed my heart with the other. "Promise."

Back at my house, I cradled the open cookbook in a clean kitchen towel and placed it on a shelf above my counter. I wasn't taking any chances. This was my opportunity to redeem myself, and I wasn't going to blow it. One by one, I measured, stirred and sifted each ingredient slowly and cautiously. Then it came time to turn the dough into a bowl rubbed with oil so that it could rise freely without sticking to the sides. With a sure hand, I unscrewed the cap. Then I lifted the bottle of oil and, in nothing short of a gymnastic maneuver, it flew from my fingers into the air and landed on top of my mother's precious cookbook.

I tried every trick I knew to minimize the damage. I mopped the pages with paper towels and placed tissues between them to stop the oil from spreading. I even dusted the book with baby powder and cornstarch to absorb the grease, all to no avail. It was ruined. I thought quickly, but could come up with no other good solutions. The only hope I had was to come clean to my mother and buy her a new book to replace the one I had damaged.

In the days long before the Internet, that required some footwork. When I finished baking my bread, I began calling bookstores in the area to see if they had a copy in stock. All too soon, I found out the sorry truth: *The Bread Book* was out of print. Furthermore, it had been a small print run, and chances were no store — anywhere — had any remaining copies.

I started to shake. And then I started to pray. Even though it seemed frivolous to make such a request in prayer, I could think of no other course of action. *Oh, Lord,* I thought. *You know my heart. I meant to do something good, yet it turned out bad. I don't want to disappoint my mother. Please help me find a way out of this mess.*

The following weekend, my mother and I had a date to do some holiday shopping. My stomach churned as I thought of seeing her again and having to tell her the truth. I would confess after we finished our errands, I decided. There was no use ruining the whole day. Besides, there was a bookstore in the mall and maybe, by some miracle, they might have a copy.

Yet, it was not to be.

On the drive home, I was getting ready to tell her when my mother pointed out a dollar store on the main road. "Let's stop in and take a look," she said. "I need some wrapping paper anyway."

So, we did. And as I walked through the doors of the most dusty, dingy dollar store I had ever seen, there, right at the first end cap, was a pile of scattered books with a copy of *The Bread Book* right on top. I can't say for certain this was a miracle, but it sure felt like one. I paid my dollar and gave my mother the book. She was happy. I was happy. And after I filled her in on the details of my story, we both agreed that perhaps no honest request made in prayer is ever too frivolous to be answered.

~Monica A. Andermann

Miracles in Paris

The universe has no restrictions. You place restrictions
on the universe with your expectations.
~Author Unknown

I firmly believe nothing gives God a greater chuckle than our shock and delight at receiving the gift of a miracle when we least expect it. In my case, it arrived even after I'd completely given up on my wish coming true.

My firsthand experience of the Divine's comedy skills took place at the end of May 2012. I had decided the month before to travel to Paris and all the pieces of my plan were falling easily and quickly into place. Flight booked? Check. Business class, no less! See some tennis at the French Open? Check. My friend had a spare ticket for the quarterfinals. Place to stay? Well, this was where it got interesting.

You see, I have a stubborn tendency to get stuck on an idea. I mean arms-crossed-feet-planted-face-pouting-I'm-not-budging stuck. This time around, I had developed a fierce determination to stay in an apartment with a view of the Eiffel Tower. How the seed of this idea came to be planted, I couldn't say. But once those roots took hold, there was no steering me off course.

Another friend had suggested renting an apartment instead of a regular hotel room. I'd have more space and amenities, and it might even be cheaper. Plus, I'd get to live more like a real Parisian. Sounded simple and perfect. How hard could it be to find one with an Eiffel Tower view? Easy peasy, right? Ha, ha, ha!

I proceeded to lose sleep over it for the next two weeks, staying up into the wee hours of the morning to scour properties and make inquiries. One request after another was met with the same response, "Sorry, we're booked." Ten days before I was to fly out, I had nowhere to stay.

Eventually, I settled on a small apartment that, while far from ideal in location, space, and price, became my final and, I figured, only option. And it did have my view, if not a great one. A five-page contract appeared in my inbox to seal the deal.

But I couldn't bring myself to sign it; I sat on it for hours. I don't often experience bells and whistles going off within my head, but every fiber of my being seemed to scream, "Don't do it!"

Thankfully, I listened. And in that moment I finally got unstuck and let go of the Eiffel Tower. With a deep sigh, I rebooted and started my search from scratch. I still wanted a room with a view, but this time I decided it simply had to be something distinctly Parisian. That opened up a slew of new choices.

One woman I contacted thoughtfully passed my name along to some people she knew who also rented apartments. Within hours, I received a link to a space they had available.

It was gorgeous. Newly renovated, it was two floors connected by a spiral staircase. The appliances were brand-new, but the décor had an artisan antique flair. There was closet space to spare, skylights in the ceiling, a large flat-screen television perched atop counters both upstairs and downstairs, and two plush, white bathrobes awaiting my use. I felt like royalty. It was first-class all the way, and I would be the first to stay there.

And the view? A door off the bedroom on the second floor opened up to a tiny terrace with a table and chairs from which I gazed upon the grandeur of the famed Notre-Dame Cathedral.

To top it off, it was only three blocks away from where my friend lived. The owners were wonderfully friendly and gave me a great deal for nine nights, all in a simple, one-page contract.

I wouldn't have found this apartment on my own. It wasn't listed on any of the sites I was using. It was only because I finally let go and opened up to another possibility that it literally fell into my lap. I knew I'd had a heavy dose of heavenly help.

But God wasn't done getting the last laugh yet.

One late evening, a couple of days into my stay, I was soaking in the bath watching a movie when a twinkling in the distance caught my eye. Slowly turning my head, I realized I was staring at none other than the Eiffel Tower's nightly light show.

My jaw hit the floor. I had looked out that window several times since my arrival and somehow had completely overlooked the famous frame of one of the most iconic landmarks in the world on the horizon.

"You're hilarious," I said aloud, shaking my head in wonder. For the remainder of my stay, I would bask in the dazzling glow of the tower's light show before bed, and grin from ear to ear.

There is a line in *A Course in Miracles* that says, "There is no order of difficulty in miracles." I hadn't even asked for divine guidance, but my hopes were heard, my heart was led, and my wish was granted in truly transcendental form.

Today, any time I need a reminder to "let go and let God," I think of the Eiffel Tower. I still fail regularly at the letting go part, but when I find myself once again stubbornly stuck, I picture those shimmering lights, imagine a gentle nudge in the ribs, and let another who knows better take the wheel. And when those unexpected miracles occur, I can only say, "Very funny; you got me again, God!"

I swear I can sometimes hear a celestial chuckling.

~Danielle Lescure

The Yellow Balloon

Hope is faith holding out its hand in the dark.
~George Iles

It was one of those Erma Bombeck days. The phone hadn't stopped ringing, I had loads of laundry to do, and Karen, my four-year-old, was my shadow, tugging at my shirttail and whining for attention.

In desperation, I rummaged through a closet and found a bag of forgotten balloons. "Yellow," she said with delight. Yellow it was. Immediately, the balloon became a favorite friend, and she latched onto it with pudgy fingers, carrying it around the rest of the day and telling it secrets.

It was, of course, my turn for carpool duty. Considering the way my day had gone, I was not surprised that I was already running ten minutes late as I backed out of the driveway. Karen chose that day to sing "It's Not Easy Being Green" over and over again. It would not have been quite so nerve-wracking had she not paused between each stanza to beat the balloon against the dashboard with agonizing regularity. Three times. Never two. Never four. Well, I rationalized, at least she could count to three.

Once the back seat was full of second graders, I was thankful for their exuberant, half-hearted bickering, which helped drown out Karen's singing. As I turned the corner, trying to keep my attention on my driving, I felt a gust of wind blow across my feet. I responded automatically, "Karen! Please. Close the window. It's freezing out!"

And then I heard the kind of shrill, panicky scream that stops the heart of even veteran mothers. Frantically, I looked over my shoulder, expecting at the least to find a gigantic tarantula, a broken limb, or a quart of blood pooling on the freshly shampooed carpeting. But it was Karen I saw, both arms extended out the window as if in supplication, as she cried beseechingly, "B'loon, b'loon. Come back! Come back!"

With the exception of Karen's heartbreaking sobs, there was not a sound in the car. We all watched mute and helpless as "b'loon" floated into the jaws of the busy intersection, miraculously surviving unscathed as it bounced between an orange VW and a white Ford pickup and then disappeared into a clump of very pointy pine trees.

By the time we reached home, the promise of a new balloon, two new balloons or even ten new balloons had failed to calm Karen. As I held her on my lap and rocked her, I wondered how to explain how far "three miles to school" was, and the inevitable consequences of frail balloons meeting concrete, grass and trees.

But that night, as I tucked her into bed and kissed her cherub cheek, she was oddly calm. "My b'loon will come back. Mommy," she said with the naïve assurance of a child taught to trust. I wiped back the tears, feeling slightly betrayed. There was no chapter in any baby book on coping with lost balloons and a child's unquestioning faith.

Three weeks later, I sat at the dining room table, watching Karen with a warm maternal glow dampened with a tinge of sadness. She was so small, trusting and vulnerable. I couldn't help but wonder how many yellow balloons life would take from her. Suddenly, she stood up and went to the front door. She tugged it open, and then Matilda, the favored doll of the day, was dropped unceremoniously to the floor as Karen bent and picked up… a yellow balloon.

The yellow balloon?

She raised it to her cheek for a moment, then kissed it tenderly and said, "I knew you'd come back." She skipped into her bedroom to talk with her long-lost friend.

Now, I will never know what caused Karen to open the door at that precise moment, nor how a balloon, a yellow balloon, came to be on our front porch steps. But what I do know is that Karen showed me, in the way of a child, what faith is. And in the future, when I find myself treading water in one of life's deeper valleys, I need only think of yellow balloons to know, with childlike faith, that tomorrow is another day. And nothing, my friends, is impossible.

~Candy Schock

A Vote of Confidence

May the miracle you need be just around the corner.
~Vicki Reece

I had quit my job as a hospice nurse in order to focus on my writing and speaking ministry, and this particular day I was questioning whether or not I had made the right decision. "I need a sign, God," I prayed as I took a walk down my street on a humid June morning. "If I'm really doing what You want me to do with my life, please give me a sign."

I had one published book out, but it wasn't doing as well as I had hoped. The feedback I received from readers was great, but the writing industry is tough, to say the least. I never fathomed how much work and stress were involved in publishing and launching a book. With more and more books, and fewer and fewer brick-and-mortar stores, it's a huge challenge to get a book into the hands of a substantial number of people. Don't get me wrong — it's an honor for me to bless only one person. It really is. But after spending countless hours — years, actually — pouring myself into something, I wanted it to spread far and wide.

For me, it isn't about the money; it's about impacting the lives of as many people as possible. Thankfully, I am blessed to have a husband whose career allows us to live comfortably without me having to contribute financially. But this particular day, I must admit that the money factor was really weighing heavily on me because I needed a new computer. Mine had been acting up for way too long.

I wanted an Apple computer, which was more expensive than any I ever had before. With so much of my time spent on a computer, it was extremely important to have one that was fast, reliable, and easy to use.

I was rather discouraged because I felt like my new career was a financial burden. It was costing me more money than I was bringing in, especially considering how much money we were about to spend on my new MacBook Air.

After praying, I tried to let go of my worries. Many times before, God had spoken to me in amazing ways, so I trusted He would come through for me again. And boy did He ever!

My husband and I spent the day at an amusement park, something I knew he would enjoy for his upcoming birthday. Then it was off to the mall — one with an Apple store — to buy my new computer.

After making my selection, my husband forked out a large sum of money, and we headed for the door. At the exact moment we walked through the door, I received a mysterious phone call from my mom. Initially, her voice scared me. She asked what I was doing, and after telling her, she told us to come by her house on our way home. I asked her why, but she wouldn't tell me; however, she did assure me that nothing was wrong.

So, after the hour-long drive home, my husband and I stopped by my mom and stepdad's house. We were both baffled, wondering why she had been so adamant that we come. Honestly, I was a little worried, despite the fact that my mom told me she didn't have bad news. As we all sat down together in the living room, the wheels in my head were spinning as fast as ever, and my heart was beating fast. What in the world was going on?

After finding out, I was in tears… happy tears. It turned out that my mom had gone to her bank to close out a safe deposit box she had had for years, and she came across a huge surprise — one for me. She and I had forgotten about the savings bonds she was storing there — U.S. bonds that my generous aunt and uncle had given me every single year on my birthday, from one year to eighteen years of age.

I was thirty-six at the time, so every one of the bonds had matured and, therefore, was worth even more than their face value. In other words,

I had hit the jackpot! My mom felt terrible that she had unknowingly kept them from me all that time. Little did she know that she couldn't have picked a better time to give them to me!

The savings bonds had crossed my mind a few years before. I had vaguely remembered that they were stored in a safe deposit box at some point, but I figured they had already been cashed out and credited to me a long time ago — long enough that the exact details had gotten lost somewhere in the sea of memories made in the years between college and the present.

I was astonished and told them the story of how I had asked — actually, *insisted* may be a better word — that God give me a sign that I was doing His will. What better sign could He have provided than by blessing me with nearly twice the amount of money I had hesitantly spent on that computer a few hours before? The fact that I received my mom's phone call only seconds after the purchase, right before stepping out of the store, was icing on the cake.

This may not constitute a true miracle, but I know it was much more than coincidence that my mom stumbled upon those bonds on a day when I most needed the confidence, encouragement, and money to continue my writing career to inspire others and deepen their faith.

~Mandy Lawrence

64

If the Key Fits

Life is a series of thousands of tiny
miracles. Notice them.
~Author Unknown

My Uncle Pat was a barber and he always had the best stories to tell at our family's Sunday dinner table. He was never short of anecdotes about the customers who came into his shop each week. Sad stories, happy stories, amazing stories — his customers had them all, and we got to hear them. Yet the story that I remember best is one in which he took center stage.

As we ate our antipasto one Sunday afternoon, my uncle told us that he had stopped at the grocery store to do his weekly shopping on his day off. After buying up his usual items, he pushed his shopping cart toward his 1970 gold Dodge Dart and noticed that an identical Dart had parked in the space next to his. Intrigued, he took a closer look, only to find a young woman alternately wiping tears from her cheeks and frantically yanking on the door of the car.

Now, my uncle had the kindest heart of anyone I ever met, so, I knew before he even told us that he went over to that woman in his quiet, unassuming way to ask her if he could help. The young woman lifted her tear-stained face and pointed toward the driver's seat. And there my uncle saw the set of keys she had accidentally locked inside.

"I ran out to get milk on my way to pick up my kids from school, and look what I did! I was rushing so much that I locked my keys in the car." She wiped a few more tears from her face. "How will I get them now?" she sobbed.

Well, my uncle may have been kind, and certainly a talented barber, but handy he was not, and opening a locked car door without a key was something way beyond his abilities. Still, he was determined to be of help. So, he did the only thing he could think of doing. He reached into his pocket and handed the woman his car key. "Here," he said, "try this."

The young woman gave him a you've-got-to-be-kidding look.

"Try it," he told her again as he offered her his key. "It might work. I mean, they're both Dodge Darts, and they're even the same color."

With that, the young woman shrugged her shoulders, took the key, slipped it into the lock and opened the door. Her tears of terror quickly turned into tears of joy. "My prayers were answered," she said, and then thanked my uncle profusely before driving off in time to fetch her children from school.

My entire family sat around the dinner table that day in complete awe of my uncle's story. Yet no one was more awestruck than my uncle himself. We tossed around the possibilities. My mother and father both agreed that certainly it was plausible, with so many cars manufactured in this world, that a lock-and-key combination could be repeated. But that two cars with the same lock parked next to each other on the same day, well, that was some coincidence. And that a kindly man with the right key showed up at the exact moment a frantic young mother was wondering how she could open her locked door, well, that was plain amazing.

We continued to mull over the situation as dessert was being served.

"Amazing," my mother muttered.

"Incredible," my father declared.

Then my uncle gave his assessment. "You know, I think it was a miracle."

We all nodded our heads. "Yes, a miracle." And somewhere out there, I'm sure one very relieved young mother agreed.

~Monica A. Andermann

65

Flying Without a License

Miracles happen to those who believe.
If you believe in something with all your
heart and mind, you bring it to life.
~Leon Brown

"I'm sorry," the attendant said. "I can't let you board this flight as your ID has expired."

I was stunned. Shocked. My good friend and I had driven two hours into Edmonton the night before and had been at the airport since 5:00 a.m., organized and ready for this 7:00 a.m. flight.

Also, it meant I had been driving without a license. That was another issue. But right then I just needed to get on this flight to Toronto.

The agent understood our dilemma but, sticking to policy, she handed us two boarding passes and smiled. "There is a flight at 10:00. You need to get another official photo ID. Good luck."

That didn't allow me enough time to go home to Barrhead and come back. While my friend and the flight agent looked over some other ID I had, I phoned my neighbour and friend who lived in the next apartment and had my key. Would she answer at this early hour, and would she answer a cell number she did not recognize?

She did.

"Rita, I need your help. Can you please go to my apartment and get my passport?" I told her where it was, and she found it.

She replied, "I have it, but I'm sorry I can't bring it to you. I have to go to work."

I said, "Can you please phone my friends, Brad and Joan?" I gave her their home number and hung up.

When I called Rita back, she said she had reached Brad and he was on his way with my passport. She gave me his cell number.

The event in Toronto that night was the launch party for *Chicken Soup for the Soul: The Spirit of Canada*, in which I had two stories. I was invited to attend, sign books, and be part of the celebration party. I had quietly planned to attend about a month prior, but since then several friends had decided to join me. Three loyal, long-time friends and my niece from Manitoba had changed their plans to celebrate with me, and two other special people I had met in Cape Breton (the experience was recounted in one of my stories) drove 2,227 miles from Florida to be there to see me again. I had to make it.

As my friends were in Toronto getting ready to go to the venue, my friend and I were still three provinces away, racing from the airport by taxi to our vehicle to meet Brad on the highway. When there was an accident that caused a big traffic jam, we thought all was lost. But we got the passport, and hurried back, getting to the gate with only minutes to spare. I texted my friends, "I missed my flight." One of them replied, "Joking I hope." But it was no joke.

We boarded the 10:00 a.m. flight still not sure how it would all play out. As I sank into my window seat, I finally relaxed, and my tears blurred the view of the beautiful green square fields and glorious puffy clouds.

Two great friends in Toronto met us at the airport, and after some brief difficulties, the four of us arrived at the book launch party. After a brief connection with my waiting guests, I guided the others to join them, ran with my suitcase to the washroom, and changed into my red-and-white Canadian outfit. When I came back, they said I looked good. Maybe I should dress all the time from a suitcase in a small washroom in one minute!

Immediately, I started signing books with the other authors.

Everyday Miracles |

Although some moaned about sore wrists and fingers after a couple of hundred books, I'm sure I could have signed a thousand.

When Janet Matthews, in her heartwarming manner, relayed the true importance of story, and when Chris Robertson, with his national enthusiasm, joined our Canadian spirits, I knew there was no better place for me that night. When Rob Harshman read his story from the chapter, "Honouring Those Who Served," and when Lesley Marcovich from South Africa read what "O Canada" meant to her, I knew there was a reason things had worked out with my flight. And as I listened to "Sid, Please Sign My Jersey," I looked around at every smiling face in that room and knew a miracle had put me there.

~Glenice Wilson

God of the Little Things

Miracles are the natural way of the Universe. Our
only job is to move our doubting minds out of the way.
~Jonathan Lockwood Huie

I was running late, as usual. I had spent the morning paying bills, and then my yard guy showed up and needed payment, too. So when I arrived at the church, I practically flew out of the car and dashed inside the chapel. Two women were waiting; it was past noon, and I was five minutes late for the prayer hour that I'd signed up for.

I sat there alone, trying to quiet my thoughts. But all my financial worries kept circling in my mind and, as always, a little self-pity inched its way in. For more than thirty-five years, I hadn't needed to worry about finances. My husband not only took care of all the bills, but he relished the task. In the year since he'd died, I'd struggled to get up to speed with all the accounts, the bill-paying schedule, and the juggling of funds from here to there. How did he do it all so effortlessly?

And to top it off, I was hungry. I hadn't had time to grab anything before I left my house, but I'd checked the bread on the counter, figuring I'd make a sandwich when I got home. As usual, the bread had started to mold, and I'd had to toss it in the trash.

Since it was just me now, I almost always threw away bread. I couldn't finish a loaf or a package of sub rolls before spoilage set in. I could put the bread in the freezer, but I hated the way the bread tasted after being frozen and reheated. So I sat there in church, worrying about bread, too. I was leaving town soon and only needed enough slices for a couple of days. Should I stop by the grocery store and buy a loaf that was sure to go bad? Or just skip the bread altogether? It was a little thing, the bread, but it was just one more reminder of the loss I felt each day.

For twenty minutes or so, the worries tumbled around. Finally, I was able to find some peace and pray. In fact, I was surprised when I looked up and realized it was 1:00 and time to go. I gathered up my purse and headed to the door.

Just across from the chapel doors, chairs were lined up against a wall of glass, and a box sat on one of the chairs. I'd been in such a rush that I'd missed it when I first arrived. A sign on the box read, "Free. Please take one."

Perfect, I thought. Our church often received booklets or pamphlets to give away, and I sure needed some spiritual reading to take with me on my trip. So I walked over to the box and peered in.

It was bread — two 12-inch sub rolls in a package from the grocery store down the street. Enough bread to make four sandwiches, which happened to be exactly the amount of bread I needed. I literally turned my head back to the chapel and thought, *Um… God? Is that You?*

Still, I didn't reach for the bread. There was only one package, and surely someone else needed that bread more than I did.

But as I stood there looking at the bread, I had another thought. Well, maybe not so much a thought — more like a message. God wanted me to know that He was taking care of me. It was a little thing, this bread worry of mine, but God had heard me. And if God could take care of my little worries, He was surely taking care of the big ones, too.

"Thank you," I said. "For everything." And I picked up the bread. I'd just have time to make a sandwich before heading out on my next errand!

~Cathy C. Hall

Chapter 8

Miracles and More

Dreams and Premonitions

67

In My Dreams

*Pay attention to your dreams — God's angels often
speak directly to our hearts when we are asleep.*
~Eileen Elias Freeman,
The Angels' Little Instruction Book

"Good morning! First, the good news: You don't have an aneurysm or a brain tumor! Now, the bad news: We have no idea what is going on with you. So today we are going to check you for cancer and spinal meningitis."

Having suffered through four days of an excruciating headache, my husband had finally agreed to let me take him to the emergency room. After a round of tests, all of which came back normal, they admitted him "for observation." The following day, they ran another series of tests with the same results, leading to another night in the hospital. They ran more tests every day. A week in, we were no closer to an answer than the day he came in.

One night, when his blood pressure was dangerously high, I collapsed in an exhausted heap in the chair by his bed. I fell asleep, but it was a restless and disturbing sleep, populated by eerie and improbable dreams. In the midst of my mental chaos, one quietly odd dream demanded my attention.

It was a dream of striking simplicity: nothing more than a stick figure of a man lying in a stick figure of a bed. That was the entirety of it, and as I stood outside myself looking in, realization washed over me. The man in the bed was my husband, and he had shingles.

The next morning, the doctor came in with his usual "Good morning!" I listened with only half a mind to his recital of the tests of the day as my dream replayed in my head. Done, the doctor started out the door to order the tests, when I surprised myself by blurting out, "Do you think he could have shingles?" The doctor came to an abrupt stop, paused a moment in the doorway, and then took off down the hall in a virtual run.

Shortly afterward, on my way home for a shower and breakfast, I walked past the nurses' station where the doctor sat at the desk with a phone to his ear. "His wife thinks he has shingles," I overheard as I walked by.

I returned later in the morning to find the doctor once again in my husband's room. The test for shingles had been ordered and… bingo! Diagnosed at last, my husband was released the next day with prescriptions and orders for a follow-up visit.

My religion has long held that God speaks to us only through the Scriptures, and at one time I think I might have been inclined to agree. But now, if anyone were to ask me if God speaks to us in dreams, my answer just might be a resounding "Yes!"

~Mary Ables

68

Swim to the Light

A dream which is not interpreted is
like a letter which is not read.
~The Talmud

I awoke suddenly from a deep sleep. My heart was pounding, and I was scared. I closed my eyes, hoping to fall back to sleep quickly. But there it was again.

I was drowning. An unknown force was pulling me straight down toward the bottom of a deep, dark ocean. I was wrapped in a twisted heavy rope from my shoulders to my ankles. My arms were pinned to my sides, and my legs were bound together.

I could feel myself sinking quickly toward the bottom. I had no oxygen left and I was starting to panic. I was going to die soon if I didn't do something, but I didn't know what to do!

I started moving my bound legs back and forth like a mermaid. All of a sudden, the ropes loosened and my feet and legs were free. I was kicking my feet and moving my upper body around sideways. The ropes fell away. I was kicking my feet even faster now, and my body started moving upward!

I was getting closer to the top and could see rays of light penetrating the water. "Swim to the light," a little voice said. "Swim to the light." I broke through the surface of the water, gasping for air. The sun was shining, and the sky was blue. I was alive, and everything was going to be fine.

I opened my eyes again in the dark room. The soft glow of the alarm clock cast an eerie light on the ceiling. I got out of bed, afraid I would have the bad dream again if I went back to sleep. It haunted me all day, making it hard to focus at work. My mind kept drifting back to the dream, wondering what it could possibly mean.

A few days later, a colleague stopped by my office. Sandy had recently been diagnosed with breast cancer and had started chemo. She was only in her thirties and had three young children. Outwardly, I tried to be positive and encouraging, but inwardly I was very upset by all that was happening to her.

That night, the dream came roaring back again. The next morning, I told my husband about it while we were getting ready for work. He speculated that I was internalizing what Sandy was going through. My husband said, "The dream might be just to reassure you that Sandy will be alright if she fights back." I liked his interpretation, but I wasn't sure if that's what it really meant.

Over the next few weeks, I had the same dream several times. I couldn't shake the dream. I became convinced that the dream was mostly about me, but somehow Sandy was very connected. Sandy was fighting her cancer. The dream was showing me that I needed to fight back and swim to the light.

I struggled to find a connection between Sandy and my dream. What was wrong? What did I need to fight? The only thing I could come up with was to make an appointment for a mammogram. A few days after the appointment, I got a call saying they wanted to do more X-rays. That same day, the radiologist recommended a biopsy, which was scheduled for a few days later.

The day finally came for me to get the biopsy results. When the doctor came into the room, he moved his chair close to mine and said, "I'm afraid I don't have very good news."

There were no tears, just a feeling of numbness. "I know," I said, nodding slowly.

"You do?" the doctor asked incredulously, sitting back in his chair.

"Yes, I had a dream," I told him. "That's why I came in for a mammogram."

I never had the dream again.

It was a long road, with surgery, chemo, and radiation, but I trusted the dream completely. It gave me hope and a positive attitude. I fought back, prayed frequently, and was finally able to swim to the light.

It's been eleven years, and I'm still doing well. Divine intervention saved my life, and cancer changed my perspective. I've met some wonderful people because of it, and I've witnessed and received unbelievable kindnesses. Best of all, I have had the opportunity to pay it forward and help others on similar journeys.

And in case you're wondering about Sandy, she is doing well, too!

~Barbara Dorman Bower

All the Way Home

*The power of intuitive understanding will protect
you from harm until the end of your days.*
~Lao Tzu

S ometimes, we just get a feeling. Whether instinct or intuition, it's a visceral jolt that sets us on guard and shapes our responses, if we are wise enough to listen. I definitely had it when I stepped out of the main building of the community college in Parsons, Kansas, at 8:30 in the evening on April 19, 2000. Having just finished an exam, I was tired and ready to go home. I looked up and noted the sky was an odd, yellowish-gray, and the air was eerily still and heavy for early spring. I thought: *Man, it looks like it's going to rain, and probably hail, any minute.*

I knew my husband would freak out if I got caught in a hailstorm in our brand-new Suburban. We lived in the country six miles away, so I knew I'd better hurry. After jogging to my car, I jumped in and headed for home. Martina McBride belted out "Wild Angels" from the CD player.

As I drove around the plaza a few blocks away, the sky grew more ominous, with low, dark clouds building to the south. The wind picked up, sending a plastic shopping bag dancing past me on the street. Rain slowly started to fall, and I knew a storm was imminent.

I quickly began thinking of places nearby to pull in for cover until the worst had passed. Two blocks away was Parsons Motors, which had a large metal awning that would shelter me. I decided I would stop to see if there was room for my car. But as I went under the underpass and prepared to turn into the drive, a strong sense of apprehension washed over me, and an inner voice said, *No, just keep going and get home as fast as you can. If the car gets damaged by hail, it's not the end of the world.*

So that's what I did. Martina kept singing, and I kept on driving. There were only a few cars in front of me, all moving west down Main Street toward the city limit, our headlights reflecting off the road as the wet patches began to broaden. With just three miles to go, I started to think I might actually make it in time.

I couldn't have been more wrong. After little more than a mile, I passed over the bridge near the country club and ran smack into a wall of blinding rain and wind so strong it caught me off guard, pushing my side mirror up against the driver's window and my vehicle hard to the right. The last thing I saw clearly were the sudden brake lights of the cars in front of me as each halted and veered onto the shoulder of the highway. I quickly followed suit. I sat stunned and somewhat frightened, gripping the steering wheel, as the wind and rain rocked my large Suburban. I could scarcely make out the hood of my car as all my other surroundings disappeared into the swirling darkness. I imagined this was as close as I could come to experiencing a hurricane in Kansas. I silently prayed it wouldn't get any worse.

Ten long minutes passed before the torrent eased and each car, in turn, pulled slowly back onto the roadway. I crept the final two miles to my house, and as I pulled into the drive the rain completely stopped. Before I could turn off the car, my husband and two young daughters came barreling out the front door. I climbed out of the car and met them at the rear. The girls threw their arms around my waist. My husband was shaking, his voice cracking as he asked, "Where have you been? A tornado just hit Parsons!"

I gasped, as I struggled to register what he had said. I looked down at my children, my eyes brimming with tears, and could only stammer, "I just came from there. I was stopped outside of town in the worst rainstorm I have ever seen."

We went inside, and my husband told me about the evening's

weather alerts. He couldn't believe that no one at the college had told us we were under a tornado warning before we left the building. He asked if I had heard the tornado sirens or a radio weather bulletin. I explained that I had a CD playing and might have gone through town right before the sirens sounded. I told him about my gut feeling that I should just go home. We were so thankful I had chosen not to stop.

The next day, I watched news footage of the destruction. An F3 tornado had torn through the center of the city at 8:50 p.m., damaging fifty-three businesses and 577 homes. I was overcome with sadness and disbelief, viewing the devastated landscape of the town where I was born and raised. It was then that I realized the full magnitude of my decision to stay my course. I stared at the TV and began trembling and crying as it flashed an image of the mangled, twisted metal building that had been Parsons Motors. That metal awning in front, where I had planned to take shelter, was completely collapsed; I would likely have been crushed beneath it.

Gifts come in many forms, whether subtle nudges to our unconscious minds or outright divine interventions. I believe wholeheartedly I was a blessed recipient that night.

~Tiffany Flynn

70

Be Happy

Unable are the loved to die. For love is immortality.
~Emily Dickinson

To say that my heart was broken was an understatement. My younger sister, Anna, who was also my best friend, had passed away from leukemia, and I was living in a fog of grief.

I got up each day, did what I had to do, came home, stared at the TV, and then went back to bed. This cycle continued for more than a year. My heart physically ached, and doing anything that I used to find enjoyable seemed wrong without my sister there to enjoy it with me.

Since I was still going through the motions, my family didn't worry about me too much. They were fighting their own battles with grief and figuring out their own lives without Anna. Since no one was worried about me, I wasn't worried about myself.

It was the second summer after her death when I had the dream.

In the dream, I was sitting at the dining room table with my family, and we were about to eat supper. Anna was gone, but not in the sense of death — more in the sense that she was out of town. The phone rang, and my father answered it.

He looked at me, phone receiver in his outstretched hand. "It's for you."

I was confused as to who would be calling me. Since my sister's death, I had turned down almost every invitation and pushed away almost all my friends.

I walked over and spoke a cautious "hello" into the phone.

"Hey, it's me, Anna."

She didn't have to say her name, I knew her voice instantly. Even though I knew I was dreaming, her voice warmed me. It was crystal clear, and I felt as if she were standing right by me, even though we were on the phone. I wanted to speak, but couldn't find my voice.

"I don't have long, but I just wanted you to know that I want you to be happy," she said.

"Happy?" I repeated.

"Yeah." Her voice was cheerful, as it always was, and I could picture her smile — her glorious smile that could lighten the darkest of rooms. "Like you were in conservation."

"Conservation?" There was so much I wanted to say to her. I wanted to tell her how much I loved her, how much I missed her, and how sorry I was for not staying longer at the hospital on the night she died. But all I could do was repeat the last words of her sentences.

"Yeah," she said. "Gotta go. Love you."

The phone went silent, and I woke up. The dream was still vivid and replayed in my mind as I lay in bed contemplating what she had said: *Like you were in conservation.*

What did she mean by "conservation"? I thought about our last six months together. Two of those months I had spent as a bear researcher in the mountains of New Mexico. It was most definitely conservation work, and as my brilliant sister had reminded me, it was one of my happiest times.

As the sun peeked over the horizon, I got up, dressed, and put on my boots. As I started toward the door, ready to go hiking for the first time since Anna's death, the phone rang.

I grabbed it quickly so I could tell whomever it was to call back later, before the motivating effects of the dream wore off and I fell back into my fog. The line was quiet, but in my mind I could hear my sister's voice saying, "Be happy."

~Jennifer McMurrain

71

Take Me Out to the Ballgame

Love recognizes no barriers. It jumps hurdles,
leaps fences, penetrates walls to arrive at
its destination full of hope.
~Maya Angelou

The divorce had been rough, and the ongoing legal struggles were exhausting. I slumped in the pew one gloomy
Sunday morning. The gray day seemed to penetrate the
inside of the church and my mood as I sat there and
prayed, "God, if you just get me out of this mess, I promise I will
never, ever get married again!"

I think God must have smiled at my offer. Immediately, I was
given a vision or a premonition—and it scared me to death!

I saw myself getting ready to walk down the left aisle of our church
with my adult children, Darren and Michele, my son-in-law, Tim, and my
grandson, Kristopher. Although Kristopher was their only child, Michele
was carrying a little, dark-haired girl about two years old. Coming down
the right aisle was a tall man holding the hand of a little girl. The altar was
filled with beautiful, pink flowers!

The vision only lasted a few seconds, but it was so real that I
was shaking and confused. I thought about it for a few days and then
forgot about it as I struggled to survive. Working two jobs, I had no
social life at all.

I did enjoy watching our local baseball team, the California Angels, on TV. Finally, at my friends' urging, I joined the Angels Booster Club. It was fun to attend the baseball games as a group and hand out giveaway items at the gates. While working the gates, I met John, one of the club members. He was so friendly, and we talked and laughed a lot.

Whenever the team was out of town, a group of us would gather to watch the Angels on TV. John was always present and hopeful of a relationship, but I told him, "I enjoy being with you, but I'm not interested in anything more." He would just nod his head and smile.

One day, John's parents invited me to their house for a party. John had an adorable daughter, Jamie, and it was her sixth birthday. I knew he had a little girl, but he was pretty protective of her and hadn't introduced us until he was sure about his feelings for me. She and I bonded immediately, but I told John, "I still don't want to get married again — ever." John just smiled and nodded his head in that infuriating way of his. I responded with an adamant, "I mean it!"

"I know you do — now," he replied, grinning.

I took the problem to God. "Why won't he believe me? I don't want to hurt him, God, but I just don't want to get married again."

One day, John and I were sitting at the park watching Jamie play on the monkey bars. "You know," John said quietly, "we might as well get married. We're together all the time, and we get along so well. I can't imagine my life without you."

I had a lump in my throat as I sat there staring at him and then at his sweet girl. Neither of us spoke for a long time, and then I said, "I can't imagine my life without both of you, either."

We decided on a February church wedding and a reception at Angel Stadium where we had met. Michele and Tim came from Minnesota to visit us in October and arrived with Kristopher, now four years old, and two-year-old, Kelly, my little, dark-haired granddaughter.

On Wednesday of their weeklong visit, Michele said to me, "Mom, we're going to start building our new house, and we won't be able to come back in February for your wedding."

"What shall we do?" I asked John.

With his usual calm, he asked me, "What's more important to

you — to have all the kids there or to have the wedding we planned in February?"

When he said that, I remembered that vision from three years before. "It's definitely more important to have all the kids there," I replied, "but how can we pull this together so quickly?"

"We'll just split up all the tasks, and everyone can help," he replied confidently.

I called my friend, Betty, who worked at a nursery. "John and I are getting married on Saturday. Can you help with the flowers?"

"Of course, I wouldn't miss it," she replied calmly. "What color is your dress?"

"I don't have one yet!" In fact, I hadn't even thought about it.

"Okay," Betty said, "your flowers will be pink. Pink will go with any color you choose."

I called our Booster Club friends to see if they could serve refreshments. They jumped right in and even planned to wear their Booster Club shirts.

Another friend, Isobel, offered to make our wedding cake. "No one else can make your cake and put all the love into it that I can," she said.

Everyone pitched in. Some made calls since we had no time to send invitations. Others offered to decorate and make punch. "I'll get napkins, plates and cups," my future father-in-law volunteered. I wondered if it would all match when the pieces were put together.

At the rehearsal, I told our pastor about my vision. "I think it was a picture from God," I explained, "so I want to walk down the left aisle with my children and grandchildren while John walks down the right aisle with his daughter. Then we can all come out the center aisle together as one family."

"I think that's a fine idea," he agreed, smiling.

On Saturday, I walked into the church reception hall, and everything looked beautiful! Everything that our friends and family had prepared fit together beautifully. Isobel's cake looked like three layers of love and deliciousness. There were the plates and napkins with our names printed on them as promised. And — everything was pink!

Dreams and Premonitions |

Just before we were to walk down the aisle, Kelly slipped and started to cry, so Michele picked her up and held her, and we walked down the aisle together just as I had seen in my vision.

The pastor even included all the kids in the ceremony. After we said our vows, he had us all clasp hands on top of my Bible and asked my children, "Do you promise to respect and honor John and this marriage?"

"Yes, we do," they promised.

Turning to Jamie, the pastor asked her, "Do you promise to respect and honor Judee as your stepmother?"

"I do," she answered in a solemn, small voice.

"Then I pronounce this family is one in the sight of God and these witnesses!" announced the pastor.

As we started our journey together down the center aisle, we laughed out loud as the organist played a dignified rendition of "Take Me Out to the Ballgame" on the church organ. We had heard that song hundreds of times, but now we would hear *our* song at every baseball game!

~Judee Stapp

72

A Single Twisted Tree

*At times you have to leave the city of your comfort
and go into the wilderness of your intuition. What
you'll discover will be wonderful. What
you'll discover is yourself.*
~Alan Alda

I had been planning this for years — I would book an extended stay in Ireland, the birthplace of my great-grandfather. I needed to get out of the rut I'd been in since I graduated from college: the sameness of my routine, and the feeling that something just wasn't right about this life I had created.

So, when the time came to take the leap, I had already sold off most of my possessions and was moving the rest into storage. My company was on notice that I would be gone at least six months, with no guarantee that I would return or that they would offer me the same job if I came back. The lease on my apartment was up, and I had enough money saved up to live on for a while.

Then, as I was about to buy the plane ticket to Ireland, I started to have vivid dreams of kangaroos and the red desert. I knew nothing about Australia. Still, those dreams continued, night after night, saturated in intense colors and a surreal silence. Finally, they were too powerful to ignore. Clearly, something was waiting for me Down Under. I bought a ticket for my new destination.

Then, with less than two weeks to go, I flopped onto the couch for a nap. Another dream arrived with all the clarity of a vision.

I was sailing over the red plains as easily as an eagle. Here and there, saltbush and spiky grasses splashed the desert a frosty, faded green. The feeling was that of utter freedom.

I felt drawn toward a single tree twisted from years in the brutal environment. In the shade beneath the thin branches lay my corpse. The image jolted me, but I moved farther ahead, just to be sure that it was me. It was, and I was definitely dead.

I lay there on the couch for the longest time thinking about the vision. This one had been by far the most clear, the one that felt as if I was actually there in some way experiencing the events. Was this a premonition, one of those gut feelings that keeps people from boarding planes that end up crashing? And if I headed into the Outback anyway, would I regret my choice?

Then the thought came to me that I was already dead. The corporate job I had worked so hard to get was killing me. Staying meant falling ever deeper into the darkness. Even if I ended up dying during the trip, I would have met my end while living fully.

A week after landing in Sydney, I purchased a twenty-year-old sedan. I geared up with forty gallons of gasoline and a tent in the trunk, and a two-week supply of dried rice, potatoes and water jumbled on the rear seat. Then, armed only with a map pulled from an old *National Geographic* magazine, I headed into the desert.

The territory was so rough that only the middle of the roads — ragged patches of asphalt the Australians called highways — were drivable. During the course of that journey, five tires blew from the extreme conditions, the hood came loose and slammed against the windshield, the car got stuck up to the axles in the talc-like Outback dust, and an untraceable short in the system occasionally left me stranded for hours before mysteriously fixing itself.

Amid these challenges there was incredible beauty. Every night, I pulled off in some lonely patch of desert where it felt like the world was devoid of other human life. I cooked over an open fire and listened to the embers crackle in the silent desert. The stars' steadfast glow made time irrelevant.

Then, one day, I was driving along a roadbed that had been raised about four feet to prevent the asphalt from washing away during seasonal flooding. The pavement was a single lane in each direction, and was barely more than a crumbling layer of asphalt. The speedometer was hovering north of 80 mph when one of the tires blew.

The car flew off the road and landed hard on the desert floor. By some slim chance, the kinetic energy did not flip the vehicle. Instead, it bounced upward, bounding again and again in hops that grew shorter but were no less dangerous. I could do nothing but wait for the car to stop.

Then a single twisted tree rose up in front of me. It was the image I had seen in that vision. I was going to die.

Suddenly, a bright hot light flashed through me, and I knew. I did not want to die this way. I looked to my right at the road. The moment I thought, *that's where I want to be,* the car was back on the road.

I had not moved the wheel. I had not blinked or even taken a breath. But the car was on the asphalt again, a little wobbly but now slow enough to control. I pulled over, parked on the narrow shoulder, and looked out at that lone tree. My arms began to shake so hard I could barely keep my grip on the steering wheel.

But I had changed the vision. I had traveled halfway around the world in order to choose life. I was not just surviving in a salaried position, keeping my head down and my mouth shut. I chose to live fully. When we leave our lives open to possibility, even something miraculous can happen.

~Laine Cunningham

73

A House with a View

*You must train your intuition — you must trust the
small voice inside you which tells you exactly
what to say, what to decide.*
~Ingrid Bergman

"**W**e can't live here."

"What?" My husband gave me an incredulous stare. "Why not?"

"I don't know," I stammered, shaking my head. "It's just… um… not right."

"What on earth are you talking about? It's perfect! A big kitchen with a view of the ocean. Three bedrooms, two baths — and I know you love that round corner fireplace in the family room!" He swept the room with his arm and then added, "Plus, it's affordable and will be ready for us to move in on time."

I nodded, tears welling up in my eyes. The house was perfect for us and all we had hoped for when we sat in our just-sold house in Illinois. Visions of a home with a view of the ocean filled our dreams as we prepared to begin a new adventure together.

Our life was going to be quite different, and not just because of the move. After eleven years of marriage, I was pregnant! The shock of it brought us utter joy as well as great surprise to our family and friends. It also meant changes, drastic ones.

As often happens, nothing was easy or logical. Bill had been waiting for the opportunity to transfer to California for five years. Word came of an opening soon after we learned of my pregnancy. The timing couldn't have been worse. I was considered "high risk" because I was thirty-one years old. Today, that would be average, but in the early 1970s it was considered late in life to be delivering a baby.

"You can't travel," said my obstetrician.

"I have to," I replied.

He argued with me, giving me all the reasons why I shouldn't go house hunting with Bill, but he finally shook his head, muttering something about headstrong, older mothers-to-be.

Finding a new home turned out to be more challenging than we expected. Day after day, we drove up and down the coast searching for that perfect house. And on the fourth day, it looked like we had found it. Except...

We wandered through the house, and a mounting sense of panic began to surround me. I thought, *Maybe it's just my "condition," or maybe I'm just tired, or maybe...* But no. There was not a single reason for my feeling of alarm. I tried to push it down, but it grew.

"Look at the size of this room! It'll easily hold our king-size bed," Bill said with enthusiasm, "and the small one next to it will be perfect for the baby." He kept his arm around me, pointing out the charms of the house as we walked through it again. I said nothing, and he was aware that I was quiet, not at all thrilled. He was confused but had gotten used to my new mood swings and endured them without comment. He knew they would pass. But this time nothing dispelled my feelings. In fact, the longer we stayed in the house, the more they grew. I felt a chill run down my entire body, and a sense of doom enveloped me.

"I'm sorry, honey. I really am." I looked up at Bill and continued, "We just can't live here."

"Aww, Jeanie." Bill's face was one of complete exasperation.

I pushed my way outside and into our rental car. Bill followed hesitantly, looking at the house with longing. It hurt me to see him so sad. We gazed at the sun sparkling on the ocean as we slowly and silently took the curves down toward the freeway.

The next day, we didn't mention the "house with the view," but continued our search. Late in the afternoon, we discovered a new community of rolling hills and a beautiful house with a sweeping view of the valley and mountains beyond. It would be ready for occupancy within six weeks and, most important, filled me with serenity.

"We'll be happy here," I said. "I can feel it."

Bill nodded and said, "I don't understand — not at all," but called to tell the agent that he'd made a sale.

A month later, we moved in, and six weeks after that the "baby" arrived — two of them! We were incredibly blessed and busy beyond belief.

More than a year went by before we were driving to San Diego with our daughters for a day at the zoo. We were passing the neighborhood where I had passed on our dream house with the ocean view because of my eerie "feelings."

"Let's go see the house," I blurted out.

"What house?" Bill said, and then almost immediately, "Oh, that one. Okay, why not?" And he took the exit that led up the hill to the neighborhood.

As we came around the final curve, we both gasped, and Bill jammed on the brakes. There were no houses. None at all. In fact, all we saw was a round fireplace standing sentinel on the corner lot. "Our" fireplace.

"Fire," Bill uttered through a deep breath.

"Fire? What fire?"

"Remember the Camp Pendleton fire, the one that got into the brush and went beyond the camp?" I nodded but didn't take my eyes off the barrenness before me as he continued. "I heard that it burned some houses, but never dreamed it was here." We stared at the bare street and that lone fireplace.

"Something bad was going to happen…" I whispered. "I knew it… I just didn't know what."

Voices rose from the back seat. The girls had been quietly complaining, but we were too stunned to take note of them until they added high-pitched whining, almost harmonized, as only they could do.

"Let's get going," Bill said, grinning at his daughters. He then reached over and hugged me. "You and your 'feelings.' I'm so grateful for them. I'll never doubt you again!"

It's been forty-five years since we found our perfect house with a view — the second one. We still live here, just the two of us again. Our daughters left for college, and then married and moved on with their own lives. They still love to hear the story of how we found the home where they grew up. And they are adjusting to the fact that it's time for us to downsize and let another family enjoy a life of love and happiness here.

Feelings. Never deny them. They don't come often, but I have experienced them occasionally, and each time learned they're meant to be heard and heeded. They are God's gifts.

~Jean Haynie Stewart

74

Phone Calls at Midnight

*Miracles, in the sense of phenomena we cannot
explain, surround us on every hand: life
itself is the miracle of miracles.*
~George Bernard Shaw

My final year of college was way more stressful than I had anticipated. With weekly essays, internship applications, and numerous exams, I barely had time to sleep.

On top of it all, my sister Sarah—a confidante I used to see every day—moved halfway across the world. She was most likely facing her own trials and tribulations, starting a brand-new job in a foreign country. With nearly eight thousand miles between us, what had started as weekly Sunday phone calls eventually diminished to only birthdays and holidays. We were both so busy. Too busy, it seemed, even for family.

The final week of the semester crept up on me without much warning. I found myself at my desk late one night, desperately cramming for an exam. I was operating on three cups of coffee, four hours of sleep, and a whole lot of adrenaline.

I must have fallen asleep in my chair.

Suddenly, I was on a beach. The sand was pearl white, the sky violet. The sea lay green and still ahead of me. The beach was empty—save for one jagged gray rock and a young woman on top of it.

The woman's back was toward me. With a start, I recognized the locks of dark hair.

"Sarah?" I found my voice too loud in the eerie quiet. "Is that you?"

The woman turned her head. It was my sister — but she was weeping bright red tears. She said, "Goodbye."

I woke with a start, my heart thundering in my chest. My mouth was completely dry. I picked up the phone and called Sarah.

It took three full rings for Sarah to answer. "Hello?"

Hearing her voice made me realize I had been holding my breath. I allowed myself to exhale. "Sarah."

"Is everything alright? It's past midnight where you are."

"Yes, I'm fine. It's just…" I was starting to calm down. I took in the books around me, the papers on which I had fallen asleep. Now that I was fully awake, I couldn't justify calling her due to a silly nightmare. "We haven't talked in a while," I said at last. The excuse, I realized, was also the truth. It had been weeks.

"You're right," she said "How are you?" A pause. "Don't answer that. I forgot it was finals week!"

And so we chatted. As the minutes passed, the anxiety within me faded away. Eventually, I glanced at the clock and realized we had been talking for almost an hour. "Oh! Sarah, am I keeping you from anything?"

I heard her laugh on the other end. "I missed my bus to grab your phone call, but that's alright. I'm waiting for the next one."

"Oh, no! I'm sorry."

"Don't be. It's not often that you call." There was a pause. "Truth be told, I was a little scared. I thought something had gone wrong."

"No, nothing is wrong." *Other than my nerves,* I thought. "I'm going to let you go. Don't miss your next bus!"

"Alright. Good luck with your studying!"

I hung up the phone and looked at the table on which I had fallen asleep. I saw piles of bookmarked textbooks, highlighted notes, and unfinished essays. So much worry and stress had plagued me these past few weeks; no wonder I was having nightmares! I decided to let myself have some rest and went to bed.

By the time my alarm woke me the next day, I had next to no recollection of the dream. I got back to work. My mind was so preoccupied, in fact, that I only remembered the phone call when Sarah's number flashed on my phone at lunch. I blinked at the screen, surprised at her calling. It was nearing midnight in Thailand. "Hello?"

I heard heavy breathing and Sarah's voice trembling on the other end. "Sabrina?"

I felt my stomach twist. "What's wrong? Are you okay?"

"Yes, I'm fine… but yesterday… " I heard more heavy breathing and what sounded like a choked sob.

"Sarah?"

"When you called me yesterday, and I missed my bus to answer your call… that bus was in an accident, Sabrina. I just found out. It ran into a truck passing the beach. There were no survivors."

Snatches of the nightmare came back to me. An impossible sky and crimson tears, the unshakeable feeling that I needed to reach out to my sister.

Sarah said what I was only beginning to realize. "Your call saved my life."

I didn't know what to say. Or how to feel. I only felt immense gratitude. I started to sob.

Sarah was crying, too. She said, "I don't know how to thank you."

"Don't," I said. "Don't thank me." I only had the universe to thank. I truly believed there was a force of good out there looking out for us. Something that kept all things in balance, and sometimes, prevented the worst things in life from happening. "But Sarah… please do one thing."

"What's that?"

"Call me more often."

~Sabrina Forest

75

The Party

*It was possible that a miracle was not something that
happened to you, but rather something that didn't.*
~Jodi Picoult, The Tenth Circle

I had tossed and turned most of the night in a restless sleep. I slowly opened my eyes and yawned as I looked out my bedroom window. It would soon be sunrise. With only a couple hours of sleep, I didn't know how I was going to get through my hectic day. It was my daughter's third birthday, and I had so much to do before the guests arrived for her party. I wanted everything to be perfect.

It was only 5:00 a.m. I needed more sleep, so I closed my eyes and managed to drift off again, but then I had the most vivid dream.

Heather's birthday party was about to begin. I was rushing around, tidying the house and preparing food for my guests. "Mom, when is everyone coming over?" "Mom, can I have just one treat?" My daughter kept interrupting me with questions.

Feeling overwhelmed, I turned to her and said in a stern tone, "Heather, enough. I have a lot to do! Go and ask your dad!" With a sad face, my daughter went off to find her father.

I called out to my husband, Harold, to tell him I was making a quick run to the grocery store for some last-minute items I had forgotten. I could feel the stress as I rushed out the door. Just then, I heard a loud crash coming from inside my house. My daughter's cries were loud and terrifying. I tried to run to see what happened, but my legs wouldn't move. My body was weighted down, and I was stuck. I stood frozen in fear. I couldn't reach my daughter to help her!

I woke up startled, confused and with my heart racing. The dream was so realistic, I thought it actually happened. I looked at the clock and realized I had only been asleep for a half-hour.

It was useless to try to fall back to sleep. I decided to begin my day and get a head start preparing for the party. I decorated the house with balloons and streamers. I made over a dozen goody bags that were filled with candy and small toys for the kids to take home. I finished making platters of finger foods, and I was very proud of Heather's Rainbow Brite birthday cake that I made!

The morning whizzed by, and soon it was the afternoon. Guests would be arriving in less than an hour. "There," I said with satisfaction as I put the finishing touches on the cake. Now I just needed to go to the grocery store to buy the birthday candles I had forgotten to purchase the day before. In a mad dash to beat the clock, I called out to Harold to let him know I'd be right back. As I headed out the door, I froze. This was just like my dream! This time, I didn't freeze. I ran back inside the house, just as my daughter was leaning on the glass dining room table to reach her drink. Everything after that went in slow motion as I saw her crash through the glass table top. I was able to grab the back of her dress and lift her up before she hit the floor.

As my daughter wailed, I searched her body to see if she was hurt. She was startled, but she didn't have a single scratch. My husband stood there in shock. The thick glass had caved in on the chrome base of the table, with huge, sharp pieces of glass and shards everywhere. One large wedge of glass had been so close to my daughter's face. I shuddered to think what could have happened if I hadn't gone back into the house, and if I didn't have that dream.

My daughter was shaken up afterward, but I've learned that kids are more resilient than adults. A few minutes later, she asked for her drink as if nothing had happened. As a mom, that was a relief. After Harold and I cleaned up all the glass, we had a few minutes to spare before the guests arrived. We sat down to compose ourselves.

The birthday party went off without a hitch. It was a wonderful diversion from what had happened earlier. That night, in the quiet of our home, I reluctantly told Harold about my vivid dream. I thought he wouldn't take me seriously, but he looked me straight in the eye and said, "Your dream saved Heather from getting badly hurt. What a great birthday gift you gave her!" I smiled up at him with heavy eyes as I drifted off into a much-needed, sweet slumber.

~Dorann Weber

76

Once Upon a Time at a Barbecue

Carve your name on hearts, not tombstones. A legacy
is etched into the minds of others and the
stories they share about you.
~Shannon L. Alder

On Saturdays, unless the weather was bad, my husband would take our little daughter Julie to the park for a few hours so "Mommy can have a break." I appreciated the time alone and tried to fill it with something that I wasn't able to do with an active preschooler in the house, like reading a good book, working on my tan, or soaking in a bubble bath.

One unforgettable Saturday, I was napping on the sofa when voices in the back yard woke me up.

Plumes of heavy gray smoke billowed past the dining room window.

Horrified, I ran for the back door, fearing that the house had caught on fire.

Instead I found a party — a barbecue.

The grill was going full blast. Hot dogs and hamburgers were engulfed in flames. There was a table piled high with food. People were milling about and filling their plates, chatting and laughing.

I nearly fainted when I realized who they were.

"Hey, kid, get over here and give me a hug!" Grandpa Charles hollered from behind the inferno.

Sporting a sauce-smeared "Kiss the Cook" apron, he held a spatula in one hand while embracing me with the other.

Grandpa Charles had died when I was twelve.

The smiling faces that surrounded me had passed away years earlier. They were all there: Those I loved and longed for. Ancestors I wished I'd known, who before that day had only lived in old photo albums.

How was it possible?

Unless...

"Am I dead?" I demanded.

"No, honey, you're very much alive," Uncle Tim stated dryly as everyone chuckled.

One by one, as they embraced me, I closed my eyes. I was immersed in scents from my childhood: pipe tobacco, lemon verbena, rose petals, hair tonic and leather.

With each passing year, I'd become increasingly aware that my immediate family was dwindling. As an only child, I feared that one day I might be the only one left.

To see them again, to bask in their love, was a miracle.

They looked younger than I remembered. Thinning hair was thick again, wrinkled cheeks were unlined and glowing, and eyes were clear and bright, no longer filled with pain. They were happy, carefree and at peace.

When the crowd parted, Grandpa Marion was waiting for me.

The last time I saw him, he was near death. The man who stood before me was robust and healthy with a mouth full of sparkling white teeth — a shock, as I'd never seen him with teeth. Grandpa insisted his dentures hurt, and he refused to wear them, stubbornly opting to gum his food for the rest of his life.

"You're so handsome!" I exclaimed.

"Must be my pretty new choppers." He laughed.

Grandpa Marion was a man of few words and only spoke when necessary. Painfully shy, he had a tendency to blend in with the furnishings unless he moved or cleared his throat. A woman once plopped down on his lap, not seeing him in the chair — an experience that mortified them both.

But when Grandpa was with me, he was rarely at a loss for words.

I adored him. When he passed away, I lost the dearest of friends.

I pulled him into my arms and held on tight. He smelled as he always had, like apple butter, soap, and coffee.

"I've missed you so much," I murmured.

"I've always been right here with you," he whispered. "I would never be far away from my girl."

"For Pete's sake, you've paid enough attention to him. I'm here, too!"

I whirled around the second I heard her voice.

It was Grandma Helen, her strawberry-gold hair glinting in the sun, her hazel eyes shining.

She grabbed me by the shoulders and squeezed the stuffing out of me. Her breathtaking hugs were the best in the world. I closed my eyes and deeply inhaled aromas of clove oil, sugar cookies, timeworn books, and antique dolls—soothing scents that were hers alone.

When I was a child, Grandma Helen was my safe place, my person, my hero. There wasn't a problem she couldn't fix, and she was fearless. A master storyteller with an infectious giggle, she was a delight and one of the most incredible people I'd ever known.

In later years, Alzheimer's had stilled the giggle. What a blessing it was to hear it again.

"I've missed you most of all, Grandma. I've been so lonely for you."

As tears rolled down my cheeks, she wiped them away with an embroidered handkerchief and kissed my forehead.

"Let's have no more crying. You've already wasted too many tears on your Grandpa and me. Look at all you have: a husband who loves you, my beautiful great-granddaughter, your parents, lots of friends and a good job."

"How do you know? Have you been watching me?"

"Of course. Just because you can't see us doesn't mean we can't see you. Heaven is closer than you think."

It was almost too much to take in at once. Everyone talked, laughed and cried. I could see bits and pieces of myself in each person: blond hair, green eyes, high foreheads, short fingers, and flat feet.

The sun had lowered, and it was getting late. I kept glancing at my watch. Where on earth were Ralph and Julie?

"Please don't leave. My husband and daughter should be back any

minute," I implored.

"Don't worry. We'll be around," Uncle Oscar said with a smile.

"I could use some paper towels," Grandpa Charles called.

"Okay, I'll be right back!"

When I returned with the roll of paper towels, no one was there.

The grill was cold, as though it had never been used.

Our barbecue was over.

Just then, car doors slammed and jolted me awake.

Oh, no. It was a dream.

My heart sank.

In the days that followed, I tried to wrap my mind around what happened, trying to make sense of it all.

I refused to believe that my visitors were an illusion, the byproduct of an afternoon nap. Our time together was as real as anything I'd ever experienced. They were here.

But why did they come?

Then I remembered their words.

"Don't worry. We'll be around."

"I've always been right here with you. I would never be far away from my girl."

"Just because you can't see us doesn't mean we can't see you. Heaven is closer than you think."

Perhaps they wanted to show me that they were well, and that I will be, too. They wanted to reassure me that no matter what, I'd never be without my family, never alone. They wanted me to realize that they were as close as my thoughts, loving me and waiting until we could be together again.

Every now and then, I get a whiff of burnt hamburgers, pipe tobacco, hair tonic, clove oil, apple butter, and soap. Every now and then, I hear their voices, along with their whispers of humor and wisdom as I watch Julie grow up, and as her dad and I grow older. They are reminders of the limitless power of love woven through the elasticity of time and space.

~Michelle Close Mills

Chapter 9

Miracles and More

Divine Intervention

77

Just Go

Not everything we experience can
be explained by logic or science.
~Linda Westphal

I'd been restless all morning, feeling uncomfortable and not able to put a finger on why. Everything seemed all right. I'd woken up that morning next to my wife, we'd had a wonderful Saturday breakfast together, but I was sitting on the sofa holding the front page of the newspaper and not really reading it. Something was wrong, but I didn't know what.

My wife didn't seem to notice my distraction. She busied herself cutting fabric for a new quilt. I sat and stared at the back yard through the French doors, trying to figure out what was bothering me.

All of a sudden, I was gripped by the feeling that I needed to be somewhere. I didn't know where, but I knew it wasn't here inside the house. I headed for the front door and my hand automatically went to my pocket for my car key. But then something told me I wasn't going to be driving anywhere. I unlocked the front door and stood there on the threshold waiting.

"Honey," my wife Ann said, looking up from her sewing machine. "Is everything all right?"

I wanted to tell her there was nothing wrong, but somehow I knew that wasn't the truth. I looked at her and smiled, and the words came from my mouth before I even had a chance to think about them.

"I need to go for a walk," I said.

Ann looked at me, studying something in my eyes. Then she nodded and said, "Well, have a nice time, dear."

I nodded and stepped out onto the porch, wondering where I was supposed to go. Apparently, my legs had an idea because I found myself starting off on one of our normal morning walks. This time, however, I turned north after going one block and walked up a street that I'd never taken before.

After I'd covered a few blocks, I began to hear two female voices, and one of them was crying hysterically. A voice in my head said *Hurry* and I found myself running toward the sound. I ran up to a house where two women stood on the front lawn. One of them was dressed in a bathing suit. She was the one crying.

"My baby!" she yelled, staring down at a small girl lying still on the green grass. "My baby's dead!"

The other woman stood there next to her, holding her hand. The color had drained out of her face. She looked up to see me approaching and said, "They were swimming in the back yard. I think her daughter's drowned!"

Years ago, in college, I'd been trained in CPR because I'd taken a summer job teaching kids how to swim at a summer camp. I hadn't thought about that time in ages, but all of a sudden the memory of my training came flooding back into my brain. I knelt by the little girl.

I began doing CPR and asked if anyone had called 911. The woman standing next to the little girl's mother nodded weakly. I checked for a pulse, found none, cleared the girl's airway and began CPR. Her mother continued to cry hysterically, but that all faded away for me as I focused on all the steps I remembered from CPR class.

I don't know how much time passed, but finally the girl coughed, spit up water, and vomited. She began to cry just as an ambulance pulled up, and the EMS crew ran over. I backed away while they went to work. Her mother sat next to her, shaking with emotion.

You're done here, the voice inside my head said suddenly. So I let my legs turn me around and I walked away, even as I heard one of the EMTs call out to me, "Thanks!"

When I got home, my wife was still working on her quilt. I walked inside on shaky legs and collapsed on the sofa. My wife looked up from her work, smiled at me, and asked, "So, how did your walk go?"

I opened my mouth and took a deep breath, intending to tell her everything that had happened, but then I heard myself say simply, "It went well, I think. Yes, I'd say everything went pretty well."

~John P. Buentello

78

A Birthday Blessing

Life is funny… we never know what's in store for us,
and time brings on what is meant to be.
~April Mae Monterrosa

I hadn't missed a single one of my grandchildren's birthday parties. There had been twenty-three of them so far. Catey was eight; Colin, seven; Landon, five; and Blake, three. Now my streak was going to end, because Landon was not having a sixth birthday party. My son and daughter-in-law had instead planned a Disney cruise that was scheduled to leave three days after his birthday.

Landon lived only five hours away in northern Kentucky, however, so it seemed strange that I wouldn't be able to at least see him on his birthday. Nevertheless, I decided to escape the February cold of West Virginia and spend four days with my brother and sister-in-law at their timeshare in Orlando. My return flight would be on Thursday, Landon's actual birthday. I had texted my son and daughter-in-law that I would call him on his birthday sometime between the end of school and his eight o'clock bedtime.

As I was waiting for my flight in Orlando, the weather app on my phone had indicated it would be windy around the time the plane was scheduled to land. I didn't pay much attention to that, and anyway, the flight took off pretty much on time.

As we approached the airport, however, it seemed like it was taking too long to land. Something was not right. Finally, the pilot came on the speakers and told us it was too windy. He reassured us by saying there was plenty of fuel so we were going to circle the airport until the wind subsided. The only thing on my to-do list that evening was that phone call, and I had hours before Landon's bedtime, so it didn't really matter to me.

As we continued to circle, though, I started to feel a little uneasy. I wondered why we didn't divert to the airport thirty minutes north. A fellow passenger stated that the runway there was too short. I knew the wind to the northeast was also a problem that afternoon, so Pittsburgh was not going to be an alternative. The pilot eventually came on again and told us we were going to divert west to Cincinnati. That was ironic. My son and his family lived fifteen minutes away from that airport.

We were going there to refuel and would then return to West Virginia when the winds died down. This would work. I just needed enough time to turn on my phone while the plane was being refueled so I could say "Happy Birthday" to Landon and let him know I hadn't forgotten. Then they changed the plan. They had us deplane and wait for further instructions. That was even better news for me. I could go inside the terminal, make my phone call in privacy, and then have a relaxing dinner before re-boarding the plane.

There was no answer to my call, however, on either my son or daughter-in-law's phone. I thought they might have taken Landon out for a birthday dinner. I left a detailed message. Then I got an alert on my phone that my plane had been rescheduled for 9:00 the following morning. I made another call to both phones with this change of plans. There was still no answer. Meanwhile, the airline was booking rooms for the stranded passengers at local hotels. Before I had finished my dinner, my daughter-in-law called me back, laughing at this turn of events and inviting me to spend the night with them instead of at a hotel.

Chris and the boys came to pick me up at baggage claim. I went home with them and watched Landon blow out the candles on his cake and open his cards and presents. I hadn't missed his birthday after all! It was such a blessing.

There may have been other airports where we could have refueled, but God was my pilot that day. He had a different flight plan in mind, taking that plane to the airport where at least one passenger preferred to be.

~Susan Hunter

79

The Rush of Angel's Wings

Prayer at its highest is a two-way conversation,
and for me the most important part
is listening to God's replies.
~Frank C. Laubach

I was bone-weary as I crawled into the vehicle. It had been several long, exhausting months at our mission in Haiti. We'd said goodbye to the last work team and now were heading home ourselves. Several projects had been completed, hundreds of hungry children had been fed, and now my husband, my cousin, and I were eager to get back to Canada. Christmas preparations would be in full swing when we returned, and that meant precious family time — something we dearly missed while working so far away. Those weeks at home would pass quickly, though, and before long it would be time to head back to Haiti, so we were anxious to be on our way.

The journey from our mission compound to the airport in Port au Prince is long and often dangerous. Travel in this third-world country is very different from what we appreciate in North America. All one needs for a driver's license in Haiti is to pay the fee — no test necessary. Lessons on road safety do not factor into the experience.

The one traffic light in the capital city is often moved around in hopes someone will actually stop for the red, but usually to no avail, making intersections a blend of confusion and terrifying close calls. While traffic on these pothole-infused roads is always heavy, there are also no speed limits or rules. Anyone can pass at anytime and the narrow road can have four or five cars abreast going in both directions and traveling at breakneck speeds. Over the years, we have become somewhat numb to it. Still, the sixty-mile drive to the airport is always a concern.

My husband and I started this mission in 2006, and after several hair-raising events on the roads we made a conscious decision to stop and pray before starting each journey across the country. This particular trip was no different. Before climbing into our chauffeured vehicle, we stood, held hands, bowed our heads and asked for God's protection — specifically requesting angels to go before us and behind us. Little did we know the incredible way this prayer was about to be answered.

As always, the roads that day were very busy. Our driver seemed quite anxious to get us through the traffic and to the airport on time, so we moved swiftly down the bumpy highway. We swerved around *taptaps* — old half-ton trucks reconstructed to seat twenty-five to thirty passengers on benches, with live goats and chickens dangling from the sides — and passed motorbike taxis with families of four or five on board, as well as the occasional beat-up school bus stuffed with people inside and cargo piled on the roof.

Suddenly, we found ourselves behind an extremely large truck pulling a long flatbed trailer. Swaying on top of the trailer directly in front of us was a monstrous machine. Through the layers of caked-on mud we saw a huge road grader, the largest we'd ever seen. It spanned our entire side of the road, and with steady oncoming traffic, there was no way around it. Although the gigantic machine did not seem to be safely secured, we had no choice but to tuck in behind it and wait for an opportunity to pass.

Conversation between the three of us had come to an abrupt halt as we focused on the unsteady piece of equipment. It pitched and swayed back and forth, and the chains that supposedly secured it flopped dangerously about. Suddenly, there was an ear-splitting explosion. We watched two huge back tires blow off the flatbed trailer, instantly becoming deadly airborne projectiles headed straight for our front windshield. In that split second, we knew we were looking death in the face.

Then the unimaginable happened. At the last minute, as though struck by an unseen hand, one tire veered off to the right side of our car, whizzing past my window, and the other tire swerved around the left side, flashing past my husband's. The force of them was so powerful and close that we could feel the gust of wind rock our vehicle and smell the burning rubber as they flew by. After they passed us, the massive, wayward tires fell on opposite sides of the road and burst into flames.

In that moment of silence, I could have sworn I heard the gentle rush of angels' wings. No one spoke for a few seconds until my husband said, "Did that really just happen?"

I could do nothing more than nod my head.

There was no denying we had just experienced a miracle, narrowly escaping death. That simple prayer spoken before we left had been answered in a most miraculous way.

Now, not only do we always pray before traveling those dangerous roads, we also pray before leaving our compound to walk through the village or to head up a mountain trail on the back of a motorbike. We ask for protection against falling mangoes, infected mosquitoes, biting dogs, raging rivers and any other dangers seen or unseen.

Praying now has a new authenticity for us, a greater urgency, and today we feel as never before that our very lives depend on it.

~Heather Rodin

80

One Rainy Morning

*Coincidence is the language of the stars. For something
to happen, so many forces have to be put into action.*
~Paulo Coelho

The beeping of my cell-phone alarm jolted me awake. Summer rain beat against the window of my friend Alice's guestroom, and I wanted nothing more than to pull the covers over my head and grab a few more winks. But home was more than a hundred miles away, and I had a full afternoon of appointments ahead of me. I needed to get on the road. I swung my feet onto the floor and picked up the phone to click on the weather app.

That's when I noticed the low-battery warning. Rats! I'd meant to attach the phone to the charger before I went to sleep. No worries, though. Charging it while I ate breakfast would give it enough juice. I plugged the cord into the outlet near my bed and laid the phone on the bedside table. Then I headed to the kitchen for a cup of coffee and one of Alice's famous blueberry muffins. We lingered longer than I'd intended in her cozy breakfast nook, chatting and watching the rain that was still coming down in buckets.

"My umbrella's where it can't do me a bit of good," I told her.

Alice raised her eyebrows. "Back seat of the car?"

"Right."

We both laughed, and she said she'd walk me out under her gigantic golf umbrella. A few minutes later, that's what we did. I gave

Alice a hug and promised to visit again soon. I knew she was lonely. Her husband had died only a few months earlier, and her only child lived clear across the country.

"I hope you really will come back soon," she said, dabbing at her eyes. "You be careful out there and take it slow around the curves. These mountain roads are slick."

"I'll be careful," I promised, and I meant it. The fifteen miles of back road that led to Alice's cabin were treacherous even in good weather. It would be a white-knuckle trip to the main highway on this rainy day, for sure.

With headlights blazing and windshield wipers slapping, I made my way slowly along. What I needed was some music to help keep me focused. I punched on the radio, but got nothing but static. I reached into my purse, which I'd set beside me on the passenger seat, for my phone, which had hundreds of songs stored on it. But the phone wasn't in the side pocket where I usually kept it. It wasn't in the main pocket with my wallet and sunglasses. It didn't take long for me to figure out exactly where it was. The phone was on the bedside table in Alice's guest room.

If it would've done any good, I'd have laid my head on the steering wheel and cried. This mistake was going to cost me at least an hour. Now, there was no way I could make it to my first appointment on time. No matter. I had to have the phone. I turned the car around and headed back along the same wet, curvy roads I'd just traveled.

I pulled into Alice's driveway and raced through the rain to the front door. She didn't answer when I knocked, so I turned the knob. It wasn't locked. "Helloooo…," I called out. "Crazy me forgot my phone." No answer. "Alice?" I said. "Alice, it's me." Silence was the only response. I made my way toward her bedroom, but pulled up short when I turned the corner into the hall. There was Alice, lying on the floor and staring at the ceiling. I dropped to my knees beside her. Her breathing was shallow, and she had welts on her neck. All the color had drained from her face. I squeezed her hand and put my lips next to her ear. "Can you tell me what happened?"

"Wasp sting," she murmured in a hoarse voice. "EpiPen's in the medicine cabinet."

I rushed to the bathroom and found the pen. "Tell me what to do."

"Take it out of the case and pull off the cap. Hold the pen in your fist and plunge in the needle." She pointed to her upper thigh. "Right there. Hold it for ten seconds. Hurry."

Plunge in the needle? I was no nurse. I'd never in my whole life given anyone a shot. It was all I could do to dig a splinter out of a finger. But I slid the EpiPen out of its plastic holder and jammed the needle into her thigh. "Now call 911," she said. I retrieved my phone from the guestroom and, with shaking hands, made the call. Within minutes, an ambulance arrived and took Alice to the hospital. I followed in my own car.

Needless to say, I missed all my appointments that afternoon. In the greater scheme of things, that didn't matter one bit. What did matter was that I hadn't remembered to charge my cell phone the night before. And that I'd left it on the bedside table. And that I'd realized — just in the nick of time — that the phone wasn't in my purse and had turned around. Alice knew she was allergic to stings, but had never, until that day, had a true anaphylactic reaction. But she kept injectable epinephrine around just in case. If I hadn't returned to her house when I did and given her the shot, she likely would have died.

A lucky coincidence? Not to my way of thinking. It was a miracle if I ever saw one.

~Jennie Ivey

81

Wrong Turn

God didn't bring you this far to abandon you.
~Author Unknown

My daughter was fragile. Suffering from severe bipolar disorder and a wicked anxiety disorder, she'd turned to drugs to ease her pain. Bad drugs.

After hospitalizing her several times, we ended up putting her in a residential facility for a year to learn to control her moods and find a way to deal with her mental illness. Since coming home, she'd been doing well. She'd stopped doing drugs. She went to Narcotics Anonymous (NA) meetings regularly. She had a sponsor whom she could call if she felt tempted. She also took her meds, saw her therapist and was attending college.

But then an old friend overdosed, and my daughter's world came crashing down. She wondered aloud if life was worth living, if anyone could really stay sober, or if her hard work was for nothing.

She stopped going to NA meetings, refused to call her sponsor, and refused to see her therapist. She began to spin out of control.

Until the day she slammed the door behind her and raced to the car. I was yelling and distraught as I tried to stop her. "Please, God," I prayed as she sped down the street. "Let her be okay."

But, despite my prayer, I was unprepared for the scene when she came home.

Less than twenty minutes later, she burst through the door, all smiles and kisses as she grabbed my shoulders and spun me around.

"Mom! Mom! It was a miracle!" she gushed.

"What?"

"I was almost in an accident!"

And while this statement did not feel like the beginning of a miracle to me, I sat down as she laid out her story.

My daughter had raced down the street intent on finding drugs. Despite so many months of sobriety, she felt she couldn't handle another minute of pain without a drug to numb her feelings.

She'd made a call, found a connection and was hurrying to the rendezvous spot. But just as she turned left onto the street, another car swerved from the right, heading in the wrong direction. My daughter slammed on the brakes and swerved to the side of the road to miss hitting the wayward car. At the same time, the errant car swerved, and the two ended up off the road, but out of danger.

As the other driver ran from her car to check on my daughter's safety, my child was shaken to her bones — for the driver of the other car was her NA sponsor — the woman she should call if she was in trouble!

"I'm so sorry!" the woman cried before seeing my daughter's face. "I don't know what happened — I just took a wrong turn."

Right then and there, by the side of the road, my daughter confessed where she was going and what she was about to do. But her confession was not just to the woman before her — it was to the universe.

"It was God!" my daughter cried into my arms. "God stopped me from making a terrible mistake. He made her take a wrong turn to keep me from taking a wrong path. He literally stopped me in my tracks and sent help."

And the message was received.

My daughter has not done drugs since that day. She finished her college program, regularly takes her meds and sees her therapist, and is finishing up an internship program that will lead to a solid career.

But more, she's gained a faith in her destiny, her ability, and her worthiness that keep her walking steadily on her path — and help her avoid wrong turns.

~Susan Traugh

82

When Grandpa Said Goodbye

If the people we love are stolen from us, the way to
have them live on is to never stop loving them.
~James O'Barr

When I was about four years old, my mom's parents moved into our house. We lived in a nice little neighborhood in El Paso, Texas. Most of my large Mexican family—both sets of grandparents, cousins, and aunts and uncles—lived in this town. Every birthday was a big hoopla attended by at least thirty people, and that was just family.

I loved my grandparents and I was particularly close with my grandma because she would often sneak me cookies and Coca-Cola when my mom wasn't around. I was very much looking forward to Grandma coming to live with us. Grandpa, on the other hand, not so much.

He was this lumbering man who towered over me. He never spoke to anyone. I was afraid of him. When attending family events, he sat on the couch without speaking and he stared into the distance. He walked with a slight limp and always had a slight smell about him because he wore adult diapers. His eyes always looked hollow and distant, like he was somewhere else. Whenever I asked my mom why Grandpa didn't talk, she would answer, "He has depression" and that was the end of the conversation. At the age of four, I had no idea what that meant. As I grew up, I thought anyone with depression would be someone who just sat with a vacant stare not talking.

My grandparents lived with us for about three years. They were present for every Christmas, Easter, birthday party, ballet recital, first day of school, and sporting event that my sister and I ever had. They were also present for the mundane, day-to-day moments — every breakfast, lunch and dinner, and every fight my sister and I ever had about some stupid toy. They were there for every tear or happy face. My grandma was an active participant; my grandpa no more than a breathing houseplant whose roots went deep into the living room couch. Eventually, I stopped noticing he was even there.

One day, our happy El Paso bubble burst because my dad got a job in Ohio. At the age of seven, I was about to face the hardest thing I had faced in my life up to that point.

On a sunny day in the fall, we packed up our house and left our family behind, my grandparents included. They were moving into my uncle's house because they didn't want to leave the only city they had ever known as home. They had already lost their house and independence; they weren't about to lose their city, too. So, we left and said we would call and visit when we could. This was way before video chatting or the Internet, so we knew a visit, or even a phone call, would be very expensive.

A few months went by, and our family of four adjusted to life in Ohio. My sister and I enrolled in a new school and made new friends. Then one day we got a very urgent phone call from my mom's brother. Grandpa had suffered a stroke and was in the hospital. He would need to have open-heart surgery. We needed to come home. We flew back to El Paso in a hurry because we didn't think Grandpa had long to live.

We stayed a few days, and in that time I got to see my extended family again. I didn't quite understand the seriousness of the situation. I was just excited to play with all my cousins. My grandpa recovered and was on his way to going home. This meant that we, too, would be going home, back to Ohio.

About a month later, we received a miracle in the form of a phone call. Grandpa had been visiting one of my mom's brothers and watching his favorite sports team — the Dallas Cowboys. At some point during the visit, he began to stand up and cheer. My uncle quickly got on the phone and exclaimed to my mom, "Dad is cured! He's himself again!"

It was unbelievable. I watched my mom's face as she spoke into the phone. I watched her utter shock as she spoke to her father for the first time in fifteen years. I watched her jump for joy when she handed the phone over to my dad to talk to Grandpa for the first time since he met my mom. I watched my sister's bewilderment as my grandpa asked her about school and her sports teams. I knew it would soon be my turn.

My mom pushed the phone into my tiny seven-year-old hand. "Grandpa is on the phone. He wants to talk to you!"

"What?" I said in return. "Grandpa? He wants to *talk*? To *me*?"

What could he possibly want to say to me? He didn't know anything about my life, or so I thought.

"Yes! Grandpa wants to talk to you," she replied.

Hesitantly, I grabbed the phone and said, "Hello?"

"Hi, Roni!" It was a cheerful voice that was slightly gruff. It was also unfamiliar because, in my whole life, I had never actually heard my grandfather utter one word.

I don't remember everything that was said in that conversation, but as soon as I got on the phone, my grandpa was at no loss for words. He knew everything about me, right down to my favorite stuffed bunny rabbit's name. I couldn't believe that the stoic houseplant on the couch could not only talk, but also had been paying attention all those years.

We all went to bed that night excited about what was to come with Grandpa. We couldn't wait to talk to him more. After school the next day, my dad came to pick us up. I knew something was wrong since he usually wasn't the one to pick us up. As soon as we got in the car, he told us that Grandpa was back in the hospital, and we had to go to El Paso again. This time, he said, Grandpa probably wasn't going to make it.

I couldn't understand what he was saying. I had just talked to him the night before, and he was fine. More than fine. I was sad and angry at the same time. It just didn't make sense.

After he died, and we went back home to Ohio, I had a talk with my mom while she was tucking me in at night.

"Mom, why would God do that to us?" I asked her. "Why would God let us finally talk to Grandpa and then take him away?"

"Because God wanted us to talk to Grandpa one last time."

"But why? Why now?" I asked.

"I don't know why," she answered with tears in her eyes. "No one knows why miracles happen. We are just lucky that we got to talk to him one last time. God let Grandpa say goodbye to all of us."

~Veronica DeSantos Ryan

Frozen

Never drive faster than your guardian angel can fly.
~Author Unknown

I adjusted the car's visor and leaned forward, straining against my seatbelt. The aviator sunglasses I wore were no match against the intense sun. I gripped the steering wheel tighter as I attempted to follow the road's yellow line. The asphalt was worn so smooth in some areas that it served as a reflective surface. No matter where I looked — up and straight ahead, or down at the road — I was blinded by the sun. I took a right at the first stoplight, and in an instant I could see again.

I pulled into the local Dollar General and ran in for a few essentials. I was back in the car in less than twenty minutes. Thankfully, the sun would be at my back for the drive home.

I sat at the intersection and waited for the light to turn. The light turned green, but my body suddenly seemed to stop working. I was completely unable to move. I stared at the green light, fully aware I needed to take my foot off the brake and place it on the accelerator, but it was as if I had become frozen in time.

This is weird, I thought. *What's happening to me? Am I paralyzed? Did I have a stroke? Should I be alarmed?* But I wasn't alarmed. I felt bewildered, but at the same time peaceful. There was no fear.

With every bit of strength in me, I willed my body to move. My efforts sent my body lurching toward the center console in a jerky motion, and suddenly I had full range of motion once again.

I was easing out into the intersection when the unmistakable roar of a diesel engine filled my car. It sounded entirely too close, and it was coming from my left side. A blur of color filled my peripheral vision. I slammed on my brakes as a large truck narrowly missed my vehicle.

The driver had blown right through a red light and never even slowed down. Perhaps he, too, had been blinded by the sun. Shaken, I pulled into the first parking lot I came to.

I sat there contemplating the "what-ifs" of my near miss. If I'd pulled into the intersection three to five seconds sooner, I could have been seriously injured or worse. I shuddered at the thought. That's when I looked up and noticed the building I'd ended up in front of; I was sitting in the parking lot of a church. As I focused on the large cross adorning the front of the chapel, I realized my unexplainable, temporary paralysis had lasted three to five seconds.

I grabbed my phone and called my husband.

"Hey, babe," he answered. "What are you doing?"

"Oh, not much," I replied. "Just hanging out with my guardian angel."

~Melissa Wootan

84

My Time to Move

Faith is not without worry or care, but
faith is fear that has said a prayer.
~Author Unknown

I always knew I was adopted. I remember obsessing over who my biological parents were, grilling my parents for information, and even, for a while, convincing myself that Bernadette Peters was my biological mom. My parents were open with me, but they also knew what would happen if they gave a Type-A teenager too much information. "When you're twenty-one, we'll tell you their names," they told me. I can't even count the number of times I heard that.

It was a private adoption, which means my parents actually got to meet the people who gave me life. They knew their names. They saw their faces. I held on to their promise of "when you're twenty-one" until the day finally came. I was in my final semester of college, working on a capstone presentation and taking seven courses. I was also working thirty-five hours a week. But I didn't wait one extra day past my birthday before asking for the names of my biological parents.

As soon as I had them, I took to the Internet. After thirty minutes, I found them. I remember calling my best friend to have her look at my biological mother on Facebook. "Do you think this is her? Do you think I look like her?"

My brain couldn't process it. I didn't sleep at all that night. In the morning, I told my parents I had found my birth parents and my dad said, "Kimberley, you have a lot going on right now. Please, for your own sake, wait until after you graduate to contact anyone."

He was right. I did have a lot going on. Then my mom made another request of me: "When you reach out, reach out to Laura first." Laura was my biological grandmother. My research showed that she still lived in the area, while my biological mother and father did not. It made sense, so I agreed to that as well.

The month that followed was torturous. I was filled with insecurity. What if they didn't like me? What if they didn't want to know me? Was I setting myself up for the greatest disappointment of my life by reaching out to these people?

Graduation came and went, as did the week after it. I barely remember that time now. What I do remember is agonizing over whether or not I should call the phone number I found for Laura. I was in church one Sunday morning in December, still thinking about it. I had been praying about whether to call or not for days. I wasn't really paying attention to the sermon because I was so distracted. Then, something registered.

The pastor said, "Sometimes, it feels like God isn't moving because he's waiting for you to move." I had fulfilled my parents' wishes and waited till after graduation. I had nothing pressing in my life now. I had Laura's phone number saved in my cell phone. The only thing holding me back from reaching out was me!

The pastor's words were life changing for me. I finally realized it was all in my hands. I prayed differently after that. I asked God for the interaction to go well. I prayed that Laura would want to get to know me, and that she would say my biological mother wanted to know me, too. I prayed for acceptance. I don't even remember walking to the parking lot and getting into my car because I was praying so hard. After fifteen more minutes of sitting in my car, staring at the number on my cell phone, I hit Call. The phone rang twice, and I hung up. It was a first step, though!

I realized I didn't know what message I would leave if she didn't answer. I mean, you can't really tell someone, "Hey, I'm your long-lost granddaughter. Wanna get coffee?" in a voicemail. I prayed again for courage and the right words to say, and hit Redial. The call went to voicemail, and I left the most awkward, vague message of my life. I think I said my name and phone number four times!

I didn't want to go to my parents' house. It just seemed weird to get that call back while I was there, so I went to my best friend's apartment. We sat there in her living room, staring at my phone. I had the ringer turned all the way up. When it actually started ringing, I almost fell over. I grabbed the phone and went outside. I was scared I'd lose the signal in the apartment, and this was one time I certainly didn't want my phone to cut out.

"Hello?"

"Hi, this is Laura. I received a call from this number."

I asked what her daughter's name was. We had a winner.

"Well, like I said in the message, my name is Kimberley Diane Sorrells, and I think I'm your biological granddaughter."

Her next words sent me into shock. She said, "I was praying for you in church this morning." A new family in her Sunday school class had adopted a baby, and she said it reminded her of the granddaughter she had never met. She prayed I was doing well with my life and was safe.

I couldn't believe it! I said, "I was praying for you in church this morning, too."

Laura and I spent the next five minutes crying, not speaking a word. We eventually got to my biological mother's contact information and how my parents were. I learned I had a brother.

Now I have two families. All because I listened to the pastor and found the faith to make the first move.

~Kimberley Sorrells

Chapter
10

Miracles and More

Signs from Above

85

Just a Rose for Mom and Me

Where flowers bloom, so does hope.
~Lady Bird Johnson

In the grand scheme of things, it was always just Mom and me. I was a child of the 1950s and the offspring of one of those typical marriages that seem to define the turbulent times that saw us through wars, assassinations, and unrecognized poverty.

Mom and my biological dad were both factory workers, and they scratched out just enough to pay the fifty-nine-dollar-a-month house payment and keep the utilities on.

I had been a hard birth for Mom. She had me when she was barely sixteen, and medical complications prevented her from having another child.

So, it was always just her, me, and "him." From the time I was six or seven until the day she finally worked up the courage to escape his drunken rages, I don't remember a single day when "happy" was a consideration for either of us.

I came in from school one Thursday afternoon. The fight had started before I got home. Just like so many times before, he hit her. I interfered, and then he hit me.

But this time, I hit him back. And when he woke up from my

enthusiastic and youthfully energetic right hook, we were already gone — packed and moved.

So, in my junior-high and high school years, it was just Mom and me. We had gone from a three-bedroom house to a tiny apartment. Mom worked two jobs. I lied about my age at fourteen and went to work after school and on weekends at a local amusement park.

But we made it. She eventually remarried, found happiness, and was left a widow way too early. I married my high school sweetheart, we had three kids, and Mom became a doting grandmother who loved my wife as much as I did.

We spent every Sunday with her at the house she had bought in the country, and life was good. Part of that time together was spent tending the roses that grew on her place. They were not prize roses — just natural-growing rosebushes that surrounded her property.

Mom loved roses. She even persuaded me to dig up a few of the scraggly wild rosebushes and transplant them in the small yard in front of our house in town.

One Sunday, two weeks before Christmas, we had spent the day with her at her country house and had eaten dinner. I had fixed yet another series of computer problems for her, and she talked about longing for spring so she could smell her roses.

We left and made the forty-five-minute drive home. As I unlocked the door, the phone was ringing. The voice on the other end was a county deputy who proceeded to tell me that Mom had called 911 within minutes of us leaving.

She was gone, dead at the age of sixty-three from an aneurysm.

The next four days were a blur. I wasn't grief-stricken or inconsolable. I was just numb. My wife and two of my female cousins basically took care of all the arrangements. I didn't have a preference on the type of service, the color of the casket or the music they played.

None of it mattered to me.

The one detail that I insisted on was simple. All I asked was that anyone sending a floral tribute please send roses. I didn't want to see any other kind of flowers at the chapel or the gravesite.

On the day of the services, I finally broke down. Before I left for the chapel, I went into a room by myself, locked the door, cried out all my tears, and asked Mom to send me a sign that everything was going to be okay.

The funeral was amazing. People from all walks of life in all sizes, shapes and colors came out to pay their last respects to this simple, God-fearing woman who had devoted much of her life to caring for and about me.

From the chapel, we went to the cemetery. The small headstone with lyrics from one of the songs my cousins picked for the service — "Angels Among Us" by the country group Alabama — said it all: "Guide us with a light of love…"

The family car took us home. I still felt lost. Confused. Dazed.

And then I saw it.

As I got out of the limo on a cold and wet December day, a scraggly rosebush in the middle of my front yard touched my soul. It was barren of leaves and just looked like a couple of twigs. But it was sporting one rose. One perfect, pink rose glistening in the sun.

And once again, it was just Mom and me.

~Dennis McCaslin

86

The Guardian

We all have a guardian angel, sent down from
above. To keep us safe from harm and
surround us with their love.
~Author Unknown

While giving my very first presentation as a sales director, I was motioned out of the conference room to take an urgent phone call. On the other end of the line, I heard my husband's shaky voice informing me that our twelve-year-old son had not returned home from walking the dog that afternoon.

I felt my knees buckle. Well, there it was, something that all parents dread. The world was full of evil people waiting to snatch unsuspecting children from their parents. Hadn't I read at least a hundred news articles about such crimes? Yet, we had always been so careful; we had taught our son about "stranger danger" and the importance of staying close to home. Still… somewhere deep inside, I knew this day was coming. I knew it in the same way I feared accidental drownings, chokings, and sudden infant death syndrome.

I told my team there was a family emergency and began the forty-minute drive to my house. By the time I arrived home, every possible scenario that my son could have experienced had played out vividly in my mind.

Because it had only been two hours since my son had put the dog back in the fence and then disappeared, the police weren't going to get involved right away. So our neighbors and family members had formed a search party and were already combing the woods around our neighborhood when I pulled into our driveway. I wanted to be out in the streets, shouting my son's name and searching the alleyways with everyone else, but I was encouraged to stay near the phone in case there was a call.

I was so deep in meditation and prayer that I nearly tossed the phone across the room when it suddenly rang. *Please don't be bad news,* I thought, and then answered.

"Hey," came the voice of my aunt, "I just wanted you to know that he is okay." The tone of her voice caused me to relax automatically. She must have learned some good news!

"Oh! Thank God!" I squealed. "How do you know?"

"I was praying, and God gave me a vision. I saw him lying in the woods, using his backpack for a pillow, and I saw a guardian angel with outstretched hands standing over him," my aunt explained.

"Asleep? In the woods? No, he would never do that. He's afraid to go into the woods, and it's getting dark. Are you sure he was asleep? Maybe he was dead. Could it have been eternal sleep?"

My aunt was considered to be a bit of a "Jesus freak" by several people in my family because of her deep faith, but so many of her dreams and visions had been eerily accurate over the years that even the most serious of doubters had to take notice.

"No, he is not dead," she assured me. "He is sleeping, and an angel is watching over him. I'm going to bed now that I know he's safe. Goodnight." The phone clicked. I sat alone in my bedroom, still holding the receiver to my ear, half-expecting to hear more, but there was only silence.

I dashed to my son's bedroom, and sure enough, his backpack was missing. Why hadn't I noticed that before? I scanned the room for other missing items, but everything seemed to be in place.

After several hours, we were informed that our son had been dropped off at the police station, alive and well. So like clowns in a circus car, our entire entourage piled into one vehicle and headed out to retrieve him.

When we returned home, my son explained that he had decided to run away because he had made his first "C" on a progress report and did not want to stick around for the consequences. So he packed his backpack with Goldfish crackers (in case he got hungry on his trip) and his collection of baseball cards (in case he needed to sell them for food), and headed into the sewers to avoid being seen by anyone. He didn't count on the sewers curving in all directions, so when he emerged, he found himself in unfamiliar territory.

He said a lady stopped her car and reminded him that he was out after curfew, but he assured her he was on his way home. By then, however, he was completely lost and running out of Goldfish crackers. Because it was getting dark, and he was in a bad area of town, my son decided to travel through the woods, rather than on the streets. So he made his way through the trails in the woods until he grew weary and decided to take a break. Using his backpack for a pillow, he curled up under a tree and took a nap.

"I don't know how long I had been asleep," my son continued, "but something made me wake up. I had the strangest feeling that someone was watching me, and when I looked around, I saw a man standing just a few feet away, holding his arms out and watching me sleep. At first, I thought he was a tree because he was so tall and he was standing so still. Plus, his arms seemed super-long like branches. But then I realized it was a man, and I grabbed my backpack and didn't stop running until I reached the street."

The same lady who had pulled up beside him a few hours earlier pulled up again and told him to get in her car.

"What! You got in the car with a stranger? Son! What have I told you about that?" I scolded.

"I know, Mom," my son answered, "but I was tired, and she seemed nice. She took me to the police station."

Even though my son had broken the cardinal rule and accepted a ride from a stranger, I was grateful for that particular stranger because she had done the right thing. I decided to call the police station the next day and get her name in order to properly thank her. When I called the station, however, I was told the only name she left was "Alpha."

Later that night, I heard my husband telling my son that he had done the right thing by "running away from the weirdo in the woods." I just smiled, and silently thanked a woman named Alpha and a very tall, weird man who watched over my sleeping boy and brought him safely home to me.

~Cynthia Zayn

87

The Dragonfly Kiss

*The relationship between parents and children, but
especially between mothers and daughters,
is tremendously powerful, scarcely to be
comprehended in any rational way.
~Joyce Carol Oates*

On August 18, 2015, my beautiful, amazing mother was diagnosed with Stage 4 lung cancer out of the blue. In the blink of an eye, our lives turned upside-down. Why did this happen to her? She never smoked, she was otherwise healthy, and she always did the right thing. People were completely shocked.

Mom was loved by so many. She had been an amazing, hard-working secretary at Melrose High School for years, and now she had to stop working and start fighting for her life.

On the day we got the diagnosis, I was sitting outside with my two older sisters. We were talking about how sick mom was, and that it didn't seem like we were going to hear good news later in the afternoon. We were all nervous and crying. All of a sudden, a dragonfly sat on my foot and stayed there throughout our entire conversation. I thought that was sort of strange, but I just smiled at the little creature through tear-stained eyes. Later in the afternoon, we got the dreaded news.

A week after Mom was diagnosed, I took a walk with my dog to clear my head. As we were walking back to my house, a dragonfly flew into my hand and stayed there. I thought this was really odd. Since when do dragonflies come around and land on us more than once? I had to call my sisters and tell them maybe it was a sign of hope that Mom would be okay. We went to the hospital to tell my mom, and she said, "Wow, that's really weird. Don't you girls remember that bag I bring to work every day? Your aunt gave it to me and it has dragonflies on it."

Over the next few months, my sisters and I saw an abundance of dragonflies around us daily. I remember walking outside and seeing way more than I had ever seen before. Some would even land on me.

Fast-forward to the morning of December 20, 2015. I woke up to a dream of dragonflies in all different sizes and colors flying around me. That day, I felt different. I was nauseous and sick to my stomach. I had a feeling that something bad was going to happen. I went to church and cried the entire time. I visited my mom in the hospital. At this point, she wasn't doing well. She had had a stroke, and the targeted treatment she was getting didn't seem to be working anymore. Before leaving the hospital, I told her I loved her, and she said, "I love you, too. I'll see you tomorrow." Those were our last words. In the early morning of December 21, 2015, she died unexpectedly.

Through all these hardships, little dragonflies kept visiting me. Every time I visited my mom's grave, they were there. On her birthday, one flew into my hands. My sisters and I ultimately decided to get matching dragonfly tattoos on our wrists in memory of Mom.

But the most amazing thing happened on September 4, 2016 — the day my mom had tried to live for. It was the day I was getting married.

It was a beautiful day. I wore the dress that Mom picked out two summers before. I lit a candle for her and had it glowing all night. I put little details throughout the venue that reminded me of her.

Then, at the end of the reception, when the last song was over, I heard a scream coming from my sister. I thought something was wrong, that someone was hurt. I saw her pointing to where she had been sitting. A dragonfly was perched right on my family's table. I went over and scooped it up. I couldn't stop crying. It lay in my hand for a couple of seconds, and before it flew away, it brushed my cheek. My photographer was there just in time to catch this amazing shot, which means so much to me.

I can't even begin to describe how I felt at that moment. I just knew my mother was there. She wouldn't have missed that day for the world. Janice Seelley, my amazing mother, came to my wedding and gave me a kiss goodnight that I will cherish forever.

~Eva Spaulding

88

Time to Reflect

They say that time heals all things, they say you can always forget; but the smiles and the tears across the years they twist my heart strings yet!
~George Orwell, 1984

We lost my brother to a heart attack early one Valentine's Day. He would have appreciated the irony in that — his own heart failing on the day when we celebrate hearts and love. He was sixty-three. Bob died alone in the ER, without hearing that we loved him, without goodbyes, hugs, or the touch of a hand. He was gone.

Growing up together, this older brother of mine was a mix of quiet genius and cheeky rascal. Never one to miss an opportunity to provoke or tease, Bob ended up creating a family legacy with our kitchen clock. Clocks that hung in people's kitchens back then were electric and plugged into a special, recessed outlet high on a kitchen wall. One of the inconveniences of this was that if the power went out, the clock would stop and wouldn't restart on its own when the power was restored. Someone would have to climb up to re-start it by spinning the shaft that stuck out the back of the clock.

This climbing task fell to my brother when he was a teenager. One day when re-starting the clock he twirled the shaft in the wrong direction. My mother soon pointed out that our clock was running backward. She thought it would be a simple thing to unplug it and restart it, but Bob was not only fascinated — he was delighted!

The clock came down off the wall. Bob re-marked the numbers in their mirror-image locations, and reinstalled that clock to run backward intentionally. Since it was well out of our petite mother's reach to change the clock herself, it continued running backward throughout the remaining decades our family spent in that house. It frustrated my mother to no end. She would glance at the clock, misunderstand the time, and have a mental stumble in the midst of her busy day. "Bob, you and your damn clock!" was often heard in our home.

Not long after my brother died, I got a phone call from our mom. "Are you sitting down?" she asked. I assured her that I was not in any danger should I faint from whatever news she had, and she continued. "My clock is running backward. I've been sitting here drinking coffee and watching it for about fifteen minutes now. It's running backward."

This news was stunning all by itself, but after more conversation I learned that the backward-running clock was a digital clock. Why and how could a digital clock run backward? Later that day, my husband and I drove over to Mom's house and saw it for ourselves. I learned that the clock was one my brother had purchased for her, a fact that strengthened the connection to him. Bob had also bought an identical clock for his own home, and my mother had brought it back to her place when we cleaned out his house.

Mom had often seemed doubtful about an afterlife, and about many things that couldn't be touched, analyzed, or scientifically explained. At some point, though, my mother accepted the clock's odd behavior as a message that her son was all right. She speaks somewhat easily of his life and his stories, perhaps more comfortably than she speaks of others who have passed. Mom soon unplugged the backward clock and replaced it with the identical clock from my brother's house. That clock is working normally and remains in her home to this day.

Meanwhile, my husband and I have the original clock that began this story. It's old and ugly, with its scrawled re-numbering that memorializes my brother's youth. I feel an instant connection with him when

I see it — his playfulness, his genius, and his absence. Evidently, clocks have become my brother's means to connect with us now — clocks that cross time and dimensions.

~Judy Bonamici Cools

89

The Sparrow

Dogs are miracles with paws.
~Attributed to Susan Ariel Rainbow Kennedy

My father-in-law was a kind and loyal man. His main concern in life was the welfare of his family, including my husband, Tal. After years of battling a terminal lung condition, he passed away peacefully at his home on a cold winter morning with Tal and my mother-in-law by his side.

Later that day, the family's Golden Retriever began barking inside the house. As Tal opened the door to let out the dog, a little sparrow flew in. Darting about the living room, the tiny bird sang an energetic song to my mother-in-law and Tal. After several minutes, the bird exited through the open door, flying away into the wintry bright-white sky. Something struck Tal as unusual about the encounter, so we researched the symbolism of sparrows and discovered a legend that they can see souls and carry them to heaven.

Two years passed, seasons came and went, and it was winter once again. On a cool and clear afternoon, Tal and I took our beloved dog, Toby, for what would be his last walk. His body was shutting down from a rare autoimmune disorder. The illness had progressed rapidly, and Toby seemed to have aged ten years in a matter of days. Our once vibrant Greyhound, who used to trot gracefully down our street, now had a heavily labored stride. Even though he was exhausted, his sweet brindle face looked happy as he took in the surrounding smells. Not even a terminal disease could take away his love of a good olfactory excursion around the neighborhood.

As we returned to our condominium's entrance, we heard a twinkling sound. Tal and I looked up and saw a wind chime made of rainbow-colored pieces dancing in the breeze on a patio above. We had never noticed it before.

An hour later, Toby passed away peacefully on his dog bed, his favorite spot in the world. He was surrounded by Tal, Redman (his brother from the same litter), and me. We said our goodbyes, and then covered him one last time with the rainbow-patterned blanket that had kept him warm on many a cold night.

Later that day, Tal and I took Redman out for a walk. Eyes swollen and hearts broken, we seemed to move in slow motion down the same path we shared with Toby only a few hours earlier. Redman also seemed to be in a haze of grief, completely disinterested in the multitude of scents hiding in the grass below.

Suddenly, a little sparrow with a brindle pattern appeared on a tree branch only a few feet away. Jumping wildly, he bounced and spun around exactly like Toby did when he was excited. Once the sparrow realized he had our attention, he hopped even closer. He sang directly to us with great intensity, leaning forward in our direction while making eye contact as if trying to communicate something.

Tal and I just stood there taking in what was happening. It was magic. The little bird's joyful song reverberated through my being, and a strange feeling of warmth washed over me. After a few precious moments when time stood still, the sparrow flew up past the barren trees. As he ascended, the bright sun obscured him from sight. His birdsong grew more and more distant until the sound faded completely. We stood there for several moments, looking upward toward the sky. Even though I could no longer hear the sparrow's beautiful voice, somehow I knew he was still singing. It was only after he was gone that I remembered the legend of sparrows carrying souls to heaven.

Was this last visit by a sparrow just a coincidence? Perhaps. But when I think about the miracle of life that shined in Toby's eyes — eyes that gazed at Tal and me with boundless affection — well, frankly, our devoted dog visiting us one last time before his soul flew to heaven just makes more sense. I say that not only because of the extraordinary timing of our encounter, but because of what I felt deep inside my being when that sparrow sang his beautiful song.

~L. Bower

90

Just the Sign I Wanted

Music is well said to be the speech of angels.
~Thomas Carlyle

It had been a birthday to remember. Two of my three grown children and their spouses, my grandson and his fiancée, and eight of my closest friends all gathered to help me celebrate at a beautiful restaurant. There was love all around, and laughter filled the room. For a while, I even managed to forget that my soul mate wouldn't be there.

Paul and I were married forty-plus years when he died suddenly. Although that was five years earlier, I thought of him every day, but this night I could be carefree. I could forget about all the birthdays that Paul had made special by arranging a surprise party or dinner.

The last birthday I spent with him, he invited thirty friends and family members to a Buca di Beppo feast in the "Pope's room" — a fun, rowdy place for Italian food. He wasn't a "diamonds" kind of guy, but more into people having fun and being loving. His personality was larger than life, and he swept me off my feet at sixteen. We grew up together, marrying at nineteen and twenty-two respectively. He learned early on in our marriage that birthdays were a special day for me.

My actual birthday was Monday, but I had decided to hold my celebratory dinner Sunday night. I wanted those who had to work Monday to get home at a reasonable hour. After the restaurant, those who could came back to my house to party and visit.

The next day, my daughter Mary and I went shopping and then to a spa. Finally, we joined her husband for pizza later at their house. It was a laidback day, but it was perfect after the dinner and party the night before.

I left Mary's house about 10:00 p.m. feeling a little dejected. As I drove home down the coast route from my daughter's house, I told Paul, "Did you forget what day this is? I haven't seen any signs that you remembered my birthday, and you always have."

In the past, he had always talked to me through my Sirius radio. It wasn't a coincidence that every time I turned it on, they played, "Earth Angel." I always felt him near when that song came on. Tonight, I yearned to hear from him. Would he come through? Would he remember?

The first song I heard was "If Tomorrow Never Comes" by Garth Brooks, one of our favorite country singers. When the kids were younger, before they married, we would all go dirt-bike riding in the desert. Garth was our go-to guy for dancing around the campfire.

I was amazed at how relevant his lyrics were that night.

If tomorrow never comes
Will she know how much I loved her
Did I try in every way to show her every day
That she's my only one

Wow. Was Paul telling me I was still his only one? I was a little sad at the next part of the song.

And if my time on earth were through
And she must face this world without me
Is the love I gave her in the past
Gonna be enough to last

Of course, Paul's love was enough to "last" for me. I was so grateful and awestruck to have "received" this song on my car radio as I finished my birthday. I dissolved into tears. I had gotten my sign.

Then, just in case I wasn't sure, the next song was "Happy, Happy Birthday Baby" by The Tune Weavers.

Okay, I had no doubts. My guy knew what day it was, and I drove home sobbing but happy. He remembered. Paul was with me in spirit once again.

~Sallie A. Rodman

91

Jake's Last Gift

I have found that when you are deeply troubled,
there are things you get from the silent, devoted
companionship of a dog that you can
get from no other source.
~Doris Day

When I was a young woman, my best friend by far was my Border Collie, Jake. He joined my family when I was fourteen years old and he was fourteen weeks, so the two of us grew up side by side. We hit our awkward adolescent phase at the same time, and while Jake naturally grew out of his much faster than I did, he never held it against me. The two of us were inseparable until he passed away from cancer at the ripe old age of thirteen.

The day we had to say goodbye was a very difficult one for me. On the one hand, I was grateful that Jake had lived such a good long life, and I didn't want to sully that gratitude with too much sorrow. But at the same time, my house suddenly felt very empty, my kitchen too quiet, and my back yard much, much too big. I managed to stand the silence for several hours. Then I got in my car and drove to Smith Rock State Park in Terrebonne, Oregon.

Smith Rock State Park is one of those stunning natural places that is hard to describe with mere words. Although the beautiful stone cliffs there are beloved by competitive rock climbers worldwide, one doesn't have to be a rock climber to enjoy them. The park also has several wonderful pet-friendly hiking trails for those of us whose athletic abilities are more, shall we say, down-to-earth. Jake and I had spent many happy hours exploring them together, and walking beneath the ancient rocks had never failed to fill me with a deep sense of peace.

That day was no exception. I spent maybe half an hour hiking up one of the easier trails, and while I missed my beautiful dog fiercely with every step, just being alone in nature helped to ease my heart. I was just wondering if it was time to turn back and head home when a little ball of black-and-white fur suddenly came streaking up the trail. It was dragging a nylon leash behind it.

The blur was moving so quickly that I didn't really get a look at it, but some dog-person instincts never fade. I knew instantly that the blur was a dog that had somehow tugged its leash out of its owner's hand, and I quickly moved to intervene. I stepped on the leash, halting the little runaway in mid-flight. And when I looked down to see what I'd caught, I couldn't believe my eyes.

It was a little black-and-white Border Collie puppy—one that could have been the twin of my Jake when we first met.

I didn't have much time to stare. A few seconds later, the puppy's human mom, red-faced and sweating, came sprinting around the bend in the trail. "Oh, thank you so much!" she said when she saw that I had caught her furry fugitive. "I don't know why Jake took off like that except that he's been cooped up in the car all day. I guess he just decided he really needed a good run."

"Jake?" I repeated. "This puppy is named Jake?" And then I burst into tears.

Looking back on it, I'm a little amazed that the woman didn't snatch up her puppy and run. Having a total stranger suddenly fall apart on you in the middle of a wilderness trail is hardly likely to inspire much confidence. But true dog people are a rare breed. The woman took one look at me, then gently took Jake's leash from my hand and guided me to a nearby picnic table. She urged me to sit down. Then she lifted the puppy onto the table and asked me to tell her what was wrong.

By the time I'd finished stuttering out my story, she was looking very thoughtful. "You know," she said, "my husband and I are driving home to Seattle — we've been visiting our daughter down in California. Normally, we wouldn't have stopped for a break until we reached Madras. But when I saw the sign for Smith Rock, something told me we needed to stop." She smiled at Jake and me, who had crossed the table and put his tiny paws on my shoulders, trying frantically to lick my face. "I think I know why now. I think your Jake is using our Jake to say goodbye."

My hands froze in Jake's soft baby fur. It couldn't be possible. Or could it? But before I could voice my doubts, the woman smiled again, laughing a little as Jake's still insistently licking tongue went up my nose. "Are you going to get another dog?" she asked.

I shook my head. "I could never," I said. "My Jake was far too special for me to ever want to replace him."

"Not replace, no," the woman said. "That would be impossible. But I still think you'll have another dog in your life one day, when the time is right." She cocked her head thoughtfully to one side. "I think perhaps your Jake will see to it that you find the right one."

"I could never," I repeated — and at that moment, I honestly believed it was true. To her credit, the woman didn't try to push. She just walked me back to the parking lot, where we spent a few minutes talking about inconsequential things with her husband before they all got back in their truck and resumed their trip home to Seattle. I never even learned her name.

But her words stuck with me anyway, as did the incredible coincidence of running into Jake at Smith Rock that day. What, after all, were the odds of meeting a puppy of the same breed, the same coloring, and even the same name as my Jake only a few hours after he passed away? In many ways, the chance encounter really did feel like my dog's final gift to me, his way of assuring me that he'd never leave me entirely. And that thought comforted me greatly during all the days and weeks ahead.

But the story doesn't end there. About a year later, I received a surprise phone call from my vet. "I don't know if you're interested," she said. "But one of my other clients just had a litter of Border Collie pups, and they're all lovely young dogs. The second that Brittney said she was looking for good homes for them, I thought of you. You might want to drive out and have a look."

"Well…" I said hesitantly. "I suppose it wouldn't hurt to visit. Where does Brittney live?"

"She has a small ranch in Terrebonne, right next to Smith Rock State Park," my vet said. "The pups were born right in the shadow of the cliffs."

~Kerrie R. Barney

92

A Miracle Made for One

In the night of death, hope sees a star, and listening
love can hear the rustle of a wing.
~Robert Ingersoll

"Good morning," I said to my daughter-in-law as I slipped into her kitchen. "You're up early. How did you sleep?"

"Okay, I guess. And you?"

"Pretty well," I said as I poured myself a cup of coffee, remembering all we had shared the previous day. "I'll be back in a little while," I said, scooping up my keys. "I think I'll have my morning coffee with Ray."

The day before, I had buried my husband of forty-two years, father of seven and grandfather to nine, the love of my life. We had enjoyed our morning coffee together for as long as I could remember. Driving away from the cemetery the previous afternoon, I vowed to share this one last ritual with him.

We chose to bury Ray in a rural cemetery with a view of the Colorado valley we love and have called home for nearly thirty years. Although he and I had recently moved to coastal North Carolina, hoping to improve his quality of life as he battled lung disease, Ray died unexpectedly two weeks after we arrived. I brought him back home for burial. And this morning was typical Colorado... sunny, still and magnificent.

I had driven past this churchyard cemetery thousands of times over the years, but now it was changed. My husband was dead. I had never done this before.

Slowing as I neared the cemetery entrance, I felt the crunch of gravel beneath my tires as I turned from the two-lane highway onto the narrow, rocky road leading to Ray's grave. Tears spilled from my eyes when I spotted the funeral flowers standing guard over the clumps of earth holding the remains of the man I loved.

I parked the car and sat motionless. I had no script for what should come next. Clutching my travel mug filled with lukewarm coffee, I opened the door, slid from behind the wheel and walked slowly to his grave.

"Baby, I'm here," I whispered. I felt bewildered, searching for something I couldn't name.

After forty-two years of marriage, we knew each other better than we knew ourselves; we could finish one another's sentences without a second guess. Ray and I had prepared ourselves for his passing and my widowhood as best we could. We said things we needed to say, forgave one another and shared heart-to-heart talks about death, dying and the legacy he wanted to leave. But way too soon, I held him as he took his last labored breath.

My greatest fear since falling in love with my husband was that he would die and leave me alone. He did. How could I survive without my best friend?

"Lord, help," I prayed. "I don't even know how to pray. But I know I'm scared and sad and overwhelmed. I need something from you, with your fingerprints all over it, to let me know I'm not forgotten, and that you are with me."

Aimlessly, I walked back to my car, slipped behind the wheel, sipped my coffee and waited. For what? Then I noticed birds. Scores of them flocked toward Ray's grave while outlying trees stood silent. They flitted from branch to branch and chirped bossily to one another while hopping on his grave or circling above it. What a party! Oh, how Ray would have loved it.

Ray had always enjoyed birds. He would contentedly sit and

watch them, fill his feeders, or patiently scatter seeds for them with the grandkids. I loved that about him. But birds were *his* thing. I'd never really taken an interest in them until they quietly morphed into part of our retirement plan.

"I'm concerned about our expectations of one another when we retire," I had shared one evening as we talked about our imminent empty nest and impending retirement. "I don't think I want to do it the way you do." We had watched countless couples stumble in this season. Some drifted apart from one another while others became suffocating and inseparable. How could we navigate this transition and do it well? Over time, we agreed we could each be boss of ourselves. We would develop our individual interests and cultivate mutual ones.

"So, what else could we do together besides golf?" I continued.

"Well, I do really like birds," he said.

"I can do that! I love how you take time to be still and notice them. I want to learn how to do that," I said.

And so I did. I began to learn the names and characteristics of common birds that visited our feeders. We identified different shore-birds when we travelled to the coast. I started to notice their beauty and individuality.

This morning, plain brown sparrows and colorful mountain blue-birds darted about Ray's grave. I watched and listened, mesmerized. Then, startled, I ducked as a bluebird dive-bombed straight toward me, veering sharply upward before smashing into my windshield. I gasped. Within a few seconds, it happened again—and then a third time, as if the birds, under someone's command, lined up, took aim and targeted me behind the driver's wheel, my peaceful cup of coffee long forgotten.

"I get it, Lord. It's my answer."

Then, punctuating the obvious, a bluebird fluttered beside the passenger window before calmly perching on my side mirror. Stealing sideways glances through soft brown eyes, he seemed to be asking, "Are you watching this?" I was, and I was captivated.

My heart raced, overwhelmed by the number of birds surrounding Ray's grave—three diving bluebirds and one perched within my grasp, engaging me, willing me to know he was an answer to my prayer.

That morning, I had returned to the cemetery to share a cup of coffee with my beloved and ask God to send a sign just for me. He did. He sent birds.

~Paula Freeman

93

Pennies from Heaven

Angels speak to those who silence
their minds long enough to hear.
~Proverb

I was at a yard sale looking through a box of old books when I saw a 1936 yearbook from Glendale High School in California. The name "Ben" was written in the upper right corner of the first page. The yearbook was full of the usual notes from classmates, as well as some newspaper clippings about Ben's academic and athletic achievements. I looked around for the owner of the house and found him carrying more boxes out of the garage with the help of his two young sons.

I asked him, "Are you selling this?"

"Yeah," he replied. "I'll take three bucks for it."

I asked if he knew who Ben was. He said he was his grandfather.

I couldn't understand why anyone would want to get rid of such a precious family memento, especially for such a paltry amount of money, so I asked if he was sure he wanted to sell it. He said yes again with a slightly impatient tone as he began talking with another customer.

Though he obviously had no interest in it, I still wanted to encourage him to keep it — if not for himself, then for his children. But then I thought maybe he had his reasons for letting the yearbook go. Family emotions are complicated. I felt sorry for his sons, who would never get to look at this window into their grandfather's life. I almost didn't buy it for that reason until I heard him tell someone, "Anything that doesn't sell is going to the thrift shop."

I handed him the three dollars, got into my car, and set the yearbook on the seat beside me. I wanted to find someplace quiet and explore every page immediately, but I had to hurry home because I was repainting the interior of my house that day. My wife had taken our two daughters to her father's house to get them away from the paint fumes. I worked all day, but the job took longer than I expected, so I called my wife and asked her to stay overnight there so the paint would be dry before she and the girls returned.

I worked through the night and looked at the yearbook during breaks. I learned that Ben, the yearbook's owner, was no average Joe. He was the Student Body President and Yell Leader, as well as a track and football star. Leadership also ran in the family because his younger brother succeeded him as president, which was a first for the high school at the time and probably hasn't been repeated since. They were both exemplary students, full of boundless energy and ambition.

The first thing that impressed me as I flipped through the pages was how well dressed and groomed everyone was. The next was the penmanship and eloquence of the comments. I had to keep reminding myself that they were written by teenagers. The language was charming and full of terms of endearment unique to the 1930s like "good egg" and "swell fellow." By all accounts, Ben was both.

But I couldn't help feeling sad as I looked at the photos of Ben and his classmates, their young faces so full of high expectations for their futures, because I knew their lives had been lived, and they were all either gone or very, very old. It was a lot like the "Carpe Diem" scene from the *Dead Poets Society* movie. Looking at photos of young people from another time has always stirred unsettling emotions in me and made me meditate on my own mortality.

Before I returned to my work, I found a playlist on YouTube of hit songs from 1936 and said, "Here's some music from when you were young, Ben. I hope you enjoy it."

As I worked, Bing Crosby crooned "Pennies from Heaven," Billie Holiday sang "Summertime," and dozens of other enchanting tunes from the brightest lights of that era such as Benny Goodman, Guy

Lombardo, and Tommy Dorsey transported me to the year when Ben was a high-school senior — on top of the world and destined for great things. As Fred Astaire sang "The Way You Look Tonight," I imagined Ben slow dancing with his girlfriend across the floor of my living room. The fact that my house was built in 1939 and hasn't been changed much in the years since only added to the ethereal effect.

With such wonderful melodies playing, work was easier, and time passed quickly. When I finished, it was 4:00 a.m. The music ended, and the house was quiet. I sat down, returned to the yearbook, found Ben's photo and said, "Thanks for keeping me company, Ben. I wish I could have known you." Using the vernacular of the era, I added, "You seemed like a swell fellow."

A few seconds later, there was a knock at the door, but not just any knock — it was a knock with the "shave and a haircut, two bits" cadence very common to the era Ben lived in — five knocks, a pause, then two more. I was startled because of the late hour, but figured my wife had come home early with the girls for some reason. I was sitting close to the door, so I rushed over and opened it. There was nobody on the porch. Thinking it might have been kids pulling a prank, I went outside and scanned the front yard. No one. I walked to the middle of the street, looked both ways and listened closely. It was as still and quiet as one would expect in the hours before dawn. None of my closest neighbors have children, so there was no chance some kid quickly ducked into a nearby house.

Completely bewildered, I went back inside and sat down with the old yearbook again. A few moments later, it dawned on me with a chill that the knock on the door was Ben's answer, his way of thanking me for playing the music of his youth, and for turning the pages of his yearbook so he could see the faces of his old friends again.

The curtain between this world and the next is thick, but every now and then, if we're respectful and receptive enough, and if all the conditions are perfect, I believe we can be given a "penny from heaven" — a greeting from someone on the other side who is determined enough to reach us somehow. I was certain in that moment that Ben had been there, and that his happy, musical knock at my door was his way of saying, "Thanks, pal. You're a swell fellow, too."

~Mark Rickerby

Chapter
11

Miracles
and More

Heavenly Strangers

94

Don't Take It Back

Give God your weakness, and he
will give you his strength.
~Author Unknown

At 1:00 p.m. on a Monday afternoon, my phone rang. "Wendy, this is Wayne, the roofer. I just put Rod in an ambulance. He fell off the roof."

I was more than 1,000 miles away. I booked a flight and rushed to the airport. I would arrive around midnight.

I got off the plane with my small suitcase in hand and took a taxi to the hospital. I was dropped off at the emergency entrance only to find that my husband Rod had been moved to the trauma ICU. I had to go back outside and walk around the hospital to the front entrance.

As I walked, I spoke out loud to God.

"God, I need a miracle. I don't want to do this alone… God, I don't know what to do… Will you take it?"

I entered the hospital security area to get a pass to the ICU. The guard recited a list of directions that I was too upset to understand. As I stared at him blankly a kind, elderly gentleman next to me said he would walk me there since he knew where to go.

We made our way down the wide hall toward the trauma unit, and he stopped to offer his large right hand. He introduced himself as Pastor Holland. I stopped in my tracks, took his hand and hugged this total stranger. As tears rolled down my cheeks, I said, "I so need a pastor right now."

"Would you like for me to go with you?"

"Please," I replied tearfully.

As we continued down the hall, he asked me what I had done so far. I told him I hadn't done anything yet as I didn't know what to do. I told him I talked to God outside the hospital, and that is when Pastor Holland stopped in his tracks.

"And what did you tell God?" he asked with an intense gaze.

"I didn't know what to say, so I just asked God to take it."

His deep brown eyes softened as he said, "And don't take it back. If you gave it to God, do not try and take it back."

We arrived at the locked double doors of the trauma center and used the outside phone to be let in. We found Rod on life support. Tubes, braces, bandages, restraints and noisy machines filled the room. Pastor Holland walked directly over to Rod's limp body, gently laid both hands on top of his head and silently prayed. Pastor Holland stayed with me the rest of the night, until we were asked to leave for a couple of hours. He asked if I had paper and a pen to write down everything, since he very wisely knew that I would not remember much that was explained to me. We exchanged phone numbers, and he gave me two Bible verses to read in Ephesians from the small Bible he kept in his right pocket. We both left the hospital about 7:00 a.m.

When I returned two hours later, the room nurse told me that I had just missed my pastor.

"Oh, he is not *my* pastor," I replied. "I thought he worked with the hospital."

"Why, no," the nurse said blankly. "We have never seen that man before. We let him in because we saw him with you and thought he was *your* pastor."

Who was the heavyset man in a gently wrinkled brown suit with a harvest gold shirt and matching handkerchief in his left breast pocket? Where did he say he came from? Was he my miracle?

It made me think back to our earlier conversation. Pastor Holland said he didn't have a brick-and-mortar church. He said he just went where God told him to go. He was to be at our hospital, and then he would go to Texas and on to Tacoma.

Had he really been sent to help us?

For six days, I did not see Pastor Holland. I went on the Internet to Google him without any success. I remembered he told me he took the bus to the hospital that night, so I thought he was local. I couldn't find his name in any local listings for clergy. I checked the pastoral sign-in notebook at the main entrance of the hospital. No "Pastor Holland" had signed the book. When I called the number he gave me, it was only a recorded message that the person was unavailable. Was he real? I must have called that number a dozen times to see if I could talk to someone but I always got the same recording.

On Sunday, Rod was being prepared for his first surgery — to place eight titanium screws in his eye socket and repair his fractured jaw and cheek. I kept reflecting on what the pastor told me. *Do not take it back... Do not take it back. If you give it to God, do not take it back.* As my cousin and I arrived at the hospital for the surgery, I saw Pastor Holland. He was just outside the hospital entrance. I had told my cousin about him, so I couldn't wait to have her meet him.

"I am here only a short time," he said. He gently took my cousin's hand and said, "Take good care of our Wendy. She's very precious to all of us."

Instantly, I knew everything would be all right. My mother, who had passed away, had written those exact words in a letter to me more than thirty-seven years ago. When Pastor Holland said "precious," I knew in my heart that it was my personal message from Mom through him. I didn't need to doubt the existence of Pastor Holland as my miracle. He was not only my angel, but also a messenger. I now felt my miracle was in place. By that afternoon, Rod's facial surgery would be described by the physician as "perfect."

It has been four years since Rod fell off the roof. He not only had that successful facial surgery, but later had a subdural hematoma that required a craniotomy and then a major shoulder tendon repair. At each step of the way, my strength came from my angel, Pastor Holland, who had gently whispered, "If you gave it to God, do not take it back." I repeated that phrase over and over for months until Rod made a full recovery.

We are so blessed to have miracles and angels around us. We never know when they will find us. Fortunately for me, I was actually able to give my angel a hug.

~W. Bond

95

AAA Angel

When we are touched by something it's as if we're
being brushed by an angel's wings.
~Rita Dove

y best athlete was being considered for an athletic scholarship to a university in the United States. It was very important for her to perform well at our Canadian Nationals in order to secure her spot on an NCAA team.

Chaynade had been injured during the first selection meet, but she performed well in the second. She would have to compete at the final selection meet in order to qualify for National Championships.

I have been involved with the sport of gymnastics for more than thirty years as an athlete and coach and I recognized talent. Chaynade was without a doubt one of British Columbia's best athletes, but she still needed to travel to Kamloops to compete at our Provincial Championships. I had recommended that she arrive the day before the competition, since a three-hour trip on the day of competition is not ideal for proper preparation. However, other commitments made it impossible for the family to comply with my recommendation, and they had to drive up on the day of the championships.

Since I had several other athletes competing at this event, I had to be in Kamloops for the entire weekend. Friday night, when we received news that many of the highways were closed due to a snowstorm, I began to worry about Chaynade making the trip the next day. I had what I would call a vision or premonition of the family's green van broken down beside the highway. I had never had an experience like this, but it seemed like I was watching a movie in my mind. I started to pray that nothing would prevent Chaynade from arriving safely and on time. I called my husband and asked him to pray, and to recruit friends who would pray for Chaynade and her family.

I anxiously awaited Chaynade's arrival the next day, and was relieved when she came to find me in the spectators' arena. However, Chaynade didn't just come to say "hi"; she had a whopper of a story to tell. The family van did break down at the top of the high mountain pass on the Coquihalla Highway. The radiator had blown when they were still an hour and a half from Kamloops.

Amazingly, they had just pulled over when a big, brand-new pickup truck parked behind them along with two other trucks loaded with snowmobiles. A man got out of the first truck and asked where they were headed. They explained their need to get to the competition in Kamloops, and then that man proceeded to hand his truck keys to Chaynade's mother! He said, "You take my truck for the weekend, and I'll stay here and wait for a tow truck." He asked where the van should be sent for repair and said, "You can return my truck to my place in Chilliwack on your way back home." He gave them his address, retrieved some items from the truck that he would need for his snowmobiling trip, and sent the family on their way.

Chaynade knew this was an extraordinary occurrence, so when we met her mom and her grandmother in the arena, I relayed my vision from the night before. I told them that I had "seen" their van break down, and that I had solicited the prayers of several others on their behalf. They were all quite animated discussing the unusual events of the morning, and Nana exclaimed, "That man must have been an angel."

We were all so grateful to the kind stranger who provided roadside assistance that we dubbed him the "AAA Angel."

Chaynade had a great competition, and our AAA Angel had the family van ready and waiting when they returned to Chilliwack the following day. After an excellent performance again at the National

Championships later that season Chaynade went on to compete for Texas Woman's University for four years on a scholarship. In 2011, she was named a USA Gymnastics All-American on the floor exercise.

~Lisa Naubert

96

Wise Words

Make yourself familiar with the angels and behold
them frequently in spirit; for, without being
seen, they are present with you.
~Saint Francis of Sales

We prowled through the secondhand bookstore the day after Christmas, just my husband, our two daughters, and me. This was a precious time for us. We would be splitting up as a family in a couple of days.

It had been a tough eight months since my husband had retired from the Navy. We had been shocked to discover that the only job available for Louie was in a city six and a half hours away from the mountains of southwest Virginia where we lived. My asthma had gotten so bad that it was impossible for me to stay with Louie in the city. We had finally settled for a temporary separation, praying that a job would become available in the beautiful region that we loved.

So there we were, delaying our departure by passing time in a secondhand bookstore before the girls and I headed back to southwest Virginia. We were so broke, with Louie supporting two households, that we had very little to spend in the store, just five dollars each.

We joked as we continued our treasure hunt, all hoping to find the oldest, least expensive book. There was a lot of a laughter and hugging and kissing as we enjoyed each other's company.

Jenny suddenly remembered that there was an ATM not far from the bookstore, and she had twenty-five dollars that she had squirreled away. We could divide it up, she decided.

"Come on, Jenny," Louie said with a laugh. "I'll drive you to the ATM." Then we did another round of hugging and kissing, not wanting to be apart for even a few minutes. It must have been a curious sight, this emotional family scene, but we were oblivious to what others might think.

Besides the proprietor, only one other person was in the bookstore—a lovely, well-dressed woman about my age. I noticed her expensive clothes, shoes, and handbag. I wondered what it would be like to be rich enough to walk into a bookstore and have the money to buy any book my heart desired. We were having so much fun, however, that I quickly forgot the woman.

Finally, I spied my perfect book! It was a hundred years old, and it was on my favorite time period—the Middle Ages. Oh, how I wanted that book! I quickly checked the inside cover for the price, and my heart fell. It was too expensive!

"Oh, I wish I were rich," I murmured, as my eyes locked with the woman's.

"It looks to me as though you already are," she said, with a smile.

There was a long pause, and then my heart filled with comprehension. I *was* rich. Very rich. I turned quickly to thank the woman for her gentle reminder, but she was gone!

Who was she? I don't know, but what she did for my outlook was nothing short of miraculous. I will never forget her. Where did she disappear to? I can't say.

Strangely enough, within days my husband received a job offer in southwest Virginia. In less than two weeks, he was hired, and we moved to the place that is now our home.

I've had plenty of time to wonder about that day, when an angel in a secondhand bookstore gave me God's rich message of love and encouragement when I so desperately needed it.

~Jaye Lewis

97

A Christmas Surprise

Be an angel to someone else whenever you can,
as a way of thanking God for the help
your angel has given you.
~Eileen Elias Freeman,
The Angels' Little Instruction Book

Due to my Conservative Jewish background, I did not believe in angels. That is, not until Christmas Eve of 1979, when an angel brought unexpected joy to my home.

As often happens in divorce, my five- and eleven-year-old daughters not only lost the security of an intact family, but they tearfully left behind neighborhood friends, a familiar school and the comfortable amenities of a large house — all replaced by a cramped two-bedroom apartment in a poorer part of town.

I arranged to take my vacation during their winter school holiday, and we made plans for the week: cookie-baking, movie matinees, arts and crafts, games, a pizza night, and evening car rides to view neighborhood holiday lights and lawn displays. The anticipation was working its magic, and my daughters' spirits seemed to brighten.

The week before the school break, however, devastating news of multiple family disasters came in faster than we could process the pain, clouding our vacation plans. By Christmas Eve, gloom enveloped our apartment. An afternoon movie did little to improve our mood.

Upon returning to our apartment, we were astonished to see a majestic six-foot Christmas tree, aglitter with metallic icicle strands, propped against our front door. In mute wonder, we looked back and forth, from the tree to each other, and around the deserted street. Excitement built, and the girls begged to keep the orphaned tree.

"Maybe it's for us," insisted the older.

"Yeah," echoed the younger. "I bet an angel brought it to us!"

I laughed out loud at the idea of an angel bringing a Christmas tree to a Jewish family. Nevertheless, I was caught up in their newfound elation, and I pronounced the tree "ours."

We dragged it inside and headed out to the only supermarket in our small town open that late on Christmas Eve. With holiday merchandise marked down to half price, I gave a nod of approval to a tree stand, two boxes of multicolored balls, a package of six Santa figurines, a 100-foot string of miniature lights, and one lone paper angel.

Back home, we maneuvered "our" tree into a place of honor in our tiny living room. The girls snipped and glued and painted paper decorations. With an exhilaration that had been absent for months, we strung the lights, placed the paper angel on top and festooned the tree with store-bought and homemade ornaments.

Finally, with a girl snuggled in each of my arms, we sat in semi-darkness, mesmerized by twinkling Christmas tree lights. Smiles and contented sighs proclaimed the end of our long emotional crises; there was joy in our new home. I sat in thankful amazement that a Christmas tree had the power to uplift Jewish spirits.

My five-year-old whispered softly, "Do you really think an angel brought us this tree?"

At that moment, I did not know the tree and its deliverer would forever remain a mystery. All I could do was answer honestly from my heart. "Yes," I whispered, holding them closer, "I'm sure of it."

Our vacation was a resounding success — fun, laughter and the nightly wonder of our flickering tree. By New Year's Day, our spirits were healed, and we were ready to face the challenges ahead, strengthened by the bond of our shared belief in angels and magical Christmas trees.

That winter vacation became an annual family tradition, complete with a "Jewish Angel Tree" in remembrance of our heaven-sent gift. For seventeen more years, we held our breath and felt the familiar tingles up our arms when the original paper angel was placed atop each tree.

Now my adult daughters have their own homes. There are no more luxurious vacation days spent together; there are no more Jewish Angel Trees. But each Christmas Eve, they phone to sigh and reminisce about our angel, and the special childhood memories intertwined in the branches of a six-foot tree.

~Lynne Foosaner

98

A Special Message from God

A guardian angel walks with us, sent from up above,
their loving wings surround us and enfold us with love.
~Author Unknown

It was one of those days. Irate customers, grouchy co-workers and gazillions of problems had dominated my husband's job as a shoe salesman that Saturday. He was eager to put an end to this workweek and start the one-hour commute home, but ten minutes before closing time, a customer walked in.

Taking a deep breath, my husband asked if he could help him. He hoped to take care of the customer quickly so that he could leave on time. However, the gentleman — who was deaf — insisted that he didn't need help and started looking around the men's department.

David hadn't always been a salesman. After several entrepreneurial ventures, he'd become the co-owner of a shoe store. It's a complicated story, but in the end, he learned that the business couldn't support two owners. With no paycheck coming in, our family had plunged into the deepest debt we'd ever known. Worse than that, the situation cast my husband into a state of depression unlike any he'd ever experienced in his life.

Months before, I'd lost my job and hadn't found a new one yet, which meant that David needed to get a job as quickly as possible. He hoped for one that would bring meaning to his life, but the reality hit him hard. No one wanted to hire a sixty-year-old has-been storeowner. With his "shoe experience," he managed to land this job selling shoes.

He focused on remaining optimistic by reading books on the power of positive thinking. Yet, he couldn't shake the storm cloud that hung over him. A spiritual man, my sweet husband pleaded with God, but as his life continued on a downward spiral, he felt as if God had abandoned him and completely ignored his pleas for help.

And on that nightmarish Saturday, unbeknownst to me, my husband hit an all-time low point in his life.

Now the minutes were ticking by, and closing time had already passed when the customer finally motioned for my husband.

David conjured up the most pleasant expression he could even though he was exasperated with the man for not accepting his help from the beginning. The customer had a tennis shoe in his hand, and when my husband explained that the shoe ran a size larger than the man would normally wear, the man put it back on the rack. He didn't want to try it, and he wasn't interested in trying on anything else either.

Even under duress, my husband had always maintained a chipper, amiable demeanor, but he could feel his patience wearing thin.

Then, the customer asked for a piece of paper and a pen.

My husband started to worry. At this rate, he'd be there all night!

When he tried to peek at what the man was scribbling, all that stood out was the word, "God."

At that moment, the word "God" piqued my husband's interest, especially since he'd been silently complaining to God already for sending this last-minute customer in to torture him further on this already horrible day.

The man finished writing and handed my husband the paper. He stood silently while my husband read it:

Recently God showed me you've been down for long while… Be cheer He knows your heart and is with you always. He loves you very much as do I, I'll pray for you to be strong and courage…

Also, He'll help you to overcome your struggles... Bless you...
Andrew W —

A warm feeling of peace and love washed over my husband. Suddenly, he felt ashamed for his impatience with this man and wondered who he was.

Blessed with a wonderful gift for faking a sunny disposition, my husband had always put on an amazing show for friends, co-workers and extended family, even during this crisis in his life. No one knew that he'd been down for a "long while." How did this stranger know?

Grabbing the pen from the messenger, my husband wrote back:

I talk to God all the time. Thank you for coming by!

Then my husband reached out and hugged the messenger, who took the pen again and wrote:

God spoke me to drive 1 1/2 hr from PA & stop by here unexpected.

That evening, with tears in his eyes, my husband shared his experience with our family. We wondered if his customer had been a heavenly angel, sent down to deliver this special message from God. I did not include Andrew's last name in his note above, but he did provide it, and my husband looked him up on the Internet and learned that the shoe-store messenger is an earthly angel who actually does live in Pennsylvania.

It's not every Saturday that God sends a message special delivery. Thankfully, the message was received loud and clear!

~Jill Burns

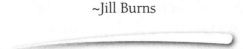

A Call Across
the Water

*I believe that tomorrow is another
day and I believe in miracles.*
~Audrey Hepburn

I zipped up my wetsuit and put my coins in the meter at the
Lake Worth Pier. It was December 23, 2010, a gray, bitingly
cold afternoon. I was off work, and so I'd driven to the beach
to surf. I locked the car, slid the key into my leash pocket,
and grabbed my red longboard and some wax before heading down
the wooden stairs to the sand. The beach was pretty empty, just a guy
ambling by with a metal detector and some kids in hooded sweatshirts. Seven or eight surfers bobbed around in the water.

I stood on the shore and watched the waves rolling in, assessing
the conditions. Wind coming from the northeast — the south side
of the pier was definitely going to be better. I walked down the sand
a few hundred feet, did some yoga stretches, and waxed my board.

In Florida, we wear wetsuits in the winter, but this was one of
the coldest years in recent memory, and I shivered as I stepped into
the water. I paddled out to the break, which can take several minutes,
depending on the length of time between waves. It was a choppy, erratic
day, with huge blasts of whitewater sending me back toward the shore.
But like a salmon swimming upstream, I soldiered on, breathing hard
as I made my way toward the end of the pier.

As the cold liquid seeped through my wetsuit — first at the shoulders, then at the chest and stomach — I thought of my surf buddy Eric's advice that it was probably time to replace my seven-year-old suit. But since I only need to wear it a few months out of the year, it seemed a pointless expense. When my dad was surfing the icy Pacific in the 1930s, no one had even heard of a wetsuit.

On a typical surf day, many things run through my head as I'm slogging my way through the breaking waves — things I need to buy on the way home, calls I have to make — but on that day, the Gordon Lightfoot song, "The Wreck of the Edmund Fitzgerald," was playing in my mind in an endless loop. Someone had posted it on Facebook that morning, and I couldn't get it out of my head — an earworm, it's called. Thinking of that song under the gray sky made my mood dark, worrisome, and I tried to un-hear it by humming a hip-hop tune.

Finally, I reached the end of the pier and sat upright on my board, breathing easier, the smell of salt and fish filling my nostrils. I thought about how I only had two days of radiation left and I'd be done. My surgery in September had been successful, and I'd gotten back in the water quickly. Now I just had to finish up my daily zaps — a fifteen-minute stop at the cancer center on my way to work — and that would be it.

I waited for a wave, and a generous-sized peeler came. I paddled for it and then promptly lost it, plunging into the water. That's when I realized how frigid it was, as my breath caught in my chest. I scurried to the surface, wanting to get out of that dark, miserable ice cavern as fast as possible. But just as I broke through the water, CLUNK, my twenty-five-pound board landed on my head. I scrambled up again, thinking, *This is why I prefer my 7'6. That board is so light I can hold it between two fingers. The 8'6 really packs a wallop.* I climbed back on the board, and that's when the lights went out.

I'm not sure how long it was. It could have been three minutes, ten minutes, or more. But then came words, young and male. "It's okay. Just stay on your board." I wasn't seeing anything, but I was hearing things — the disembodied voice, the lap of the water. I opened my eyes and found I was lying with my cheek on the board, bobbing along with the movement of the ocean.

And then it became clear what had happened. I'd been knocked on the head and had gotten back on my board just before losing consciousness. Until the boy had shouted to me, I'd been floating on my giant red clunker, waiting to be either woken or plunged back into the sea by an oncoming swell. Just as I began to grasp this, I turned my head and saw a wave coming toward me. On instinct, I paddled for it, got up, and rode it to shore.

A teenage boy with a shortboard under his arm climbed out of the water and walked toward me as I stood on the sand. "Are you okay?"

"I, I…" I couldn't speak, completely baffled at what had happened, and how I'd seemingly just picked up where I'd left off, taking the next available wave.

"I saw you get hit. You got on your board, but then you must have passed out."

"But how could I…"

"I paddled over and called out to you. The next thing I see is you're up and riding the wave."

I looked at him, then looked around; the world seemed different, not possibly real anymore, not with what had just happened.

"If you hadn't called to me, I could have fallen in the water and… you know, you saved me."

He shook his head, his wet blond curls flopping across his face. "It's nothing," he said with an embarrassed grin as he edged back into the water.

"Thank you."

"No problem." He threw his board in front of him and paddled out to catch another set.

I caught a few more waves that day before realizing I should go to the ER for a CAT scan. I had a head injury, after all. As I sat in the hospital waiting room, thoughts ran through my head. *How did I get back on my board before passing out? It was so gusty and rough, how did I not get tipped off the board, fall into the water unconscious, and drown? How did I stay safely floating on my old clunker until a call across the water saved me?*

The CAT scan came back clean, and over the next few days I told the story to several people.

"I don't see how this could have happened," my friend Eric said at the bagel shop the day after Christmas, his hands splayed on the table.

"It really did happen. I can't explain it. It's either an amazing stroke of luck or divine intervention."

"Sounds more like the second. It wasn't your time."

I looked out the window. "I guess not."

"Radiation's over?"

"Tomorrow's the last day."

Eric smiled and stood up. "Looks like you might be around a while. Let's get to the beach."

~Anneke Towne

Solidarity

*Without a sense of caring, there can
be no sense of community.*
~Anthony J. D'Angelo

I had already dubbed it the "Worst Week Ever," and it was only Tuesday. My almost two-year-old had a nasty case of croup. He sounded more like a barking puppy than a toddler; a doctor's appointment was necessary. I called out of work (again) and mentally prepared myself for a solo trip to the pediatrician and the subsequent tantrums in the waiting room.

As we were en route, speeding down a busy highway to make our appointment on time — or at least get there a respectable five minutes late — I heard a faint gurgling sound coming from the back seat. My son was still rear facing in his car seat, so I called out his name. He didn't answer. I called his name again, and all I heard was a distinct choking noise.

I screeched over onto the shoulder of the road, got out and ran to his side of the car. In the short seconds it took me to reach him, I prayed. Little did I know how much harder I would have to pray by the end of that week.

Thankfully, my son was not choking. But he *was* vomiting. Everywhere.

He was covered in large chunks of curdled milk, Puffs, and barely digested chicken nuggets. The smell was enough to make me dry heave.

There was vomit in his hair, vomit caked in the straps and buckle of his car seat, vomit on his stuffed Elmo, and vomit on the dry cleaning I had picked up a few days earlier but had never bothered to bring in the house. It was a disaster.

Carefully, I took him out of his seat and stripped off his clothes on the side of the road. That's when *she* appeared. Seemingly out of nowhere, a concerned woman wearing nurse's scrubs was standing beside me, asking if my son was okay. I looked behind me and noticed that she had pulled her SUV right up behind my car.

"He's okay. The poor thing has croup, and we are actually on our way to see his doctor. I just need to get him cleaned up. Oh, God. And his car seat. I need to clean that, too." I was babbling.

"Been there," she said with a smile. "Do you have an extra set of clothes for him?"

I nodded.

"Why don't you take him to my car and get him changed? I'll take care of the car seat for you."

Tears welled in my eyes. In that moment, I was so overwhelmed with motherhood. A sick baby. A pile of work that I continued to neglect at my corporate job because of said sick baby. A back seat covered in vomit. And here was this woman, this complete stranger, taking away some of that burden.

I protested half-heartedly, "You really don't have to do that. His car seat is disgusting."

"Oh, it's nothing. I have little ones. And I'm an ER nurse. I'm practically immune to puke."

"You're a mom?" I asked.

"Sure am," she said. "Us moms gotta stick together."

***

Five days later I was strolling through Trader Joe's, blissfully alone. My husband had offered to take my son for the morning and give me a break — if one considers a kid-free grocery shopping trip a break. I do; I might as well have been in the Bahamas.

I purposely left my phone in the car so I could float through the aisles and not be distracted by social media posts from lucky people who were *actually* in the Bahamas.

I had only been gone about forty-five minutes, but when I got back to my car, I had seven missed calls from my husband, a dozen more missed calls from my mom and an ominous text from my dad: *Emergency. Call when you can.*

Something was very, very wrong.

I called my husband, and I knew by the tone of his voice that something tragic had happened. He didn't want to be the one to tell me. He pleaded with me to call my mom. After he reassured me repeatedly that our son was okay, he delivered the most horrifying and unexpected news I have ever received — my sister's husband, my beloved brother-in-law, had dropped dead of a heart attack. He was thirty-nine.

I had just seen him two days earlier when I stopped by their house for a visit. He was having a dance party with his kids in the living room. My sister and I had stood in the kitchen, sipping our iced coffees and gossiping. I was there to help her pack for a long-awaited trip. Eventually, we joined in the dance party.

And now he was dead? Nope. Not logical. No way. Too unbelievable. No. No. No.

I called my mom next, and she gave me the facts as she knew them: My five-year-old niece and seven-year-old nephew, his children, were the ones who found him. They couldn't wake him, so they ran and got a neighbor. By the time the ambulance arrived, he was gone. There was nothing anyone could've done. My sister was on a girls' weekend away in Florida for her best friend's bachelorette party. She couldn't get a flight home due to bad weather. The situation couldn't have been worse.

My reaction was guttural — a blur of hysterical screaming.

I must've fallen to the ground because I felt someone physically pick me up off the cold pavement.

I heard a voice. "Honey, I think you're in shock. Hold onto my hand. I'm going to walk you to my car where it's warm."

I looked up to see a woman with kind, gray eyes. I will never forget those eyes.

She sat me down in her passenger's seat. She removed her coat and draped it across my lap.

"I read somewhere that when people go into shock, they get very cold. I'm going to keep you warm. Is there someone I can call for you?"

"Please call my mom. I was just on the phone with her. Wait, where is my phone?"

I realized then that she was holding my phone.

"I saw you drop your phone when you collapsed," she said.

"I collapsed?" I was so confused. Was this a weird dream?

She found my mother's number on her own and called her. I could only hear her end of the conversation.

"Yes, hi. I'm with your daughter... She appears to be in shock... Oh, I'm so sorry to hear that... That's just terrible... My condolences to your family... No, I won't let her drive... I'm going to treat her as if she's my own daughter... You don't have to worry about a thing... I'll stay with her until her ride gets here."

She hung up.

"I'm so sorry for your loss," she said. "Your mother is sending your brother to pick you up."

I nodded. Numb. None of what she was telling me made any sense. I think she could tell that I was delirious with grief, so she started to ask me questions about my life.

I told her about my son. I told her about his croup and how I thought that was the worst thing that could happen to me — a sick toddler. And now I felt so stupid because, in one sickening instant, life was infinitely worse. My sister was a thirty-seven-year-old widow, and my niece and nephew no longer had a father.

She listened and pretended I was making perfect sense. She told me about her own grown children.

She never once let go of my hand.

Again, here I was babbling to a complete stranger who had appeared out of nowhere to rescue me in my time of need.

And again, this stranger was a fellow mother.

***

In less than one week, I met two angels. Two real-life angels who are also mothers. Two women who saw something in me that they recognized as fragile, as worrisome, as worthy of their time.

It's been over a month since the Worst Week Ever. My son is fully recovered. On the other hand, I am still healing, still grieving. I look for my angels everywhere I go — both the ones on this earth, the other mothers, and the ones who left this earth entirely too soon.

~Kaysie Norman

The Eleventh Hour

There is always another layer of awareness,
understanding, and delight to be discovered through
synchronistic and serendipitous events.
~Hannelie Venucia

There is never a good time for a Category 5 hurricane to roar through our lives, but for me the timing could not have been worse. After months of unrelenting conflict with my landlord, who threatened to have me deported for refusing to pay his electric bill, I announced that I would move out of my rented bungalow on November 1st and see him in court. Then, on October 23rd, Hurricane Patricia battered my isolated little fishing village in Mexico, shredding my plans.

It took almost an entire day for neighbors to free my pets and me from our refuge, which had held its own against the storm. A rooftop water tank blocked the only door, power lines choked the vegetation, and the contents of someone's art studio fluttered around my yard. Picking my way through the debris, I headed for the beach in the fading light to see if my home-to-be — a funky trailer — had weathered the storm. Along the way, friends and strangers shared the news: No potable water. No telephone service or cell-phone signals. No way to get money, an essential in a cash economy. And no way for delivery trucks to bring in supplies, as the road into town was blocked by boulders and mudslides as well as the army, which had been charged with clearing the highway and maintaining order along the coast.

Hot, dirty, and dazed, I walked along the beach, aghast at the devastation. The Bambu Bar was gone. My favorite restaurant was gone. Josie's sweet little house was gone. The structures that remained upright appeared to be askew without their signature palapa roofs, as did the palms without their fronds. The trailer I was going to move into had been totally demolished by Patricia's fierce winds, its parts and pieces buried beneath five feet of sand.

I had only a week to find another home at a time when virtually everything had been booked in advance for the upcoming tourist season. It was impossible to communicate with absentee owners, and much of the housing stock was no longer habitable. On my way back to the bungalow, I could see that locals were already moving together into the most stable building occupied by an extended family member. My prospects were bleak. I would need a miracle.

While awaiting it, however, I could help in the cleanup and reconstruction effort. Given the unrelenting heat, no electricity, and no way to flush a toilet, staying indoors was unbearable; rinsing off in the Pacific Ocean was the only way to bathe. So I joined every other able-bodied person who took to the muddy streets from dawn to sunset — making towers out of rubble, reinforcing tipsy structures, and delivering donated food, water, supplies, and mattresses as soon as the road into town was clear.

Power was restored late on the fifth night to elated shouts of "*Hay luz!*" ("There is light!") But the joy of whirling fans, dry bedding, and running water was extremely short-lived. Only two days later, the Costalegre was drenched by torrential rains that closed the airport and flooded the town ten miles away on the next bay — the site of the nearest bank and gas station and source of our food, drinking water, and provisions. The downpour was another major setback to the local economy, which had come to depend on income earned during the winter high season. Village residents were already racing against the clock, and so was I. The word-of-mouth culture had turned up no leads; in just one more damp day, I would be homeless.

Weariness gave way to despair the next morning as I set out, past heaps of trash and cars disabled by broken glass, hoping to find friends who might agree to shelter my pets and possessions while I camped out on the beach. The beach was the shortest route to everywhere, so I traipsed along the shore. Soon I heard English-speaking voices spilling down from the roofless top floor of the town's most luxurious beachfront complex. I looked up to see two blond women sitting on the open deck, engaged in conversation as they stared forlornly out to sea. "Did you just arrive?" I called. "Can I help you with anything?"

The younger woman motioned for me to climb up the exterior stairs. We introduced ourselves and briefly shared our stories. As soon as the airport was operational, the mother, who owned the multi-unit rental property, had flown in with her daughter from Los Angeles to assess the damage and decide what to do. They didn't know where to begin.

"Do you speak Spanish?" the mother asked me.

"Yes," I replied. "I've lived in Mexico full-time for more than thirteen years."

"Can you use a Windows 10 computer?"

I nodded. "I'm a translation editor, so I have two of them — one programmed in English, the other in Spanish."

"Do you know any construction workers or landscapers?"

"In the past week, I've met everyone in town that I didn't know before."

"Could you give us a minute, please?"

After a self-guided tour of the spacious, soggy rooms, I rejoined the women on the deck.

"Well," the mother began, "I need a personal assistant, and I'd like someone to maintain my deceased partner's home. If it suits you, would you be willing to help me a few hours a week during the high season? In exchange, you could stay there rent-free. The housekeeper lives across the street." I nearly fainted.

Nothing could be accomplished on a wet Sunday afternoon, so she drove me to the house in one of the few cars with inflated tires that still had gas. Embraced by a verdant tropical forest on the banks of a stream, the house was quirky, charming, nicely furnished and, except for several scratches from toppled trees, unscathed by Patricia. In the back were a lovely covered porch and a huge, walled-in patio — a pet playground extraordinaire. And it was located only two short blocks from my makeshift animal sanctuary, whose occupants included twenty-one cats, six dogs, and a ninety-year-old widower who was no longer able to care for them. I could easily walk over to their sprawling, dilapidated quarters to feed the critters and check on Don Luis.

Trying not to gush, I said, "I absolutely love this house... but I have pets."

"How many?"

"Three rather traumatized cats."

"That's fine with me. When can you move in?"

"Tomorrow, November 1st, would be great."

"And when could you begin assisting me?"

"November 2nd is the Day of the Dead. All of the usual events have been canceled because the cemetery is inaccessible, but the locals will gather in the church plaza at noon to praise the town's patron saint because everyone survived the hurricane. I'd like to join them and come to your place after that."

We shook hands.

Then I headed back to the car with my fairy godmother, dressed in her clever disguise as a wealthy American businesswoman.

"By the way," I said, "thank you for the miracle."

~Lynne Willard

Meet Our Contributors

Mary Ables grew up in Europe and South America as the daughter of an itinerant geologist/civil engineer. She homeschooled her four, now adult, children and is the grandmother of ten. She currently helps her husband run his air care business.

Devora Adams is a writer and life coach who lives in New Jersey with her husband and four daughters. She is the author of *Amazing Women: Jewish Voices of Inspiration*, published by Menucha Publishers, as well as a proud contributor to the *Chicken Soup for the Soul* series. E-mail her at the_write_direction@yahoo.com.

Monica A. Andermann lives and writes on Long Island where she shares a home with her husband Bill and their little tabby, Samson. Her work has been included in such publications as *Woman's World* and *Guideposts* as well as many other *Chicken Soup for the Soul* books.

Dr. Ruth Anderson is a lifelong student, teacher, and award-winning author. Retired after a satisfying career in education, she embraced her second calling: that of an intuitive reader, spiritual counselor, and author. Ruth's writings can be found at www.theministryonline.com and www.facebook.com/theministryonline1/.

Kerrie R. Barney lives in Albuquerque, NM, with her beautiful new Border Collie, MacKenna. She is a full-time student at Central New

Mexico Community College. (Go Suncats!) Kerrie's book, *Life, the Universe, and Houseplants*, about her inspiring adventures growing common houseplants, is for sale online.

Nancy Barter-Billard is a journalism graduate who works as a marketing professional in Brantford, ON, Canada. In addition to spending time with her three grown children and volunteering in her community, Nancy enjoys golfing, gardening, playing online *Scrabble*, and watching *MasterChef* with her daughter, Olivia.

Michael Bisbano is a loving husband, father, and veteran of the United States Navy. When Michael is not on his radio speaking to other ham operators around the world, you can find him in his garden or helping a neighbor mow his or her lawn. Michael wants to thank his wife, Cherrilynn Bisbano, for writing the story for him.

Michelle Blan is a freelance writer located in South Florida. God has blessed her with a very full life — her spouse (Tina), kids, and fur babies. She enjoys the beach, a good book, and time with family and friends. She is currently working on an inspirational novel. Her favorite Bible verse is James 4:7. E-mail her at michelle@michelleblan.com.

W. Bond received her Bachelor of Arts and Master's degrees from Lewis and Clark College. Wendy is a retired teacher and enjoys volunteering in her community, sewing, cooking, and spending time with family and friends.

Barbara Bower is retired from the Financial Services industry. She enjoys traveling and playing cards. She has met many wonderful and very kind people because of cancer, and enjoys helping others who find themselves unexpectedly facing a similar type of journey. E-mail her at bdbower@live.com.

L. Bower is a professional graphic designer and writer who resides in Los Angeles, CA. Favorite hobbies include museums, the arts, and caring for two wonderful Greyhounds — one of whom is a new adoption.

Ellie Braun-Haley's career began as a journalist; she was motivated to write children's books and a book of miracles. Today she speaks on "miracles that changed my life" and enjoys time with her husband. She feels her greatest accomplishment is parenting her wonderful children. E-mail her at milady@evrcanada.com.

Connie Brown is a professional tourist who enjoys traveling, writing, and spending time with family. E-mail her at coswim@gmail.com.

John Buentello has published fiction, nonfiction, and poetry in many anthologies, book collections, and magazines. He's the co-author of the novel *Reproduction Rights* and the short story collection *Binary Tales*. He's completing a new picture book and a mystery novel. Reach him at jakkhakk@yahoo.com or @JackBuentello1.

Jill Burns lives in the mountains of West Virginia with her wonderful family. She's a retired piano teacher and performer. She enjoys writing, music, gardening, nature, and spending time with her grandchildren.

Bonnie Campbell received her Bachelor's degree in Education from SUNY Oswego. She is an avid reader and lover of animals. She enjoys writing, crafts, and serves on the Service Team for Girl Scouts.

Dr. Heather A. Carlson-Jaquez is an educator and Christian who has dedicated her life to teaching others. In January of 2010 Heather lost her first husband, Matt, to a ruptured brain aneurysm. While tragic, this event brought her closer to God and helped her to grow in and share her faith with others.

Danny Carpenter is the pastor of a non-denominational church in Tomball, TX. His hobbies include golf, playing the ukulele, writing and sketching. His passion is family.

Sara Conkle is a wife, mother, grandmother, and nurse. She lives in Ohio and enjoys writing and reflecting about the experiences of her life.

Judy Bonamici Cools received her Bachelor of Arts degree at the University of Michigan and is a loyal Wolverine fan. She's had regular columns in several local newspapers, as well as a column in *Herald of the South*. She and her husband make their home in rural Michigan. E-mail her at Moonlighting19@yahoo.com.

Laine Cunningham writes speculative and historical literary fiction. Her novels and stories have received two Hackney awards, the James Jones Fellowship, awards from Writer's Digest, and honors from art councils worldwide. She has been published by *Reed Magazine*, *Birmingham Arts Journal*, and *Writer's Digest*.

Elaine D'Alessandro enjoys writing fiction for children and nonfiction for adults. Her stories have appeared in children's magazines and children's anthologies. She lives in New Hampshire with her husband, and has four children and five grandchildren. She enjoys gardening, snowshoeing, power walking, and mountain climbing.

Maya DeBruyne earned her Master of Arts in Pastoral Theology from St. Joseph's College of Maine. She works as a hospital chaplain and inspirational writer from her home in Oklahoma City, OK. E-mail her at debruynemaya@gmail.com.

Sylvia Diodati is a pianist, music teacher, and writer from Canada who loves sharing her passion for creativity, and thrives to inspire others. With many manuscripts and song projects always in the works, she considers her greatest accomplishment her family: a husband and two children who light up her soul!

Rhonda J. Dragomir is a pastor's wife, writer, and speaker living in Wilmore, KY. This is her third story published in the *Chicken Soup for the Soul* series. A research geek, she is currently engrossed in all things

Scottish as she writes a historical romance novel. Contact Rhonda at The Dragomir Group: www.dragomirgroup.com.

Jenny Filush-Glaze is a licensed counselor who specializes in grief support and all aspects of death and dying. She writes a weekly column for two newspapers and her book, *Grief Talks: Thoughts on Life, Death and Positive Healing*, provides ongoing support for those on their grief journey.

Judy Fleming is a retired home health aide. She has been married for thirty years and has four grandchildren. She enjoys her home in the woods of Northwest Wisconsin with her husband, Dan. While the experience was Judy's, she would like to thank her daughter, Cassandra Kyser, for putting it on paper.

Jen Flick is a #1 bestselling author and inspirational speaker. Her essay, "Seek Heal Grow," was selected by Elizabeth Gilbert for the commemorative book, *Eat Pray Love Made Me Do It*. When not writing, Jen enjoys spending free time with her family and being outdoors in nature. Learn more at www.JenFlick.com.

Tiffany Flynn enjoys helping others as a Physical Therapist Assistant. She is passionate about her family, which includes three daughters, a granddaughter, a grandson, and one spoiled dog. She loves to read and exercise, as well as write about her experiences. Tiffany is a life-long resident of Parsons, KS.

Lynne Foosaner is a political activist, freelance writer, and grandmother, not necessarily in that order.

Sabrina Forest received her Bachelor of Arts from the University of Minnesota in 1998. She is a freelance writer who alternates living between her home in Minnesota and her second home in Canada with her husband. Sabrina is an avid baker and a keen lover of all things outdoors. She plans to write young adult novels.

Paula Freeman is founder and former executive director of Hope's Promise, a Colorado adoption agency and orphan care ministry and author of *A Place I Didn't Belong: Hope for Adoptive Moms*. Widowed with seven grown children, she lives in Colorado but gets to the beach as often as she can. Learn more at www.paulafreeman.org.

K. Drew Fuller has written all kinds of things and has all kinds of stories still to write. He likes short stories because life is made of moments. "Turn Around" is the story of the only moment in his life beyond his explanation.

Cathy C. Hall is a humor writer and children's author. Her stories, essays, and poems have been published in all kinds of interesting places, and her leveled readers are available in South Korea. So really, Cathy's like the *Where's Waldo* of the writing world, only much better dressed. (Okay, a little better dressed.)

Kathy Lynn Harris is the author of two Amazon bestselling novels: *Blue Straggler* and *A Good Kind of Knowing*, one of which earned the 2013 NFPW literary award. She has also written children's books, essays, short fiction, and poetry. Kathy enjoys Colorado mountain living with her husband, son and two untrainable hoodlum dogs.

For over thirty years **Rob Harshman** taught secondary school. He currently lives in Mississauga, ON, Canada with his wife, Susan. He loves to spend time with his two daughters, sons-in-law and three grandchildren. Rob enjoys travel, gardening and photography. He also finds time to write stories, both fiction and nonfiction.

A freelance writer from upstate New York, **Wendy Hobday Haugh** enjoys writing short stories, poems, and articles for children and adults. She recently finished writing a novel for middle grade readers and now begins the challenging search for an agent and publisher.

Linda J. Hawkins taught elementary school, was a volunteer crisis counselor for abused women/children for ten years, taught cooking classes, and is the author of thirteen books. She loves doing anything that helps families be healthier and happier. Life's pleasures: photography, tea-time, creating/cooking beautiful meals. E-mail her at hawkinslindaj@yahoo.com.

Carolyn Hill is an avid reader and writer of romance and historical fiction. Recently retired from thirty-five years as a professional interior designer, she enjoys life with her husband of forty-six years, Mical, in New Orleans. E-mail her at hill6911@msn.com.

Susan Hunter received her Bachelor of Arts in psychology and elementary education from Muhlenberg College in 1970. She is currently a financial advisor with a Fortune 500 company. She enjoys spending time with her two sons, their wives, and four grandchildren. She also enjoys travel, reading and volunteer work.

Jennie Ivey lives and writes in Tennessee. She is the author of several works of fiction and nonfiction, including stories in numerous *Chicken Soup for the Soul* books. Learn more at jennieivey.com.

Jeanie Jacobson is on the Wordsowers Christian Writers leadership team, and is published in eleven *Chicken Soup for the Soul* books. Jeanie loves visiting family and friends, reading, hiking, praise dancing, and gardening. Grab her fun book, *Fast Fixes for the Christian Pack-Rat*, online. Learn more at jeaniejacobson.com.

Leslee Kahler received both her BS and her BA from Eastern University, and her Master's from Villanova. She has a son and a daughter and lives on a small farm in rural Pennsylvania with her family and eight rescue cats. She works as the ESL assistant at the local high school and hopes to be a novelist one day.

Elizabeth Anne Kennedy received her Bachelor of Science degree from Southern Illinois University. This is her second story published in the *Chicken Soup for the Soul* series. Elizabeth is also an artist. Her inspiration comes from the simple and intense splendor captured in a moment of time. Learn more at www.elizabethannekennedy.com.

L.A. Kennedy writes from her studio in Northern California. Her stories have appeared in *Guideposts* publications and various other magazines. An artist, she has created clay, mâché, floral and fabric projects for magazines, retail stores and private sales. She enjoys theater, gardening, and creative art. E-mail her at elkaynca@aol.com.

Kelly Kowall founded a nonprofit called My Warrior's Place after her son, SPC Corey Kowall, was killed on a combat mission in 2009 while stationed in Afghanistan. She is a certified grief support provider and life coach. She is also a published author, inspirational speaker, and artist who resides in Apollo Beach, FL.

Joyce Laird is a freelance writer living in Southern California. Her features have been published in a wide range of consumer magazines and she is a regular contributor to both *Woman's World* and the *Chicken Soup for the Soul* series. Joyce is also a member of Mystery Writers of America and Sisters in Crime.

Charlotte A. Lanham wrote her first "life stories" in a weekly, home-town newspaper near Dallas, TX in 1999. Nearly 100 columns and two years later, she was hooked! Currently living in St. Louis, MO, she continues collecting the stories that have enriched her seventy-three years. She has six beautiful grandchildren!

Mandy Lawrence is a registered nurse who considers writing to be her true calling. She is a Christian speaker and the author of *Wisdom From Wilbur: How My Dog Has Brought Me Closer to God* and the novel *Replay*. Mandy loves animals, chocolate, and traveling. She and her husband Shane live in Lexington, NC.

Danielle Lescure is a singer, writer, aspiring voiceover artist, and freelancer in Los Angeles. She loves traveling, tennis, hiking, and exploring the big city. She plans to continue using her voice and personal stories in hopes of creating a compassionate global community offering support and encouragement to others.

Jaye Lewis is an award-winning inspirational writer who lives with her two daughters, five rescue dogs, and one rescue cat. She loves gardening, writing, and especially encouraging people to celebrate the miracles within their own lives. E-mail her at tekewitha@gmail.com.

Maureen Longnecker is the author of *The Other Side of the Tapestry: Choosing to Trust God When Life Hurts.* She speaks at women's retreats/ events and writes nature articles and puzzles for children's magazines. She enjoys her family, friends, reading, photography, nature, fishing, and learning. E-mail her at maureen.longnecker@gmail.com.

Lisa Loosigian has a BA in English. Her writing background includes greeting card verses, news headlines, ad copy, essays, reviews, interviews, and fiction. She works with her husband and has one handsome son. She enjoys needlepoint, Bonsai, antiquing, time spent at the ocean, and of course… writing.

Dennis McCaslin is a hometown newspaper reporter with over thirty years of writing experience, including award-winning columns and articles recognized by the Arkansas Press Association. He has also worked in television and radio and does play-by-play announcing for local high school games. E-mail him at todayinfortmith@gmail.com.

J.P. McMuff is the pen name of the married writing team, Melissa McCoy and Paul Muff, who live in Lincoln, NE with their dog Desi. Melissa is completing a Ph.D. in English and works at the University of Nebraska. Paul is a full-time general contractor. Their story is about Paul's father.

Jennifer McMurrain has won numerous awards for her short stories and novels, including hitting #1 on the Amazon Best Seller list with *Quail Crossings*. She has eleven novels and collaborations published. She lives in Bartlesville, OK with her husband and daughter. Learn more at www.jennifermcmurrain.com.

Michelle Close Mills' poetry and short stories have appeared in magazines, anthologies and several *Chicken Soup for the Soul* books. Michelle resides in Florida with her husband and is owned by two Cockatiels and two rescue kitties. Michelle's work can be found at www.michelleclosemills.com.

Marsha Warren Mittman is an award-winning writer (U.S./Ireland) of both poetry and prose. She's had numerous short stories and poems published in journals, magazines and anthologies in the U.S. and England, including six *Chicken Soup for the Soul* stories. She is the author of three chapbooks, and a humorous memoir has just been accepted for publication.

Keith Nano is an aspiring writer and poet. He has served for more than thirty years in Law Enforcement and Corrections and is a veteran of Operation Desert Storm. In addition to writing, he enjoys fishing and baseball. He lives in Central Massachusetts with his wife, Alethea, and has five children and a grandchild.

Lisa Naubert lives on the Canadian West Coast with her husband and young son. She is involved in many artistic endeavors including writing, painting, pottery, sewing, and dance choreography. She hopes to publish her first children's book in 2018.

Kaysie Norman lives at the Jersey Shore with her husband, two-year-old son, and dog. She has an MA in creative writing, and her work has been published on many popular motherhood blogs and websites.

Julie Osborne is a contributor to the *Chicken Soup for the Soul* series and former editor and feature writer for Current Publishing. Her blog,

Tales of Oz, became *Tales of Oz with Julie Osborne (and Toto Too!)* after adopting a rescue — his name, of course, was Toto. Follow Oz and Toto's tales at www.OzandToto.com or e-mail them at info@OzandToto.com.

Larraine Paquette has a BA degree in English literature from UBC in Vancouver. She is a mother of six and a grandmother of thirteen. She and her husband, Ken, live in a small city in Western Canada where they work from home and enjoy playing acoustic guitars together and going on long walks. She also enjoys playing the piano.

Amy Rovtar Payne lives on a hobby farm with her husband and an assortment of animals. She holds a degree in education, and is a certified horseback riding instructor. Amy enjoys competing in dog agility with her rescue dogs, working with her American mustang horses, and showing Rhinelander rabbits.

Fay Peterson worked in bookselling and publishing most of her career. For the past five years, she has been writing metaphorical stories for therapists and specializes in hypnosis for teenagers. Fay lives in the eastern suburbs of Melbourne with her two Burmese cats. E-mail her at Faypetersonhypnosis@gmail.com.

Connie K. Pombo is an inspirational speaker, freelance writer, and frequent contributor to the *Chicken Soup for the Soul* series. She enjoys traveling with her husband of forty-two years and writes for *International Living* magazine about her adventures. Learn more at www.conniepombo.com.

Sheila Quarles worked in corporate sales until an accident resulted in a traumatic brain injury. Determined not to use western medicine, she traveled the world for twenty years to study indigenous healing techniques. She became a Reiki Master and partnered with Kathy Morris to establish Inner Journeys, LLC. E-mail her at innerjourneys@att.net.

As the editor of four magazines, **Sheri Radford** spends her days wrestling with commas, taming adjectives, and banishing adverbs. As the author of five silly books for kids, she spends her evenings playing, imagining, and creating. She lives in Vancouver with her husband and Chairman Meow, the world's most photogenic feline.

Denise Reich is still a fervent *Star Wars* fan. Her writing has appeared in many books in the *Chicken Soup for the Soul* series, *Santa Monica Review, Huffington Post,* TheMighty.com and the Canadian magazine *Shameless,* among others. May the Force serve you well!

Mark Rickerby is co-creator/head writer of *Big Sky*, a western TV series in development. He co-authored his father's memoir, *The Other Belfast: An Irish Youth*, and wrote/sang fifteen songs on *Great Big World*, a CD inspired by his daughters Marli and Emma. This is his nineteenth contribution to the *Chicken Soup for the Soul* series.

Heather Rae Rodin serves as Executive Director for the mission Hope Grows Haiti. An award-winning writer, she has always had a passion for personal stories and often writes from experiences in Haiti. When home in Canada she enjoys time with her husband, her family, and her Great Dane, Bogart.

Sallie A. Rodman got her Certificate in Professional Writing from Cal State University, Long Beach, CA. She truly believes in signs and miracles from the other side. Sallie lives in Los Alamitos, CA with her three cats and Mollie the Beagle. E-mail her at writergal222@gmail.com.

Veronica DeSantos Ryan is a mom, writer, and performer in community theater groups in Austin, TX. She enjoys blogging, running, and life in Central Texas. She taught middle school English for seven years, including two years with Teach For America. She holds a degree in journalism from Ohio University.

Candy Schock is a Registered Nurse, having worked in surgery and the emergency department. She is the former editor of a parenting magazine as well as a writer for a seminar company. She has published over sixty of her poems and many articles. She enjoys her grandchildren and volunteering at the local school twice a week.

Julieann Selden is a blogger, chemist, mom, and nonprofit volunteer. When her husband was diagnosed with sarcoma cancer, she learned to cope through writing. On her blog, contemplatingcancer.com, she explores how life can be both beautiful and difficult at the same time.

C. Solomon grew up overseas while her father served in the United States Army. She has a love of travel and foreign culture, which led her to the study of Anthropology. In her spare time she enjoys crafting and writing.

Kimberley Sorrells is a grad student studying Linguistics at the University of North Texas. She is a textbook editor for charter schools in Texas and enjoys every aspect of learning. She plans to change the world someday.

Eva Spaulding is a graduate of Merrimack College and resides in Saugus, MA. She is pursuing a career in teaching special education. Eva enjoys hiking with her husband and their two dogs. She is passionate about keeping her mother's legacy alive through cooking delicious food and telling amazing stories.

Judee Stapp is a speaker for women's events and retreats and has written for the *Chicken Soup for the Soul* series and other publications. Through speaking and writing, her dream is to inspire people to recognize miracles in their own lives. She is a wife, mother, and grandmother. E-mail her at judeestapp@roadrunner.com or visit www.judeestapp.com.

Jan Steele is a wife and mother of three who developed a passion for writing in the midst of raising her kids while living in Asia. She loves to travel, read, write, volunteer, and watch college basketball and sunsets. Above all, she cherishes time with family and friends. Visit her blog at killingjunecleaver.blogspot.com.

Clearing out their home with a view to move to a "closet with 1 1/2 baths" in a retirement community, **Jean Haynie Stewart** and Bill will carry sweet memories of their home with a view with them. Her stories have been published in twenty *Chicken Soup for the Soul* books as well as magazines and newspapers.

Annmarie B. Tait lives in Conshohocken, PA with her husband Joe Beck. Annmarie has been published in over twenty *Chicken Soup for the Soul* books as well as various other magazines and anthologies. Annmarie and her husband enjoy singing and recording Irish and American folk music. E-mail her at irishbloom@aol.com.

Anneke Towne splits her time between New York City and coastal Florida where she writes web content for a variety of clients. She enjoys sporting activities, live music, and photography.

Susan Traugh is an award-winning author whose stories have appeared in several *Chicken Soup for the Soul* books. Her young adult novel, *The Edge of Brilliance*, is about the heroism of a bipolar teen and is available at www.susantraugh.com. Susan lives with her family in the San Diego area's incredible beauty.

Vicki Van Grack received a BA in Theatre from the University of Maryland. She acted and sang her way to New York where she met her husband. They are the proud parents of a son and a wire-haired Dachshund. Vicki has taught children, is a jewelry artist and is waiting for her first Young Adult novel to be published.

Miriam Van Scott is an author and photographer whose credits include children's books, magazine articles, television productions, website content and reference books. Her latest titles include *Song of Old: An Advent Calendar for the Spirit* and the *Shakespeare Goes Pop* series. Learn more at www.miriamvanscott.com.

Patti Wade's stories have been published in multiple *Chicken Soup for the Soul* books beginning with her story "Real" in *Chicken Soup for the Adopted Soul*. An avid writer, reader, and cat lady, she is an especially proud mother of three wonderful adult children.

Since the death of her husband in 2015, **Beverly F. Walker** is still writing heartfelt stories and is active with senior citizens in her small community. She and her cat, Maya, love it when the grandchildren come visit!

Dorann Weber is a freelance photographer for a South New Jersey newspaper and a Getty Images contributor. She has a newfound love for writing, especially for *Chicken Soup for the Soul* books. She lives in the Pinelands of South New Jersey with her family and many critters, which include chickens and ducks.

LJ Weyant is a creative type, through trial and error, with no professional instruction or training in any of the various art mediums she enjoys. She is the mom of a grown daughter and wife to her "Mister" of twenty-plus years. She enjoys traveling, creative writing and laughter… lots and lots of laughter.

After stateside careers as a journalist and cross-cultural sociologist, **Lynne Willard** now edits academic documents and translations from multiple languages to English from her "miracle house" on the Pacific coast of Mexico. A world traveler, tennis coach, and tango dancer, she also rescues animals in distress.

Glenice Wilson enjoys nature, travel, humour, cross-country skiing, writing, visual art, and music along with the people and surprises they all offer. She grew up on a farm in big-sky prairie Manitoba and ventured out to Alberta, living in Edmonton, Jasper and now in a farming community again in Barrhead, Alberta.

Pat Lay Wilson has three children and six grandchildren. She has been writing since she was eight years old — poetry, memoirs, short stories. She was a puppeteer for forty years, and now enjoys being with her family, reading, travel, and her parrot Eggbert Wertenberger. She's currently working on a romance (novel, not husband).

Dallas Woodburn is a writer, editor, and teacher living in the San Francisco Bay area. A proud contributor to more than two-dozen *Chicken Soup for the Soul* books, she blogs about simple, joyful, healthy living at DaybyDayMasterpiece.com. Her new collection of short stories is available through her website at WriteOnBooks.org.

Following a career in nuclear medicine, **Melissa Wootan** is joyfully exploring her creative side. She enjoys writing and is a regular guest on *San Antonio Living*, an hour-long lifestyle show on San Antonio's NBC affiliate, where she shares all of her best DIY and decorating tips. Contact her at www.facebook.com/chicvintique.

Cynthia Zayn lives in the Atlanta area, and is the author of *Narcissistic Lovers: How to Cope, Recover, and Move On*. Before retiring, she taught in public and private schools in the U.S. and Mexico City. She works as a freelance writer/editor, and is a frequent contributor to the *Chicken Soup for the Soul* series.

Meet Amy Newmark

Amy Newmark is the bestselling author, editor-in-chief, and publisher of the *Chicken Soup for the Soul* book series. Since 2008, she has published more than 150 new books, most of them national bestsellers in the U.S. and Canada, more than doubling the number of Chicken Soup for the Soul titles in print today. She is also the author of *Simply Happy*, a crash course in Chicken Soup for the Soul advice and wisdom that is filled with easy-to-implement, practical tips for enjoying a better life.

Amy is credited with revitalizing the Chicken Soup for the Soul brand, which has been a publishing industry phenomenon since the first book came out in 1993. By compiling inspirational and aspirational true stories curated from ordinary people who have had extraordinary experiences, Amy has kept the twenty-four-year-old Chicken Soup for the Soul brand fresh and relevant.

Amy graduated *magna cum laude* from Harvard University where she majored in Portuguese and minored in French. She then embarked on a three-decade career as a Wall Street analyst, a hedge fund manager, and a corporate executive in the technology field. She is a Chartered Financial Analyst.

Her return to literary pursuits was inevitable, as her honors thesis in college involved traveling throughout Brazil's impoverished northeast region, collecting stories from regular people. She is delighted to have come full circle in her writing career — from collecting stories "from the people" in Brazil as a twenty-year-old to, three decades later, collecting stories "from the people" for Chicken Soup for the Soul.

When Amy and her husband Bill, the CEO of Chicken Soup for the Soul, are not working, they are visiting their four grown children and their first grandchild.

Follow Amy on Twitter @amynewmark. Listen to her free inspirational podcast, The Chicken Soup for the Soul Podcast, at www.chickensoup.podbean.com, or find it on Apple Podcasts, Google Play, or your favorite podcast app.

Thank You

We owe huge thanks to all of our contributors and fans. We were overwhelmed with fabulous stories about the miracles that have happened in your lives, and it was hard to narrow down the list to 101 from the several thousand stories that were submitted. Our excellent editorial team, consisting of Elaine Kimbler, Ronelle Frankel, Susan Heim, Senior Editor Barbara LoMonaco, and Associate Publisher D'ette Corona spent many weeks each reading these stories and narrowing the list down to several hundred finalists.

Amy Newmark chose the final stories and created the chapters, and Susan Heim did her normal, fabulous first editing pass, followed by Amy's deep dive into editing and shaping the stories for this inspiring collection.

D'ette Corona continued to be Amy's right-hand woman in picking the quotes that add so much richness to each story and in working with all our wonderful writers to make their stories just right. Barbara LoMonaco and Kristiana Pastir, along with Elaine Kimbler, jumped in at the end to proof, proof, proof. And yes, there will always be typos anyway, so feel free to let us know about them at webmaster@chickensoupforthesoul.com and we will correct them in future printings.

The whole publishing team deserves a hand, including Executive Assistant Mary Fisher, Senior Director of Marketing Maureen Peltier, Senior Director of Production Victor Cataldo, and our graphic designer Daniel Zaccari, who turned our manuscript into this beautiful book.

Sharing Happiness, Inspiration, and Hope

Real people sharing real stories, every day, all over the world. In 2007, *USA Today* named *Chicken Soup for the Soul* one of the five most memorable books in the last quarter-century. With over 100 million books sold to date in the U.S. and Canada alone, more than 250 titles in print, and translations into nearly fifty languages, "chicken soup for the soul®" is one of the world's best-known phrases.

Today, twenty-four years after we first began sharing happiness, inspiration and hope through our books, we continue to delight our readers with new titles, but have also evolved beyond the bookstore with super premium pet food, television shows, podcasts, positive journalism from aplus.com, and licensed products, all revolving around true stories, as we continue "changing the world one story at a time®." Thanks for reading!

Share with Us

We all have had Chicken Soup for the Soul moments in our lives. If you would like to share your story or poem with millions of people around the world, go to chickensoup.com and click on "Submit Your Story." You may be able to help another reader and become a published author at the same time. Some of our past contributors have launched writing and speaking careers from the publication of their stories in our books!

We only accept story submissions via our website. They are no longer accepted via mail or fax. Visit our website, www.chickensoup.com, and click on Submit Your Story for our writing guidelines and a list of topics we are working on.

To contact us regarding other matters, please send us an e-mail through webmaster@chickensoupforthesoul.com, or fax or write us at:

Chicken Soup for the Soul
P.O. Box 700
Cos Cob, CT 06807-0700
Fax: 203-861-7194

One more note from your friends at Chicken Soup for the Soul: Occasionally, we receive an unsolicited book manuscript from one of our readers, and we would like to respectfully inform you that we do not accept unsolicited manuscripts and we must discard the ones that appear.

Chicken Soup for the Soul

Angels and Miracles

101 Inspirational Stories about Hope, Answered Prayers, and Divine Intervention

Amy Newmark

Paperback: 978-1-61159-964-0
eBook: 978-1-61159-263-4

More angel and miracle

Chicken Soup for the Soul.

Touched by an Angel

101 Miraculous Stories of Faith, Divine Intervention, and Answered Prayers

Amy Newmark
Foreword by Gabrielle Bernstein

Paperback: 978-1-61159-941-1
eBook: 978-1-61159-243-6

stories to inspire you

Chicken Soup for the Soul®

Miracles Happen

101 Inspirational Stories about Hope,
Answered Prayers, and
Divine Intervention

Jack Canfield,
Mark Victor Hansen
& Amy Newmark

Paperback: 978-1-61159-932-9
eBook: 978-1-61159-233-7

More classic tales of faith,

Hope & Miracles

101 Inspirational Stories of Faith, Answered Prayers & Divine Intervention

Amy Newmark
and Natasha Stoynoff
Foreword by John Edward

Paperback: 978-1-61159-944-2
eBook: 978-1-61159-246-7

hope and divine intervention

The **National Bestseller** with Real Stories from Real People

Chicken Soup
for the Soul®

Messages from Heaven

101 Miraculous Stories of Signs from Beyond, Amazing Connections, and Love that Doesn't Die

Jack Canfield,
Mark Victor Hansen,
and Amy Newmark

Paperback: 978-1-935096-91-7
eBook: 978-1-61159-205-4

Love that doesn't die...

Miraculous
Messages
from Heaven

IOI Stories of Eternal Love,
Powerful Connections, and
Divine Signs from Beyond

Jack Canfield,
Mark Victor Hansen
& Amy Newmark

Paperback: 978-1-61159-926-8
eBook: 978-1-61159-228-3

in these bestselling classics

Changing your world one story at a time®
www.chickensoup.com